JOE BOB BRIGGS

PROFOUNDLY DISTURBING

Shocking Movies
That Changed History!

D1568572

THE FOLLOWING **BOOK**
DISTURBED

AND HAS

PD | PROFOUNDLY

SHOCKING MOVIES THAT CHANGED

HAS BEEN APPROVED FOR

AUDIENCES

BEEN RATED

DISTURBING

HISTORY! | BY JOE BOB BRIGGS

UNIVERSE

THANK YOUS • No one was allowed to work on this book without an obsession for movies. • First of all, I want to thank my patient editor, Christopher Steighner of New York, who helped conceive the idea and worked it through several wild variations, supervised the design, then handled the thankless task of gathering photos. • Maggie Ragaisis of Chicago runs my Web site (www.joebobbriggs.com) and somehow keeps track of the thousands of press kits, capsule reviews, newspaper and magazine articles, photos, and movie-memorabilia oddities that have accumulated over the years. • My agent, Vicki Eisenberg, not only made the book happen, but also she is well known in Dallas as a longtime publicist and advertising representative for some of the scuzziest films in exploitation history and thereby introduced me to *The Grim Reaper*, the first film I ever reviewed, which is mentioned in the chapter on

The Texas Chain Saw Massacre. • My assistant, Mary Koon of Londonderry, New Hampshire, helped coordinate all the far-flung storage spaces from which we had to retrieve information. • Special thanks go to Fred Williamson, Herschell Gordon Lewis, and the cast and crew of *The Texas Chain Saw Massacre*—Tobe Hooper, Ronald Bozman, Marilyn Burns, Allen Danziger, John Dugan, Gunnar Hansen, Kim Henkel, Robert Kuhn, Teri McMinn, Edwin Neal, Paul A. Partain, and Jim Siedow—who graciously agreed to personal interviews in the past. • Finally, I would never have finished the project without the assistance of Rebecca Brock of Mt. Gay, West Virginia, and the resources of the West Virginia Library Commission. As my research assistant, she tracked down literally thousands of obscure references and put them into a coherent form, often helping with her own vast knowledge of genre films.

"PROFOUNDLY DISTURBING"
IS WHAT THE BEAK–NOSED PRINCIPAL
SAYS WHEN HE HAULS YOU IN FOR
WRITING OBSCENITIES ON THE BLACKBOARD.

"PROFOUNDLY DISTURBING"
IS WHAT THE MATRON IN A FLOWER–PRINT DRESS
TELLS THE PREGNANT DAUGHTER WHO
LOST HER VIRGINITY TO A RENEGADE BIKER.

"PROFOUNDLY DISTURBING"
IS WHAT THE ASYLUM DIRECTOR SAYS TO
AN UNREPENTANT PATIENT FOUND
DISEMBOWELING HIS PETS.

"PROFOUNDLY DISTURBING," IS, IN SHORT, what authority figures solemnly intone whenever the messiness of the world intrudes too far on to what we have come to think of as order, sanity, decorum, or just simple peace and quiet. It's both a judgment and an expression of uneasiness. The subtext of it is, "I would really rather not see this."

Films are all about seeing, though, and all the films I've chosen for this book have been banned, censored, condemned, or despised because in one way or another they expanded what the camera sees into some area that was previously verboten.

These films disorient, confuse, stun, horrify, and ultimately rearrange our whole view of what constitutes reality—sometimes in a literal way (the hacked limbs of *Blood Feast*, the ripe "do me" body of Bardot), sometimes in an aesthetic way (the lush colors of *The Curse of Frankenstein* set off against its horror, the dead calm of *Crash*), sometimes in a cultural way (the in-your-face freedom of *Shaft*, the exposure of teen sex to the middle class in *Mom and Dad*), and sometimes in a psychological way (the depraved moral code of *The Wild Bunch*, the adolescent sexuality of *The Creature from the Black*

Lagoon). You could take all the lurid one-sheets created for these films and add a line at the bottom: "Like you've never seen before!"

These are more than movies then. They're shows. They're spectacles. They required ballyhoo and audiences that were willing to immerse themselves in the unknown. They're so much a part of their times that they sometimes have the character of live plays or carnival attractions. They were designed for a specific audience at a specific place and time. When I say that they changed history, in some cases I mean only film history (*Reservoir Dogs*, *The Exorcist*), but even the lesser ones had some effect on the culture, even if it was passed along subterraneously through music, fanzines, or the Internet. And in some cases—notably *Deep Throat* and *The Cabinet of Dr. Caligari*—they marked such a sea change in popular culture that we could never return to what existed before.

You'll notice that the bulk of them are bunched in the sixties and seventies, especially between 1971 and 1974. There's both a practical reason and a cultural reason for that. The week that *Shaft* opened, in 1971, for example, was the same week that the first multiplex theater opened. The public had started to desert the big downtown moviehouses that had been the principal cathedrals of popular art almost since film began. It was a time of massive uncertainty, when many of the major Hollywood studios were facing bankruptcy and all of the popular genres were failing. It was one of the few times in film history that the untried, the unproven, and even the bizarre were welcome in a

studio executive's office. These were also years when the nation was digesting a slew of social and political changes from the sixties that hadn't yet been worked out in our subconsciouses. The market was open for spinners of new dreams, and many of those dreams were very dark.

Five of these films are from foreign countries, and it's interesting to note how quickly and greedily Americans are able to absorb anything exotic that throws us off balance. Germany sent *The Cabinet of Dr. Caligari*, and its cockeyed angles, skewed perspectives, and the language of inner psychological turmoil have infected our films ever since. France sent *And God Created Woman*, and Bardot's tomboyish barefoot liberation invented a style that leads in a direct line to Susan Sarandon and, for that matter, Britney Spears. England scavenged among our old cast-off monsters and came up with *The Curse of Frankenstein*, reinventing the Gothic for a younger American generation. Canadians created *Ilsa, She-Wolf of the SS*, which dove straight down into the worlds of punk rock, fetishism, and dark fantasy, embedding itself in those secret places where *Crash*, another Canadian import, added death itself as a sexual game. Yet even when the imported film touches our sense of the forbidden, it's still the American market that absorbs the new idea, stretches it, adds to it, and reexports it to the rest of the world—often, admittedly, in a watered-down form.

The makers of these films are all outsiders. With the exception of the two most recent films—directed by Quentin Tarantino and David Cronenberg—

these filmmakers were chewed up by the markets they created. Most of them never had the respect of their peers, or, if they did (I'm thinking of Sam Peckinpah), it came long after it could do them any good. Some of them came from obscurity, made their hit movie, then returned to obscurity so rapidly that only a devoted film geek would even know their names. When that happens, there's a tendency to think that they were untalented, and that the film's success had as much to do with them as the success of a lottery winner has to do with the ability to pick random numbers. I don't think this is the case. A film—any film—is too huge, too energy-draining, too demanding of insane levels of concentration to be random. It's a mix of the technological, the psychological, the literary, and the cultural, and the wonder is not that we have so many one-hit wonders, but that we have so many people who are able to make more than one film in a lifetime. The reason those guys fight for their multimillion-dollar budgets is not because they want a bigger trailer, but because they don't want to die early.

The only other observation I would make about these men is that there was an immediacy to their work, a disregard for history. Their motives were often mercenary. Certainly Kroger Babb (*Mom and Dad*), Herschell Gordon Lewis (*Blood Feast*) and Gerard Damiano (*Deep Throat*) had their eyes firmly on the bottom line. The creators of *Caligari* were bitter young men who wanted to make a political statement. The directors of *The Creature from the Black Lagoon* and *Ilsa, She-Wolf of the SS* were hired guns. Roger Vadim made *And God Created Woman* because he wanted to turn his wife into a movie star. *The Curse of Frankenstein* was conceived out of financial desperation. *The Texas Chain Saw Massacre*, *Drunken Master* and *Reservoir Dogs* were made only so that the filmmakers could establish their careers and work in the future. The only exceptions to this prove the rule. David Cronenberg could make virtually any movie he wants but is so introspective and oblivious to the marketplace that, when a dark fantasy forms in his mind, he makes the movie in spite of all evidence that to do so is suicidal—hence *Crash*. William Friedkin (*The Exorcist*) is such a monomaniacal egotist that he doesn't see the forces around him that could destroy him. And Sam Peckinpah must have been in some sort of fatalistic state when he made *The Wild Bunch* his way, uncompromising, knowing that even if it were successful, he could still be barred from ever working again.

What I'm trying to say is that most of these guys would be more likely to brawl over a single frame of film removed from a secondary scene than to bridle at a slight by the *New York Times*. They're obsessives. They're unhealthy. They look at the world and ask, "What has it never seen before?" And then they attack it, with guns, chain saws, forbidden stories, and good old-fashioned sweaty sex. It just might be that, in order to be profoundly disturbing, you must first be profoundly disturbed.

— **Joe Bob Briggs**
New York City
September 2002

The depraved Egyptian caterer Fuad Ramses in *Blood Feast*.

DU MUßT

STARRING WERNER KRAUSS   FRIEDRICH FEHER   CONRAD VEIDT   LIL DAGOVER

ORIGINAL MUSIC BY GIUSEPPE BECCE   CINEMATOGRAPHY BY WILLY HAMEISTER   SET DECORATION BY HERMANN WARM   COSTUME DESIGN BY WALTER REIMANN

ALIGARI WERDEN!

The CABINET of Dr. CALIGARI

WRITTEN BY HANS JANOWITZ AND CARL MAYER   DIRECTED BY ROBERT WIENE

RODUCTION DESIGN BY WALTER REIMANN   WALTER RÖHRIG   HERMANN WARM   PRODUCED BY RUDOLF MEINERT AND ERICH POMMER

World War I created the modern horror film.

That war was a nasty, relentless, mind-numbing slaughter churning out maimed and mangled bodies that, thanks to modern medicine, were sent home to their communities instead of being buried on the battlefield as they would have been in past wars. Many soldiers were treated for insanity for the rest of their lives.

OTHERS WERE HORRIBLY DEFORMED AND crippled, and lived out their lives as freaks. In Germany the carnage was worse than anywhere else, and the country itself was in a deep depression over what Germans considered a humiliating defeat made worse by the Treaty of Versailles.

In the midst of this gloom there appeared two angry, bitter ex-soldiers, Hanz Janowitz and Carl Mayer, who wrote a screenplay that they didn't regard as a horror story at all. *The Cabinet of Dr. Caligari* was intended as a political allegory about the way powerful men hypnotized helpless millions into doing their bidding, even if it meant turning them into killers and then murdering them. It was a revolutionary film about totalitarianism, directed at Kaiser Wilhelm but eerily prophetic of Hitler. In later years, it would become a standard "required text" in film schools, mostly because of its bizarre stylistic effects, and under the weight of academic

criticism it would lose its power to shock or thrill. Unfortunately, it has rarely been seen in its original form. For one thing, modern prints don't show the color of the original: It was tinted in shades of brown, green, and metallic blue. For another, it was designed to be seen with a full orchestra playing modernist music—Debussy, Schoenberg, Stravinsky—but most of its rereleases used one of those silly American-style melodrama scores for piano or organ, so all the atmosphere was destroyed. It was like trying to watch *Schindler's List* with "Turkey in the Straw" playing in the background and a professor pointing out every shaft of light as a pivotal moment in German Expressionism.

But on February 6, 1920, when *Das Kabinet des Doktor Caligari* was brand-new, the premiere audience at the Marmorhaus Theater in Berlin was stunned. Janowitz and Mayer thought the film had failed, because when it ended the crowd didn't move or make a noise. A few moments passed, and then a roar erupted. The crowd stood, applauding and screaming, shouting for curtain calls. A year later, the same thing happened in New York, when the film's opening at the Capitol Theatre—complete with full orchestral accompaniment, stage tableaux, and "cubist" posters—created a sensation that made the film a must-see for both the intellectuals and the lower classes who represented the principal moviegoing public at the time. It was hailed as, among other things, the first "art film"—the first movie to bring the ideas of Picasso, Braque, and Duchamp to the screen—even though it had very little to do with modern art. It was almost as though everyone was searching for a new vocabulary to describe it. "Gruesome," "macabre," and "morbid" were just a few of the words used. Like most New York sensations, it was alternately praised and condemned, with one critic calling it "the first significant attempt at the expression of a creative mind in the medium of cinematography" and another saying, "It has the odor of tainted food. It leaves a taste of cinders in the mouth."

For better or worse, the film was now world famous, scoring its greatest successes in the very capitals—London and Paris—that had so recently despised all things German. (It was less popular in Germany, where it was considered too highbrow.) When the film opened in Los Angeles, though, the American Legion was so outraged by the idea of a German film in their backyard that they organized a demonstration of two thousand people outside Miller's Theater, many of them holding placards reading "Why Pay War Tax To See German-Made Pictures?" The demonstration disintegrated into a rotten-egg-throwing riot, with police being called in to keep order, and by day's end the owner of the theater had agreed to drop the picture and replace it with another. The Legion had been fired up by the motion-picture industry, which feared a rash of cheap European movies flooding the market, and for a time there were editorials calling for an import ban on all German films. (The idea was quickly discarded when it became obvious that a trade war would only hurt Hollywood since 95 percent of the movies playing in Germany came from the States.)

THE REASON *CALIGARI* WAS SO SHOCKING IS THAT it was the first psychological horror film. The lighting was weird and unearthly—what critics called "the scenery of the soul." It was artificial and stylized, without even the slightest pretense of realism. And it was full of jagged shadows and unsettling perspectives. Even the opening title is bizarre: "A Modern representation of an eleventh century myth in which a Mountebank monk bears a strange and mysterious influence over a Somnambulist." The film proper opens with the camera irising in on two hollow-eyed men sitting together in a gauzy atmosphere that can't be placed: heaven? hell? a dream? "Everywhere there are spirits," says one man to the other. "They are all around us. They have driven me from hearth and home, from my wife and children." A woman in white, walking like a zombie, passes them as if she's an apparition. "That is my fiancée," says the man. And here, even before the movie has begun its story, we feel cut off from reality, a little claustrophobic, unable to get our bearings in time or place. If she's his fiancée, why doesn't she look at him? Is she dead? Disruptive dream narratives are not that odd for the modern viewer, but for audiences of 1920, who had seen mostly strict documentary realism, it was both confusing and fascinating.

AND THEN THE MOVIE GETS EVEN STRANGER. We're introduced to the town of Holstenwall, where a curious fair is going on, established by a shot of a creepy organ-grinder and a cockeyed merry-go-round, both moving in endless circles. The festivity of the fair is broken by an old man in a stovepipe hat, walking with a cane, his wild white hair splayed out from his head, looking very grim. "That's him!" says the narrator. It's Caligari, although we don't know that yet. Two scenes later we see the old man being humiliated by a town clerk in a high-backed chair as Caligari seeks a license to present his exhibit at the fair: a somnambulist. (The old-fashioned term had the double meaning of a sleepwalker and a psychic medium in an era that still ascribed supernatural properties to hypnotism.) Caligari gets his license, but that night the town clerk is murdered—"the first," we're told, "of a series of mysterious crimes."

At the fair, our narrator, Francis, and his breezy young friend Alan are attracted by the advertising for The Cabinet of Dr. Caligari—the unveiling of a young man who has been sleeping for twenty-three years but will awaken that night. Caligari drums up a crowd, then presents an upright coffinlike chamber. He swings open the door to reveal Cesare, who continues to sleep in a standing position. Caligari bids him to awaken "for your master," and as first his lips, then his eyelids move, we get one of the few closeups in the movie. What we see would become in later years the standard for the zombie look: a pasty complexion, dark circles under the eyes, and, when he starts to walk, a jerky step. He moves a few feet and poses like a ballet dancer as Caligari says, "Cesare will answer all your questions. Cesare knows every secret, past and future."

Alan goes to the stage and, just for fun, asks Cesare, "How long do I have to live?" The somnambulist hesitates, then answers: "Till dawn tomorrow." He says it with such certainty that Alan begins to shudder and has to be helped out by Francis. In fact, that very night, Alan is strangled and stabbed, fulfilling the prophecy and setting up the movie's suspense: Did Cesare commit the crime? Did Caligari? Or was Cesare truly a medium who saw into the future?

The reason we can't be certain whether we're watching a supernatural thriller, a dream vision, or a whodunit is that everything about the film throws us off balance. This was one of the earliest films to be shot entirely on sound stages, and all of the sets were built with *Alice in Wonderland* perspectives—only harsher and more unsettling. The actors are almost swallowed up by the sets, as though they're mere pawns in the grip of some greater force. The set designers were hired from a group called the Berlin Sturm, who had invented a new style of painting that had elements of the Gothic and the surreal. Windows were shaped like arrows. Chimneys were slanted like bent pipes. Details were either painted onto a flat plane or greatly exaggerated, making the streets and buildings of Holstenwall nightmarish. There's not a single blade of grass or warm hearth to give you any relief from this strange world that seems not quite earthly. In future years, this would be called expressionism, and it would influence films as disparate as *Citizen Kane*, *Vertigo*, *The Trip* (it does resemble an LSD vision), and numerous 1950s films noir. At one point, when Caligari is lurching through the streets, we even see literal words superimposed on the film: "I must become Caligari" floats before his eyes. What the filmmakers had done was to create an interior world of insanity with exterior sets.

Or was the movie about insanity? Director Robert Wiene and producer Erich Pommer would have said yes indeed, the narrator is insane and the movie is a record of his madness. The writers, on the other hand, would have said no, it's Caligari who's insane, along with the cruel world he lives in, but that the narrator is perfectly sane. It's one of the oddities of the movie's creation, and perhaps what gives it its peculiar charge—the creators had virtually opposite views of what the story meant.

The genesis of the movie, first revealed by film historian Siegfried Kracauer in 1947, was a trip to a fair in Hamburg taken by the film's cowriter Hanz Janowitz in 1913. He was attracted to a beautiful girl there and followed her. After he lost track of her, he could still hear her distinctive laugh, and he followed the noise into a dim park, where the sound seemed to vanish into the shrubbery. He gave up the chase, but when leaving the fair he saw a shadow emerge from the bushes and got a glimpse of an average-looking German burgher. The following day, he picked up the newspaper to discover a screaming headline: "Horrible Sex Crime on the Holstenwall! Young Gertrude Murdered!" Wondering if it could possibly be the same girl, he attended her funeral—and while there he had the sensation of seeing the very same man, the shadow, the burgher. And he felt as if he knew the murderer.

Janowitz went on to serve as an infantry officer in World War I and emerged from it a zealous pacifist. Settling back into the Berlin theater world, he met Carl Mayer, the man who would become his cowriter. Mayer was equally disenchanted with war; he was examined repeatedly for mental illness while a soldier and hated the military psychiatrists. Mayer was also probably still traumatized by precipitating his father's suicide. (As a sixteen-year-old boy, he had taken a "scientific" gambling system to Monte Carlo and had gone broke with the family's money. His father turned Mayer and his three brothers into the street, then killed himself just as the war was beginning.) When Janowitz and Mayer eventually met, they decided to do an antiwar film together, often strolling through the fair at Kantstrasse while working out their story. One day, Mayer dragged Janowitz to a sideshow called "Man or Machine," which consisted of miracles of strength performed by a man in an apparent

Following pages: Cesare abducts Francis's fiancée Jane from her bedroom.

They invented a word,
caligarisme,
to describe
a dark, sadistic world with
an appetite for destruction—
especially a world of
insane Germans.

stupor who would also utter foreboding prophecies. It brought back memories for Janowitz of the strange man in Hamburg who may or may not have killed the girl—and they knew they had their movie. They wrote *Caligari* in six weeks, taking the name from a story by Stendhal.

To Janowitz and Mayer, Caligari was a symbol of totalitarian power, made all the scarier by the fact that he turns out to be the eminent director of the local insane asylum. Cesare, the sleepwalking fake prophet, was a symbol of compulsory military service—simple people turned into automatons that will do the most barbaric crimes without even realizing what they've done. The script was intriguing enough to be accepted by Erich Pommer, chief executive at the Decla-Bioscop studio, and he actually wanted Fritz Lang to direct it. When Lang was called away to another project, he assigned it to Robert Wiene, whose own father had become insane near the end of his life. Wiene sympathized with the premise of the film—he blamed Kaiser Wilhelm for Germany's humiliation at Versailles—but he made a big change. Instead of the film being about real horrors, he wanted it to be an illusion narrated by a madman. (Hence the framing story of the two men sitting in the strange, gauzy netherworld.) Predictably, Janowitz and Mayer objected. If the story was told by a madman, and if Caligari was in fact a kindly, benevolent doctor, then the whole purpose of the movie had been perverted. It now glorified authority and made the hero into a lunatic.

But that's how they filmed it, concluding with Francis in a straitjacket screaming, "You all think I'm insane! It isn't true! It's the director who's insane!" And even though various film critics have criticized the framing story, I actually think it improves the film. The final image is of the asylum director giving Francis a kindly pat on the head and assuring everyone that he knows how to cure him—which, to me, is more chilling than if the doctor had been caught and punished. When will the director transmogrify back into a monster? How long will his expression be kindly? We've seen too much of Francis to think he can be wholly insane. I think the way Wiene did it makes it more subversive rather than less. The ending creates a shock similar to what audiences would feel decades later at the conclusion of *The Sixth Sense* (1999). It actually dupes the spectator and makes him feel a little crazy himself.

Confusing matters even more, the poster for the movie's first release screamed "You Must Become Caligari!" Of all the possible reactions to it, identifying with Caligari would seem to be the least credible—but then this was Germany, a country that would elevate Hitler to dictatorship a little more than a decade later when millions of Germans were so mesmerized by a madman that they identified with his every scheme. The French were so enamored of this film that they invented a word, caligarisme, to describe a dark, sadistic world with an appetite for destruction—especially a world of insane Germans.

Meanwhile, the film made permanent stars of virtually the entire cast. Werner Krauss, as Caligari, looks like an old man, but he was actually only thirty-six when he did the role. He would remain in Germany throughout the war years, where he was recognized as an artist of National Socialism by Hermann Goering, and he would star in one of the most notorious films in history, *Jud Süss* (1940), the ultimate anti-Semitic movie. The film was never shown in the states, of course, so he was still known mostly for the Caligari performance, which influenced Boris Karloff when he did *The Bells* in 1926. After the war, Krauss understandably had trouble getting work, and he died in 1959.

Conrad Veidt, as Cesare, had an almost opposite career, fleeing Germany in the late twenties—because he was Jewish—to become a Universal contract player in Hollywood. One of the most prolific of all German actors, he made 118 movies, of which only 49 survive, including early German exploitation films on subjects like venereal disease, prostitution, drugs, homosexuality, and sex education. Nicknamed "the man with the wicked eyes," he had several other classic silent-film roles—including *The Hands of Orlac*, *Waxworks*, *The Student of Prague* and *The Man Who Laughs*—before the advent of sound sent him scurrying back to Europe with many other foreign actors. (Universal wanted him for the lead in *Dracula*, but he was still insecure about his accented English.) He worked in London on German projects, occasionally shuttling back to Germany (where he also appeared in *Jud Süss*), then eventually perfected his English to the point where he could play sinister Teutonic villains. He moved back to Hollywood during World War II and worked almost constantly in Nazi roles, the most

famous of which is, of course, Major Strasser in *Casablanca*. He was only fifty years old in 1943, when he collapsed on a golf course and died of a heart attack, but toward the end of his life he said, "No matter what roles I play, I can't get Caligari out of my system."

Lil Dagover, the beautiful girl carried off by Cesare through a zigzag maze in the film's most memorable sequence, also remained in Germany and made films throughout the Nazi era. She tried Hollywood in 1931, making only one film there, *The Woman from Monte Carlo*, in First National Pictures' attempt to create "the next Garbo." When the experiment failed, she returned to Germany and after the war was able to avoid the stigma of being a Nazi sympathizer, mostly by appearing in harmless costume dramas and comedies. She remained popular in the post-war years and made her final movie, *End of the Game*, four years before her death, in 1980, at the age of eighty-six.

Producer Erich Pommer would settle in London during the Nazi years, where he founded Mayflower Pictures with Charles Laughton. Only Robert Wiene, the director, would struggle. The founder of Expressionism would never have another hit, although his *The Hands of Orlac* later became well-known. He fled to France in the early thirties and, cut off from the German studio system, died in virtual obscurity in 1938.

Wiene's legacy lived on, though, in films like *The Golem* by Carl Boese and Paul Wegener, *Nosferatu* by F. W. Murnau, and *Metropolis* by Fritz Lang. Expressionism flourished only from 1919 to

1924, but like the films of D. W. Griffith, its techniques would be used well into the next century. *Caligari* today is regarded not only as the first horror film, but also as the film that defined the idea of the monster itself. "Whether Americans liked it or not," wrote David J. Skal in his definitive work on the period, *The Monster Show*, "an enormous westward expansion of horrors was taking shape, a manifest destiny of the macabre. The dark beings that had used the European avant-garde to find a modern expression would soon begin crossing the Atlantic, in film canisters instead of coffins, waiting to be animated in darkened rooms through the application of artificial light. Their secrets had everything to do with light and shadow, projections, reflections, and doubles. The dark gods knew that the republic founded on principles of rational enlightenment would have a more than ample shadow-side, where monsters might flourish and be free. Shaken out of their ancient crypts and castles by the modern concussions of war, they began seeking a new resting place, slouching inexorably toward Hollywood to be born anew."

Caligari has problems for the modern viewer. For one thing, the Germans had not yet seen the films of D. W. Griffith, so they were unfamiliar with the new style of closeups and intercutting within scenes that we now expect in all films. As a result, the movie looks stagey and static. Even more off-putting is the exaggerated acting style, including bug-eyed reactions and the overuse of the hands to express emotion. I can only assume that the Berlin theater world had not yet been exposed to Konstantin Stanislavsky's acting theories, or else they would have chosen a much more understated style for the first purely psychological film. In order to appreciate the film at all, you need to think of it as a ballet or opera, in which the posturing and overacting is a sort of emotional semaphore that guides us into the minds of the performers. By regarding it as an elaborate work of choreographed movement, it will start to make emotional sense.

Perhaps the youngest director with a direct link to *Caligari* is Tim Burton, who in films such as *Edward Scissorhands* uses almost all of Wiene's techniques, including skewed perspective, lurid lighting, and the total construction of a psychologically warped world. In *Beetlejuice* (1988), he even uses some of the same makeup effects first seen on Cesare. If anyone were ever to remake *Caligari* with the full impact of the original, Burton would seem to be the ideal choice. *Caligari* has been breaking out of its film-school crypt lately, emerging in the summer of 2001 as an off-Broadway musical written by Richard Lawton and Douglas Hicton. Perhaps it was just a hundred years ahead of its time. As critic Thomas Nunan wrote in the *San Francisco Examiner* at the time of *Caligari*'s debut there, "I do not think the weirdest picture in the world a good one to see." It takes time to appreciate weird.

FOR FURTHER DISTURBANCE

The next major Expressionist classic was *Nos-feratu, eine Symphonie des Grauens*, or **NOSFERATU, A SYMPHONY OF HORROR** (1922), directed by F. W. Murnau and based on Bram Stoker's *Dracula*. Best known for the performance of Max Schreck as Court Orlock, the rodentlike recluse who hypnotizes

The Cabinet of Dr. Caligari gave birth to supernatural horror in the cinema and led to many works in the twenties that used the same Expressionist techniques. The first was *Der Golem, wie er in die Welt kam*, a precursor of **FRANKENSTEIN** (1931), which premiered in Germany in 1920 and was released in the states in 1921 as **THE GOLEM**. Noted for the set design of Edgar G. Ulmer, who would still be making B movies in America as late as the sixties, it's the story of a seventeenth-century rabbi who sees dark omens in the stars and summons the elders to pray for deliverance. The emperor, fearing a plague, orders the Jews out of Prague, but the rabbi builds a monster called a Golem out of clay in a secret cellar. The creature (Paul Wegener) starts roaming the streets, terrifying the populace. When a little girl befriends him, she removes his magic amulet, rendering him lifeless. The rabbi eventually gets an audience with the emperor and uses the Golem to perform magic, creating a panorama on the wall of a coming earthquake. When the earthquake does occur, the Golem prevents the ceiling from collapsing and saves the emperor's life, resulting in his rescinding his edict. *The Golem* was a huge hit worldwide and had been filmed before with Paul Wegener, but the 1920 film is the only one that's survived.

Max Schreck as *Nosferatu*.

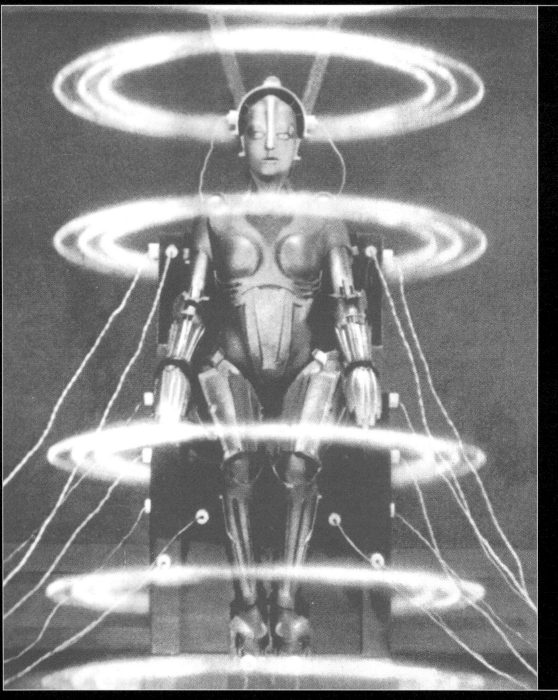

The lifelike robot in *Metropolis*.

his victims, it was tied up in legal battles with the Stoker estate for years and wasn't really appreciated as a masterpiece until after Murnau's death in 1943.

The cast of *Caligari* became famous as a result of the film, and Krauss would be seen again in JUD SÜSS (1940), the most notoriously anti-Semitic film ever made, while actors in Hollywood would look to his performance as the beginning of a horror style. Specifically, Boris Karloff modeled himself after Krauss in THE BELLS (1926). Veidt went to Hollywood and became immortalized as the sinister Major Strasser in CASABLANCA (1942), but he was starring in American films as early as 1928 (in THE MAN WHO LAUGHS). Nicknamed the Man with the Wicked Eyes, Veidt's German hits included WAXWORKS (1924) and THE STUDENT OF PRAGUE (1926). He also appeared in *Jud Süss*, even though, ironically, the Nazis objected because he was Jewish. His last film was ABOVE SUSPICION (1943). Lil Dagover's one American film, THE WOMAN FROM MONTE CARLO (1932), was a flop, but she continued to make German films for the rest of her life, the last of which was *End of the Game* (1976). Robert Wiene never directed another film as famous as *Caligari*, but his THE HANDS OF ORLAC (1927), also starring Veidt, has recently acquired a cult following.

Scary German films would continue to dominate screens around the world throughout the twenties, including Fritz Lang's METROPOLIS (1926) and Carl Dreyer's THE PASSION OF JOAN OF ARC (1928). Descendants of Caligari in the sound era include CITIZEN KANE (1941), with Gregg Toland's cinematography making extensive use of Expressionistic lighting, Tim Burton's EDWARD SCISSORHANDS (1990) and SLEEPY HOLLOW (1999), David Cronenberg's CRASH (1996), and M. Night Shyamalan's THE SIXTH SENSE (1999)—but it could really be said to have influenced every horror film of the past eighty years.

Extra!

IN PER
ELLI

"WHAT IS THIS WORLD

Many parents are making the sam
trying to keep their Boys and Gir
This story was ripped from the pag
It will awaken you.

HYGIENIC PRODUCTIONS

MOM and

with an ALL-STAR

Produced by
J. S. Jossey
and Kroger Babb
Original Screen Story by
Mildred Horn :: Supervised by
Barney Sarecky :: Directed by Wm.
Beaudine : Musical Score by Eddie Kay

ON OUR STAGE ★ RADIO'S HYGIENE COMMENTATOR
FORBES on "SECRETS of SENSIBLE SEX"

COMING TO ?"
...istake Mrs. Blake did—
...nocent thru ignorance.
...everyday life.

Fearless! Powerful!
This Picture Speaks Out! You See For Yourself Blazing Truths . . . Amazing Statistics . . . ALL The Facts About Life! Praised by Health Officials, Civic Leaders, Mothers and Parents organizations from coast-to-coast. . . . . Simply Don't Miss It!

LEAVING FOR THE DANCE

SHE MEETS A NEW BOY

CONFIDES IN MARY LOU

HER LIFE IS SPARED

presents
DAD"
HOLLYWOOD CAST

DID YOU HAVE A NICE TRIP, JOAN?

Youth deserves attention . . .
Boys and Girls are entitled to know the Truth before their bodies are wrecked and their lives ruined!

That's why this is a Tremendously Important Event!

SHOWN TO SEGREGATED AUDIENCES ONLY. NO CHILDREN ADMITTED!

WOMEN ONLY!
AND HIGH SCHOOL GIRLS
at **2** and **7** P. M.

MEN ONLY!
AND HIGH SCHOOL BOYS
at **9** P. M.

"Once in a lifetime comes a presentation that truly pulls no punches!
Now you can see the motion picture that dares discuss and explain
sex as never before seen and heard!
The one, the only, the original . . . MOM AND DAD
. . . Truly the world's most amazing attraction!
No one under high school age admitted unless accompanied by parents!!

Everything shown!
Everything explained!"

IF YOU LIVED IN A SMALL TOWN IN THE FORTIES OR fifties, it was virtually impossible *not* to know about a film called *Mom and Dad*. Sooner or later, a flamboyant publicity man would drive into town, the ads would appear, and the tempestuous debate would begin. Plastered on every available storefront, barn, bus bench, and shoeshine stand was a poster seducing you with an attractive couple in mid-kiss and black bold-faced ballyhoo exploding all around them. And in a black box in the lower left-hand corner:

"Extra! In person: Elliot Forbes, The secrets of sensible sex."

If it sounds more like the circus than the movies, that's because it was. The film's promoters came from the worlds of carnivals and burlesque houses, and they were under marching orders from a P.T. Barnum–type figure named Kroger Babb, whose motto was "You have to tell 'em to sell 'em."

Alarmed letters to the editor would appear in the local newspaper. Clergymen would express opinions from the pulpit. (If you were Catholic, you were banned from attending the movie.) In some towns, the police would send men to check the film for violations of the obscenity statutes. (Of course, the print would be "unavailable" until opening day.) And as soon as the first women-only matinee was screened, at 2 P.M. on a Friday afternoon, the town would blaze with *Mom and Dad* gossip. Though all but forgotten today, *Mom and Dad* was so heavily promoted that *Time* magazine once remarked that the ad campaign "left only the livestock unaware of the chance to learn the facts of life."

But this was not Hollywood promotion. In fact, Hollywood spent twenty years campaigning to get rid of movies like *Mom and Dad*. This movie was the last wave of the nineteenth-century medicine shows—part biology lesson, part sideshow, part morality play, part medical "shock footage"—and to this day many old-timers regard it as the purest and most successful exploitation film in history. It played continuously for twenty-three years, still booking drive-ins as late as 1977, and grossed an estimated $100 million.

Kroger Babb, who billed himself as "America's Fearless Young Showman," ruled over a vast army of *Mom and Dad* "road-show units" from his head-quarters in Worthington, Ohio. (At one time, he had twenty-six of them traveling the country.) He used a form of exhibition that has all but disappeared today, called "fourwalling." Instead of booking his film into theaters for a percentage of the box office, he would simply rent the theater outright and take it over for the week or, in smaller markets, for just one or two days. He would pay for all the advertising and promotion, put his own banners and marquees out front, and turn the theater into a midway attraction, complete with lobby curiosities designed to lure customers. But because he was a pariah in Holly-wood, he had to use independent mom-and-pop theaters that weren't part of the big chains like Para-mount and RKO, and he had to fight censorship boards, police forces, judges, clergy, and outraged newspaper editors everywhere he went. (The film was in 400 separate court proceedings during its life.)

Babb portrayed himself as a tireless battler for sex education and public morals, saving young girls from unwanted pregnancies and young boys from the ravages of venereal disease. His critics portrayed him as a huckster with a gimmick. David Friedman, a rising young public-relations executive at Para-mount who gave up a lucrative career to go on the road with Babb, called Babb's promotion "the biggest and best-organized bunko game in American show-business history."

Babb was an expert at creating a kind of mob psychosis that peaked at the moment the projector started to roll. Watching the film today, it's all but impossible to re-create the atmosphere of a capacity audience waiting breathlessly to see things they knew were forbidden and shocking. (They were tit-illated by a lobby card that promised "You actually see the birth of a baby!") It was Babb's peculiar genius that he was able to evoke the emotions of a horror movie using what is actually one of the blandest formulaic stories ever concocted. The main characters in *Mom and Dad* are named Carl, Sarah, Dan, Joan, Dave, Jack, Allen, Mary Lou, Virginia, and Junella. (Junella, the only minority in the film, is the family's black maid, who serves but-termilk pancakes and acts as a confidante to the troubled teenage daughter.) The film was designed, in fact, to portray such a typical and unremarkable Middle American town (Centerville, it's called) that when disaster strikes—in the form of pregnan-cy and the specter of venereal disease—everyone feels that the very bedrock of the American middle class is threatened.

THE WHOLE FIRST HOUR OF THE MOVIE IS DEVOTED to showing how a sweet, pretty young girl like Joan Blake could easily have her life ruined by pregnancy. She goes to a local dance where she's swept off her feet by a handsome and worldly pilot who steals a kiss as they walk outside. They hold hands and make eyes at each other while watching a jitterbug contest, a torch singer, and a teenage acrobatic act—all the usual padding found in exploitation films of the period. The next night, he takes her to a smoky nightclub in his roadster, overwhelms her with sweet talk on a moonlit Lover's Lane, and convinces her that two people as much in love as they are should definitely go all the way. Slow fade as the young lovers descend into the front seat.

Shortly thereafter, the handsome pilot has to leave town on business, but he continues to write to her. When he mentions in one of his letters that it's been four weeks since he left, Joan suddenly becomes concerned. She checks her calendar and is obviously worried. She goes to her mom and asks if she has any "hygiene books," but her mom is flabbergasted by the request. "You're not married yet," says the mother. A short time later, Joan's father notices an article in the newspaper: A young man named Jack Griffith—the pilot who took her virginity—has been killed in a plane crash. Joan drops a dinner plate when she hears the news, goes to her room, tears up the love letter she's just written, and puts her head down on her desk.

At this point, the film would stop entirely and the house lights would come up. Elliot Forbes, an "eminent sexual hygiene commentator," would stride onto the stage and deliver a twenty-minute lecture on the need for openness in sex education, the morality of the times, the biology of the body, and what the community can do to avoid the ruination of its youth.

If anyone had ever checked the credentials of Elliot Forbes, he would have discovered that Forbes was the busiest man in the history of the lecture circuit, appearing seventy-eight times a day in cities scattered from Maine to Oregon. There were, alas, twenty-six Elliot Forbeses, one for each road show, and Babb hired most of them from the ranks of retired or underemployed vaudeville comedians. They knew how to work crowds with a combination of earnestness, humor, and down-home "just folks" patter that would always crescendo the moment they held up two paperback books—one called *Man and Boy*, the other called *Woman and Girl*—and make the following spiel:

"They cannot be obtained on newsstands, or at booksellers, or anywhere else. No, these books are offered exclusively to the patrons of this presentation at a slight charge over the actual costs of printing and distribution. That price: one dollar. One dollar a copy, two dollars for the set. Now think of it—for less than the cost of a carton of cigarettes, you can have a set of these vitally important books to be read in the privacy of your own home, and I believe with all my heart that a set of these books belongs on the bedside table of every home in this great land. They will be offered for sale at this time. Attendants will pass among you in the audience. Simply raise your hand, and please, if possible, give the attendant the exact amount of your purchase. Thank you for your kind attention. In closing, I'd like to wish each of you a very long life, a very happy life, but above all—a very healthy life. Thank you, good night, and God bless you."

Two women in nurse uniforms—supposedly stationed in the theater to take care of people who fainted or had heart attacks—would then pass among the crowd collecting money and distributing the books. The books themselves were rehashes of venereal disease and pregnancy information that could be obtained at any public-health agency. But the Elliot Forbes speech was what is known in the carnival world as a "blowoff," long used in ten-in-one freak shows to hustle additional money from people who had already paid an admission price. And in any good blowoff, there's the constant implication that the "good stuff" is in the attraction you haven't yet paid for—in this case, the book. Elliot Forbes's main job was to sell the books, which frequently augmented the box-office take by as much as 50 percent. In 1957, for example, at a four-week showing of *Mom and Dad* in Baltimore, the box-office gross was $82,000, but 45,000 copies of the books were sold, resulting—after deducting printing and expenses—in a $31,000 additional profit.

Most of the Elliot Forbeses passed into history without credit for their performances, but one, named Wally Nash, was so talented that film showmen still remember his real name. "He was the crudest human being who ever lived," said Friedman, "but God, could he sell books!"

After Elliot Forbes had left the stage and all the money had been collected, the film would resume with our heroine sick to her stomach, sleeping late, and discovering that her clothes no longer fit her. (The word "pregnant" is never used by the actors.) "Mary Lou, I think I'm in trouble," she tells her best friend. After a few scenes of dramatic desperation—including an apparent off-screen suicide attempt—Joan's brother forces her to tell him the truth. Knowing he can't trust their strait-laced

parents, he seeks advice from Carl Blackburn, a kindly teacher who, we know from an earlier sequence, was fired from the high school for teaching sex education and now sells insurance. After a night of agonizing, Blackburn calls on Joan's mother and informs her that "your daughter is going to have a baby."

The mother has been the busybody villainess of our story all along. As the member of a women's club that constantly crusades against public lewdness and drinking—the same club that got the science teacher fired—she believes that sex should never be discussed in the home. Her reaction to the news: "Who was the boy? I'll have him arrested."

"They didn't tell me his name," replies the defrocked teacher. "After all, why blame the boy?"

"But you wouldn't blame such a scandalous thing on an innocent young girl like Joan!" shrieks the hysterical mother.

"No, I wouldn't blame her any more than I would the boy."

"Then who would you blame?"

"I'd blame you, Mrs. Blake, you and every parent who neglects the sacred duty of telling their children the real truth. Why were your children afraid to come to you in their trouble? Why did they have to come to me for advice? Remember this, Mrs. Blake, when your children have to go to someone else for advice, you've fallen down from your job."

"I'll never be able to face the women of my club again!" says the still unrepentant mom. "We'll be ruined."

In the next scene, Joan and Mrs. Blake are riding the train to Boston, where Joan will finish her pregnancy in secret under a doctor's care, but the grim faces of mother and daughter tell us all too plainly that their lives will never be the same.

AT THIS POINT THE MOVIE IS, FOR ALL PRACTICAL purposes, over. There's one point of minor suspense—will Joan be OK? What will she do with the baby?—but very little is made of that. In fact, the entire first ninety minutes has been a setup for three films-within-the-film that everyone will remember long after they've left the theater. If these films had been shown at the beginning, the audience probably would have walked out in disgust, but now everyone has been so massaged with guilt—the future of the race depends on getting this information out!—that they eagerly brace themselves for the graphic medical detail that follows.

With his wife and daughter packed off to Boston, Mr. Blake is suddenly roused out of his blasé attitude and tells Carl Blackburn that he intends to go to the school board and get him rehired. Now more than ever, "They need that class in social hygiene!" Cut to the principal's office, where the teacher is being rehired. Then, in one of the more forced segues in screenwriting history, Blackburn tells the principal, "I was talking with Mrs. Hayworth yesterday. You know, she's the sister of the famous Chicago specialist Dr. Ashley. She tells me he has some wonderful films explaining childbirth. But best of all, she says he's due here for a rest in October!"

"Do you suppose we could get him to talk to a small group like ours?" asks the principal.

"Well, I'll ask her to write to him about it. You never know until you try!"

In the next scene, Blackburn is introducing Dr. John D. Ashley, an obstetrician, to a class of high-school girls. Dr. Ashley has been kind enough to bring along some films made in his hospital. The first one is called *The Facts of Life: An Explanation of Sex Cycles*. An authoritative narrator begins: "Every girl should know the functions of the female body." He continues to explain as charts are revealed, showing the female menstrual cycle, drawings of the genital organs, how ovulation occurs, how spermatazoa impregnate an ovary, time-lapse depictions of the growing fetus, and then suddenly—almost without warning—graphic footage of a live birth!

But scarcely has the umbilical cord been snipped and the audience been told why silver nitrate is used in a newborn's eyes than the second film commences: *Modern American Surgery*, with a subtitle promising that a "famous American Surgeon" will perform a cesarean section on camera. Before you see it, in all its bloody closeup glory, the film assures you that "the Operation was highly successful. Both mother and baby are healthy today." And then, in an operating theater full of white-masked attendants and spectators, we watch as the incision is made ("from pubis to umbilicus"), as layer after layer of the skin and womb are cut open, as water and other fluids spray wildly, and then—as all the observers in the amphitheater stand up—the baby is removed with forceps. The film lingers for the sewing up and a few injections "to relax the mother," followed by an encomium to "one of the great miracles of modern surgery."

But wait! There's more! Two scenes later, the social hygiene teacher welcomes an all-male class, this time with an expert on venereal disease named Dr. Burnell. And now comes the pièce de résistance. The third film-within-the-film is called *Seeing Is Believing*, and it's every teenage boy's nightmare, showing grainy footage of syphilis victims struggling to walk, blinded, horribly scarred, teeth rotting, their bodies oozing with chancres and open sores, and, in one case, a fleeting image of a person whose feet have been eaten away by disease. Throughout the film, there are silent-movie-style caption cards: "Millions learn these facts the hard-way . . . by bitter experience!" "The Price of Ignorance!" "These Pictures Speak the Truth!" "Self-Styled MORALISTS Would Like To Keep These Facts A Secret!!!" "Is The Gamble Worth the Price?" The audience sees crippled and blind crying babies, horrible pox-ridden arms and legs, a festering sore where someone's eye used to be, and the big payoff, introduced by the title card "Doctors and Health Officials Agree—These shocking pictures of infected genital organs will awaken you!" What follows are fully naked bodies, but so bruised and disease-ridden that they're anything but attractive. The film concludes, oddly enough, with images of track and field athletes, healthy young swimmers, and the U.S. Army marching in formation, as though to say "This is what Americans should look like."

The narrative of Joan's story has three more brief scenes, concluding with a doctor coming into a waiting room where the nervous Blake family is pacing and praying, to say "It's all over." Joan has a good chance of recovery. And the baby? In the version I saw, the doctor says the baby has just barely survived—presumably to be adopted by a childless couple—but I've also seen accounts by *Mom and Dad* viewers who claim the baby is stillborn. The fact is, there were dozens of versions of *Mom and Dad*, including some versions that didn't have any of the three graphic films-within-the-film, so that the movie could still play in markets with strict obscenity laws. Babb was not above showing his "cold" version to local authorities and screening the "hot" version in the theater. He also always carried with him a "square-up reel." In cases where he was forced to show the "cold" version, he would sometimes be faced with an angry audience that felt cheated by the absence of what they felt they had been promised by the advertising. To appease them, he would quickly rack an additional reel of what the carnies called "pickles and beaver"—footage of full-frontal nude bodies. Remarkably, it worked! The audience left feeling they had experienced at least a little of the "good stuff."

There's one additional piece of film after the story ends. The final screen image is Kroger Babb himself, sitting at his desk and speaking directly to camera. "And now, friends, you've seen the entire production," he says. "If you agree that these pictures have been bold and shocking enough that you've learned a very worthwhile lesson from them, I wish you'd show the management your appreciation at this time. By your applause."

And, of course, the theater, so prompted, would erupt in applause, thereby cutting down on the possibility of anyone ever asking for his money back. But this brief coda is actually the essence of Babb's shell game. He says "if you agree that . . ." and then includes two reasons to like the movie—that it was shocking, and that it was educational—but speaking as though they're one and the same thing. He was such an astute student of human nature that he knew everyone needed both—you bought the ticket because you wanted to be exposed to the forbidden, but you told yourself and others that you had no choice but to be educated. It was actually a movie that could be marketed with a straight exploitation campaign when it played in grind houses and all-male theaters, or an "educational" campaign that would have entire high schools buying tickets for its students.

MOM AND DAD WAS NOT THE FIRST SEX-HYGIENE film, but it was by far the most successful. When Babb raised $62,000 from investors and filmed *Mom and Dad* in 1944, he was actually exploiting a showman's tradition that had started a full thirty years earlier. Although America had been periodically ravaged by syphilis and gonorrhea throughout the nineteenth century, the subject had never been dealt with on stage or screen until 1913, when Eugene Brieux wrote a play for the New York stage called *Damaged Goods*. In it, a young lawyer gets syphilis from a streetwalker while drunk at his bachelor party. Ignoring the advice of his doctor, he goes ahead and marries his fiancée in order to collect her dowry, thereby infecting his wife and baby. Described by critics as a "preachment" or "medical sermon," it avoided censorship by being sponsored by a medical organization and exploiting a common fear of the time—that the upper classes were in danger of strange diseases brought to America by the hordes of lower-class immigrants. When the play was made into a Mutual film in 1914, it took in $2 million at the box office, a virtually unheard-of amount at the time.

Damaged Goods marked the birth of the sex-hygiene film. A ripoff called *A Victim of Sin* came out almost immediately, and there were at least twenty more films about VD before 1920. But the real birth of what producers would come to call the "clap opera" occured at the end of World War I, when a man named Isaac Silverman purchased two films that the armed services had used to train soldiers about the dangers of venereal disease. *Fit to Fight*, the story of five young men in an army training camp, and *The End of the Road*, the story of two women in trouble, included explicit medical footage showing the ravages of gonorrhea and syphilis, complete with pus-filled open sores. What could be better for a film-hungry public constantly in search of new sensations? Silverman booked the films all over the country, where they played to capacity audiences, including twelve weeks (!) at the Grand Opera House in Brooklyn, New York. But the films also attracted the attention of local morals crusaders, who managed to get them banned in many cities. The Catholic Church, upset by the films' advocacy of "chemical prophylaxis," organized a pamphlet campaign to get them stopped.

And from that time forward, a new kind of film exhibition would arise. Silverman showed his films to "adults only" (no one under sixteen), a phrase that would become code for titillating subject matter, and he also segregated the screenings by gender. Babb would later codify this tradition in every contract he ever signed, specifying that the words "adults only" must be on all advertising and barring any distributor from showing *Mom and Dad* to mixed audiences. Women would be too embarrassed to watch a sex-hygiene film in the company of men, so he would have two women-only screenings per day, one at 2 P.M. and one at 7 P.M. The men wouldn't be allowed to see the film until 9 P.M., and by that time, they were so overwhelmed with curiosity, wanting to know what the women were talking about, that his late-night males-only screenings came to be called "the Thundering Herd."

Back in the twenties, though, Silverman made such a killing that the industry took notice and started churning out a steady stream of melodramas about heedless young people who don't learn about the dangers of sex until it's too late. In 1919 alone, there were eight sex-hygiene films, with names like *Wild Oats* and *The Solitary Sin* (about the evils of masturbation). *The Scarlet Trail* had a typical plot for the time: A doctor heads a sinister medical group that sells fake VD cures. His son is born with syphilis. When the son grows up and gets engaged, he learns of his fate and commits suicide. Even the Warner brothers got into the act, producing a film called *Open Your Eyes*, which showed syphilis rising from the lower class to attack the middle class.

It was the sex-hygiene film, in fact, that contributed greatly to the notorious Production Code that would muzzle Hollywood studios for decades to come. The first motion-picture-censorship law had been passed in Chicago in 1907, and by 1921 seven states had censorship boards, with new ones sprouting all the time. In an effort to head off government control of movies, Hollywood adopted "Thirteen Points or Standards," forbidding such things as the on-screen exploitation of sex, white slavery, nakedness, "illicit love and vice," narcotics use, vulgarity, ridicule of authority, miscegenation, profanity, and disrespect for religion. This list evolved into the "Don'ts and Be Carefuls" of 1927, which specifically added sex hygiene and venereal disease, childbirth scenes, and children's sex organs.

Remarkably, the Production Code Administration eventually issued policy statements saying that the purpose of motion pictures should be pure entertainment, and that education had no place in theaters!

And all of this was consolidated into the Production Code of 1930, after which 98 percent of all movies released were judged and censored by the office headed by Joe Breen.

But there was still that 2 percent of movies made outside the Hollywood system, and they not only defied the Production Code but used it as a sort of manual for subjects that could be exploited. In the twenties and thirties there was a boom in exploitation films dealing with crime, white slavery, and drug addiction. Louis Sonney, an Italian immigrant who was sheriff of Centralia, Washington, became nationally famous when he captured a railroad bandit named Roy Gardner and used his reward money to make a movie called *The Smiling Mail Bandit*, including footage of the real Roy Gardner telling viewers that crime doesn't pay. He took the film on the road, lecturing on the "Dangers of Crime" in theaters, saloons, Elks lodges and, when all else failed, a tent erected on the edge of town. Eventually Sonney and his sons set up Sonney Amusement Enterprises in Los Angeles, where they produced more than 400 exploitation films. At the same time, a woman named Florence Reid hit the road with a film called *Human Wreckage*. She was the widow of Wallace Reid, a film star who had made tabloid headlines in 1922 when it was revealed that he was a morphine addict. After he died, in 1923 (in a padded cell!), she accompanied the film everywhere it went, talking about the dangers of drug addiction and selling her own paperback books. After hitting virtually every city in the country, she made a second film, *Broken Laws*, and started all over again—then a third, *The Road to Ruin*.

The high Brahmans of mainstream Hollywood despised these films, mainly because they feared they would create more government censorship, but in their efforts to run the exploitation producers out of business, they had to argue against what were always presented as educational films. Remarkably, the Production Code Administration eventually issued policy statements saying that the purpose of motion pictures should be pure entertainment, and that education had no place in theaters! Perhaps this is the main reason the Louis Sonneys, Florence Reids, and Kroger Babbs of the world could so easily make the Production Code look idiotic—and continue their booming business.

Eventually the carnies on the exploitation circuit—guys with flashy names like S. S. "Steamship" Millard and Howard "Pappy" Golden—banded into a sort of informal trade association. Calling themselves the Forty Thieves, they essentially became a vertically integrated outlaw studio, using something called the "states rights" system. In the 1890s, licensing for the Kinetoscope and Vitascope had resulted in the United States being carved up into thirty-two exhibition territories, and this system of subdistribution lasted well into the 1980s. Hence, a producer could sell his film territory by territory, allowing the local "thief" to market it any way he knew how. He could even re-edit the film, shoot additional scenes, design his own ad campaign, and create any kind of come-on. (Lobby displays of drug paraphernalia were common in the thirties.) The result was a boom in exploitation, especially in the thirties, when nudist-camp films first appeared, along with films about white slavery, drugs, and always-popular sex-hygiene stories. In 1936, President Roosevelt's Surgeon General, Thomas Parran, initiated a public information campaign to stamp out VD, making Hollywood look more and more silly as it tried to ban the films. The studios were especially incensed in 1938, when a film called *Sex Madness* showed up as the second feature with Shirley Temple in *Wee Willie Winkie*, but by the following year the government had filed an antitrust suit against the studios—the famous Paramount case—and Hollywood pretty much abandoned its crusade against the exploitation films for fear of looking like monopolists.

One of the most foolproof gimmicks in the business was live-birth footage. No one knows exactly where the footage came from—some say medical-training films, some say it was paid for overseas—but within the world of the Forty Thieves, it was constantly recycled into movie after movie so that posters could be used in advertising campaigns. "See a baby born before your very eyes!" was the come-on for *The Birth of a Baby* (1938), which startled its producers by occasionally getting good reviews. "The beginning of life itself before your eyes" was the tagline for *We Want a Child*. Perhaps the ultimate live-birth promotion was for the film *No Greater Sin* (1941), which advertised "See the actual birth of triplets."

By the time Kroger Babb came along, the formula for the sex-hygiene movie was so well established that all he did was incorporate every single element of every sex hygiene movie in history into a single film. But in search of even bigger profits, he changed the rules slightly. Many of the old sex-hygiene films had played in grind houses or marginal theaters—or even bars or restaurants. He wanted to break through to the biggest theaters in the country. Perhaps the most revolutionary thing he did was to give his film such a bland and praiseworthy title: *Mom and Dad*. Who could object to a movie called *Mom and Dad*? This wasn't a movie about crazed sex maniacs or loose women or pregnant girls or the vice rackets. It was a movie about the education of all the moms and dads in the world, and, in fact, he wanted every mom and every dad to see it. His principal weapon when he came under attack was the very ordinariness of his story. When the opening titles come up and the lush strings of the orchestra play the *Mom and Dad* theme music, the first thing you see is a type crawl that reads as follows:

"Foreword. Our story is a simple one! It happens every night, somewhere. It is the story of Joan Blake—a sweet, innocent girl growing up in this fast-moving age. The temptations which she faces are as old as Time itself. But Joan is no better fortified against them than was the girl of yesteryear, because her mother—like many mothers—still thinks that ignorance is a guarantee of virtue. 'IGNORANCE IS A SIN—KNOWLEDGE IS POWER.' In this modern world, Youth is entitled to a knowledge of Hygiene—a complete understanding of the Facts of Life. Boys and girls of today aren't bad! But millions of them are becoming sexual delinquents and the victims of venereal disease, simply because they do not know the Full Truth about these subjects. This problem is a challenge to every Mom and Dad. If our story points the way to a commonsense solution . . . and saves one girl from unwed motherhood . . . or one boy from the ravages of social disease . . . it will have been well told! THE PRODUCERS."

Every road-show film included some version of this type crawl, called "the square-up" (not to be confused with the square-up reel), and it had two functions: to lessen the chance of obscenity prosecutions and to make the film palatable to women. In fact, women tended to like the film more than men, who were often a little disappointed by the lack of sex and nudity.

HOWARD W. BABB HAD GOTTEN THE NICKNAME Kroger from the name of the grocery store where he worked growing up in Lees Creek, Ohio. Born in 1906, he was a sportswriter, a newspaper reporter, an ad manager, and, by his late twenties, publicity manager for the Chakeres-Warners theater chain, where he distinguished himself with publicity stunts such as having a man buried alive in front of a theater. He got the exploitation road show bug when he hooked up with an outfit called Cox and Underwood, who were peddling an aging sex-hygiene film called *Dust to Dust* that was actually a 1934 film called *High School Girl* with a live-birth reel slapped onto the end. (Howard Russell Cox of Cox and Underwood, lectured at each performance on the "Evils of Sex Intolerance.") Proving

that he was born to be in the business, Babb must have stored this plot away in his mind for future use in *Mom and Dad*. (The Forty Thieves frequently quarreled over territories, but oddly enough, they never sued for copyright infringement. Of course, many of them were carnival men who regarded all cons as ancient and passed down from generation to generation, but they may also have simply sold stories in the same way they occasionally sold sideshow acts.)

Anxious to go out on his own, Babb got twenty investors to put up the money he needed to make *Mom and Dad*. The script was written by Mildred Horn, who would later become his wife, and who would also write the books he peddled, *Man and Woman* and *Boy and Girl*. To direct he hired William "One Shot" Beaudine (so named because he never did a second take), who dated back to the "Bowery Boys" serials and had made more than 200 B movies. Three of the actors were veterans of exploitation films, though they're not really known to the public: Hardie Albright as the sympathetic teacher Carl Blackburn, Francis Ford as the country doctor, and John Hamilton as Mr. Burnell, the guest speaker at the boys' hygiene class. Babb rented the Monogram Studios in Los Angeles and made the whole film in six days.

Babb was not only prepared for the inevitable censorship battles he would face—he egged them on. He stirred up the Catholics at every opportunity, capitalizing on the church's "C" rating (for "condemned") of his film. He wrote fake letters to the editor in advance of the film's arrival in town, hoping there would be controversy. His most successful letter was supposedly written by the anonymous mayor of a small town. The "mayor" explained that he had opposed the showing of *Mom and Dad* in his town, too, but then the 17-year-old daughter of a local churchgoing couple found herself "in trouble." She saw *Mom and Dad* with a friend, and as a result had the courage to tell her parents about her predicament. They were shocked but forgave her. The girl gave birth to a healthy boy, which was adopted by a childless couple. The girl then completed high school and got engaged to a fine young man. The "mayor" went on to thank Babb for having the courage "to tell young people what their parents didn't." And the letter ends: "P.S. That girl was my daughter."

Babb's company, Hygienic Productions, sent out an advance man to place letters such as this, buy advertising, do mailings, and hold screenings for town fathers and religious leaders. (If the town's leaders liked the film, a "soft" campaign would be used. If they didn't like it, a "hard" campaign— advertising it as "the movie self-styled moralists don't want you to see"—would be used. Both campaigns worked.) The advance man would be followed a week later by a crew of four—including "Elliot Forbes" and two "nurses"—to actually manage the film during its run. The crews would stay on the road for twenty weeks at a time. Babb even had one all-black crew for black theaters, led by Olympic champion Jesse Owens, who substituted for Elliot Forbes.

As the *Mom and Dad* exploitation scheme evolved over time, it attracted imitators. Universal

Pictures was so impressed with Babb's box office— he was becoming a very wealthy man—that in 1948 they tried to match *Mom and Dad* with their own sex-hygiene picture, *The Story of Bob and Sally*—but of course the Production Code wouldn't approve it. Universal sold it instead to one of the Forty Thieves, Gidney Talley of Dallas, who road-showed it with the ad campaign "Just How Much Truth Can You Stand?" using "Roger T. Miles" as his guest lecturer. Chicago showman Floyd Lewis produced *Street Corner* the same year, about a botched abortion, pretty much following the *Mom and Dad* model. *Because of Eve* also followed the Babb paradigm, using gender segregation, attendant nurses, and a book pitch. Between 1944 and 1949, there were ten new sex-hygiene films released, all featuring nurses and lecturers, but *Mom and Dad* was by far the most successful. In its first five years, it was seen by twenty million people. By 1950 there were so many sex-hygiene road shows that they were starting to get in each other's way, and after a town was "scorched" by a promotional campaign, it would be spoiled for any film arriving later. So in 1950, four of the films—*Mom and Dad*, *Street Corner*, *Because of Eve* and *The Story of Bob and Sally*—banded together to form Modern Film Distributors, carving out territories and agreeing not to steal markets.

But the days of the sex-hygiene film were already numbered. The irony of the sex-hygiene explosion, which steadily declined through the fifties, is that it depicted a world that never existed in the first place. The communities depicted in *Mom* and Dad, *Hometown Girl*, and *The Miracle of Life* had more in common with turn-of-the-century towns that had passed away with the Roaring Twenties. As the Kinsey Reports proved in 1948, premarital and extramarital sex was not the exception but the rule. Millions of young men had already been exposed to venereal-disease films during World War II, and millions of women had been touched by out-of-wedlock births, abortions, or abandonment. Perhaps the films succeeded because they gave a comforting message to panicked moms and dads, promising that, with just a little more education, these things could be eradicated. But many of the problems had already been eradicated, first by penicillin, which had made new syphilis cases virtually unheard of by the time *Mom and Dad* came out, then by more sophisticated forms of birth control that gave young girls more control of their sex lives. The biggest irony of all is that public schools actually did follow Kroger Babb's example and started showing sex-education films not unlike *The Facts of Life: An Explanation of Sex Cycles*. And once the information was available in schools, Babb was out of business.

The immediate cause of Babb's declining box office, though, was the burlesque film, which showed up in the early fifties. Crudely made movies filmed in aging burlesque halls, featuring strippers and comedians doing what they'd been doing for decades, these offered titillation and a hint of nudity without any of the scarifying disease subtext. By the time the second wave of nudist films came along, in 1959, it was all over for sex hygiene.

But none of them had the peculiar combination of timing, titillation, and horror that *Mom and Dad* contained. Even as the courts were loosening restrictions on obscenity—*Mom and Dad* finally played New York in 1956 when the Appellate Division of the State Supreme Court ruled that human birth was not "indecent"—Babb went off on tangents, such as a pyramid scheme called "The Idea Factory," a live horror show called *Dr. Hassam's Chasm of Spasms*, and an Ingmar Bergman film called *Summer with Monika* that he retitled *Monika, the Story of a Bad Girl*. He never showed much interest in producing nudie films—after all, if it's already on the screen, there's nothing to promote— and he seemed lost in the changing sixties. His last gasp before retiring in the seventies was *Walk the Walk*, a 1970 film starring Bernie Hamilton as a young black theological student battling both heroin addiction and alcoholism.

Kroger Babb died on January 28, 1980, in Palm Springs, California, at the age of seventy-three. And now, friends, you've seen the entire production. If you have been shocked and educated, please show the management your appreciation. By your applause.

FOR FURTHER DISTURBANCE

The first exploitation movie is generally believed to be DAMAGED GOODS (1914), a sex-hygiene film starring George Dupont, based on the popular 1913 Broadway production of Eugene Brieux's preachy play. It was widely copied before World War I, notably in A VICTIM OF SIN (1913), but was popular enough to be rereleased in 1917. The identical plot was used in Edgar Ulmer's DAMAGED LIVES (1937).

After the war, the sex-scare film was more popular than ever, beginning with THE SPREADING EVIL (1918) and THE SCARLET TRAIL (1918), in which Ezra Grafton heads a syndicate of quack doctors selling VD cures, and continuing with OPEN YOUR EYES (1919), THE SOLITARY SIN (1919), and WILD OATS (1919). The most successful hygiene films of this period were three clinical armed-service training films—FIT TO FIGHT (1919), FIT TO WIN (1919), and THE END OF THE ROAD (1919)—which a showman named Isaac Silverman used to develop the prototype for the sex-hygiene road shows, segregating screenings by sex, barring admission to children under sixteen, and ballyhooing "actual views of diseased men and women with the ugly sores open to view." The narrative sex films and the clinical medical documentaries were com-bined for the first time in THE NAKED TRUTH (1924), which took footage from *The Solitary Sin* and mixed it with clinical reels showing the effects of VD.

The exploitation road show originated in the twenties, and the first one is believed to have been Louis Sonney's THE SMILING MAIL BANDIT, which included former sheriff Sonney's lecture on "The Dangers of Crime" and his first-person retelling of how he personally arrested railroad robber Roy Gardner, who appears in the film.

Florence Reid followed Sonney's pattern with HUMAN WRECKAGE (1923), a film she made after her husband, actor Wallace Reid, died of morphine addiction in an asylum. She accompanied the film and lectured on the dangers of drug addiction, eventually producing two sequels, BROKEN LAWS (1924) and THE ROAD TO RUIN (1934).

S. S. "Steamship" Millard, one of the independent road-show producers and distributors known as the "Forty Thieves," produced early versions of *Mom and Dad* in the form of PITFALLS OF PASSION (1927) and IS YOUR DAUGHTER SAFE? (1927).

The first nudist camp film appeared in the thirties, with ELYSIA (1934), screened for men only. These films tended to be more imaginative than their cousins in the early sixties, the "nudie-cuties." TEN DAYS IN A NUDIST CAMP (1935) was a fairly straightforward documentary, while NUDIST LAND (1937) featured documentary footage of Africa, Bali, and Samoa. RED HEADED BABY (1931), on the other hand, was a pastiche of every kind of nudity, from strip poker games to artist's models to childbirth to straight nudist-camp footage.

Dwain Esper, one of the most idiosyncratic of the early road-show producers, trafficked in drug addiction, venereal disease, and insanity with films like NARCOTIC (1933), THE SEVENTH COMMANDMENT (1933), the cult classic MANIAC (1934), MODERN MOTHERHOOD (1934), HOW TO UNDRESS IN FRONT OF YOUR HUSBAND (1937), and MARIHUANA (1936), which was an anti-dope film financed by a Los Angeles church that he recycled with an exploitation campaign, retitling it *Reefer Madness*. In one of his most notorious

stunts, he accompanied *Reefer Madness* with the mummified remains of outlaw Elmer McCurdy, claiming he was a victim of drug use.

Sex-drenched vice-racket pictures began in the twenties with RED LIGHTS (1923), but flourished a decade later in the wake of Hedy Lamarr's nude appearance in ECSTASY (1932). Among the moneymakers were SEX MANIAC (1934), GAMBLING WITH SOULS (1936), SMASHING THE VICE TRUST (1937), SLAVES IN BONDAGE (1937), THE WAGES OF SIN (1938), and ESCORT GIRL (1941). CHILD BRIDE (1939) is an oddity that would probably be illegal today, because it used a minor female in nude sexual situations.

Notable "clap operas" that paved the way for *Mom and Dad* were UNWELCOME CHILDREN (1926) and HIGH SCHOOL GIRL (1934), also known as *Dust to Dust*, which Howard W. "Kroger" Babb would steal almost scene for scene. The first live-birth film was THE BIRTH OF A BABY (1938). It was copied by NO GREATER SIN (1941), and live-birth footage was inserted into some of the older sex-hygiene films after closeup obstetrics were shown to be such a crowd magnet.

After the success of *Mom and Dad*, Universal Pictures tried to match it with THE STORY OF BOB AND SALLY (1948), but the Hays Office wouldn't approve it, so they sold it to Texas states-rights distributor Gidney Talley, who road-showed it for years. STREET CORNER (1948) was another movie about an out-of-wedlock pregnancy that closely parallels the *Mom and Dad* plot and was promoted by Floyd Lewis out of Chicago. BECAUSE OF EVE

(1948), which David Friedman promoted in New England, had full-frontal nudity for the first time (but the nudes were riddled with venereal disease). Other road-show competitors to *Mom and Dad* included Canadian import SINS OF THE FATHERS (1948), the all black FEELING ALL RIGHT (1948), HOMETOWN GIRL (1948), TEST TUBE BABIES (1948), the dubbed German film STREET ACQUAINTANCE (1949), MIRACLE OF LIFE (1949), MATED (1952), and CHILDREN OF LOVE (1953).

Kroger Babb never again equaled the success of *Mom and Dad*, but he kept trying, with PRINCE OF PEACE (1949), also called *The Lawton Story*, a documentary about the Lawton, Oklahoma, Passion Play; ONE TOO MANY (1950), an antialcohol morality tale starring Ruth Warrick and Lyle Talbot; and WHY MEN LEAVE HOME (1951), a "women only" film about preserving your marriage, complete with beauty-hint books for sale. (Sometimes it was called *Secrets of Beauty*.) THE BEST IS YET TO COME was his cancer-scare film, and SHE SHOULDA SAID NO (1949) was an antidrug film starring Lila Leeds, who had been arrested for drug possession, along with Robert Mitchum. (It was retitled *Wild Weed* and *The Devil's Weed*.) In 1953, he tried to cash in on anti-Communist hysteria with HALF-WAY TO HELL, then bought the U.S. rights to Ingmar Bergman's SUMMER WITH MONIKA (1953) and retitled it *Monika, the Story of a Bad Girl*. Two of his strangest promotions were UNCLE TOM'S CABIN— he bought a 1928 silent film and put a soundtrack on it—and KARAMOJA (1954), a documentary about an African tribe that drinks blood and urine.

In the fifties, the sex-hygiene genre was steadily in decline, but there was a burst of new childbirth films from Europe, including France's CHILDREN OF LOVE (1953), Denmark's WE WANT A CHILD (1954), and Italy's THE MOST WONDERFUL MOMENT (1957). THE CASE OF DR. LAURENT (1957) was a French film with Jean Gabin that was road-showed in the states under the title *Wages of Sin*.

Kroger Babb's last film was WALK THE WALK (1970), starring Bernie Hamilton in a combination of three exploitation themes: drugs, alcohol, and black pride—a full year before SHAFT.

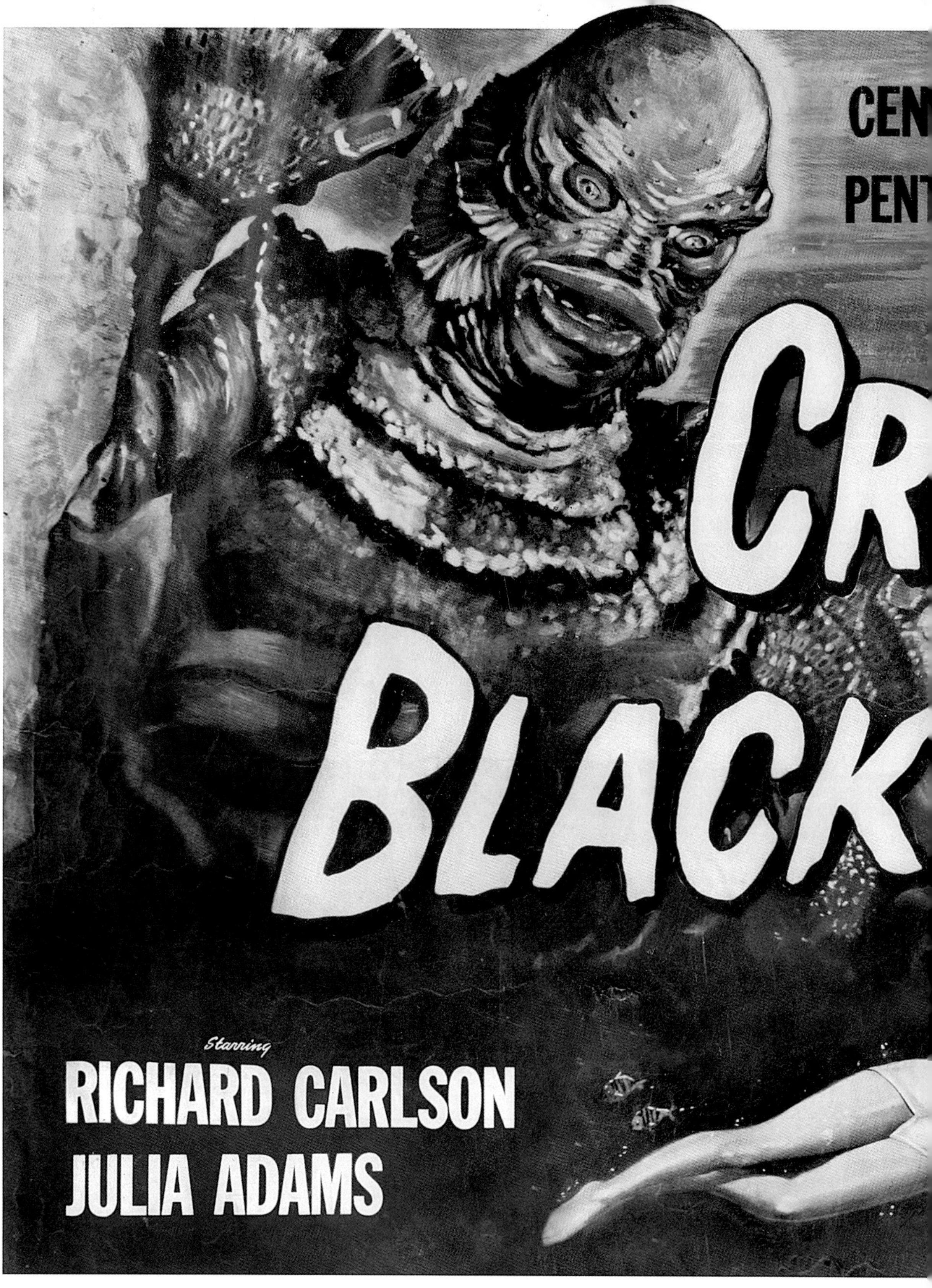
CEN
PENT
CR
BLACK
Starring
RICHARD CARLSON
JULIA ADAMS

RIES OF PASSION
P IN HIS SAVAGE HEART!

EATURE FROM THE LAGOON

AMAZING!
STARTLING!
SHOCKING!

IT'S THE CLASSIC MONSTERLAND PLOT AND THE OLDEST FORMULA IN THE WORLD:
A MISUNDERSTOOD CREATURE
AND
A BEAUTIFUL GIRL
HAVE A PSYCHIC CONNECTION
VERGING ON LOVE.

IT'S AT LEAST AS OLD AS *KING KONG*, BUT THE 1954 version that became a surprise hit for Universal-International was destined to be the ultimate fantasy for two generations of American teenage boys. *Creature from the Black Lagoon* wasn't the kind of movie that stirs the masses. Its influence was slow and subtle. Because it was only seventy-nine minutes long, the perfect length for TV syndication, it was a staple of late-night horror shows and afternoon "creature features" well into the eighties, and it was just all-American enough to escape the attention of the concerned moms who probably couldn't figure out why their sons were so obsessed with it.

What was the main attraction? Was it the Gill Man, the king of all rubber-suit monsters, who survives from the Devonian Age in an Amazon lagoon and preys on a ship full of scientific investigators? Or was it Julia Adams, the only female in the movie, whose curvy, leggy body and perky breasts are poured into a white, French-cut, crotch-enhancing swimsuit as she plunges into the lagoon, Esther Williams–style, and performs her seductive underwater dance?

It was both, of course. The one sequence that sticks in the mind long after the details of the movie are forgotten shows the gill-faced creature swimming below the back-stroking fantasy woman, studying her, following her, yet never approaching as she performs her underwater spins and turns. The monster may or may not be falling in love—the movie is short on exposition in this department—but the fourteen-year-old boys in the audience definitely are. It doesn't take a master psychologist to see how a pubescent boy, struggling with feelings of being ugly, unloved, and half-formed, would not only identify with the creature (who has acne-like protuberances on his face) but imagine a girl just like Julia Adams, who would finally come to rescue him from the lonely black lagoon called his room. This masterfully directed underwater sequence would later be copied by Steven Spielberg, almost shot for shot, in the opening sequence of *Jaws*—but in that case the creature obviously has lunch, not love, on his mind. The beautiful thing about the original is that we somehow sense, in spite of the ominous music, that the girl is safe and in fact belongs here instead of in the arms of the man she thinks she loves, the handsome but boring Richard Carlson.

Of course, like so many stories in movie history, the creators had only a vague idea of what a powerful property they had. Unlike *Frankenstein* and *Dracula*, *Creature from the Black Lagoon* had no literary pedigree. It was the result of a cocktail-party conversation at Orson Welles's house. One of the guests was a South American director who told a story about prehistoric fish-men living in the Amazon who would appear once a year to capture a village maiden. B-movie producer William Alland was intrigued by the tale and told it to screenwriter Maurice Zimm, who was hired to write a treatment called *The Sea Monster*. Four rewrites later—after Leo Lieberman, Arthur Ross, and Harry Essex all struggled with it, trying to come up with what Alland wanted—a shooting script emerged called *Black Lagoon*. The lagoon was, in fact, about the only thing that set the movie apart from other lovesick monster and science-fiction–miracle plots, with the writers borrowing liberally from *King Kong*, Sir Arthur Conan Doyle's *The Lost World*, and H. P. Lovecraft's mythical town of Innsmouth from the story "The Shadow over Innsmouth," which was full of brackish half-amphibians, half-humans who wore high collars so that no one could see the gills protruding from their necks.

The big selling point, when Alland got *Creature* approved for production at Universal's B-movie mill, was that the film would be shot in 3-D. It is, in fact, probably the finest 3-D movie ever made, thanks to a single-strip process that had been recently perfected to get rid of the headachy blurred effects of the early entries in the 3-D craze. The film was written at the height of the 3-D boom—a total of sixty-nine 3-D features were made in 1953 and 1954, and Alland had just had a minor 3-D hit with *It Came from Outer Space*—but by the time *Creature* was released in theaters, 3-D was all but over. Only a handful of people have seen it in its original format—a format that explains otherwise strange moments in the film, such as when the Gill Man seems to be walking toward the camera or waving his arms in a menacing manner for no apparent reason.

HE CAST WAS DRAWN FROM AVAILABLE CONTRACT players on the Universal backlot, but the intended star of the movie was to be the creature itself. Bud Westmore, the makeup chief for Universal-International, who had created hundreds of science-fiction and horror images, spent eight-and-a-half months researching the Gill Man and used 200 pounds of foam rubber designing the gills, fins, scales, and claws to get a half-man, half-fish look. Millicent Patrick, famous as the first female animator at Disney, did the original sketches from which Westmore worked. And Jack Arnold, the same director who had scored with *It Came from Outer Space*, contributed his own idea: He wanted the creature to look like the Academy Award "Oscar" statue, but with gills and fins.

Julia Adams was not particularly happy about being cast in the film. She was twenty-eight years old and getting desperate to escape the low-budget world. An Arkansas beauty who moved to California to become a movie star, she got her break in 1949 with a small role in *Red Hot and Blue*, but was quickly consigned to a series of quickie B westerns. Her claim to fame was having the best legs in Hollywood, but because she'd appeared exclusively in westerns, they had never been seen on screen. (The daring white swimsuit would change all that.) *Creature* would turn out to be the most memorable role of her career. After *Slaughter on Tenth Avenue*, in 1957, she semiretired to raise two sons, although she never stopped acting and later had a recurring role on *Murder, She Wrote* (as Eve Simpson) for five seasons in the nineties.

Her leading man was technically Richard Carlson, a forty-two-year-old journeyman whose career had been interrupted by World War II but who had used the 3-D craze to mount a minor comeback, first in *The Maze* and then *It Came from Outer Space*. But her real leading man was, of course, the Gill Man, and the actor in the rubber suit was considered so unimportant that he was more or less hired on impulse. His name is Ben Chapman, although he's not listed in the credits and for years nobody knew who he was. He was a twenty-five-year-old stunt man and wrangler, a roustabout from Tahiti who had appeared in some Polynesian shows as a singer and dancer and now lived in Malibu, where he went diving every day and worked as a bartender at a hangout frequented by Peter Lawford, Rod Taylor, and Frank Sinatra. One day he happened to be in the Universal casting office when they were looking for someone athletic to deal with the heavy rubber suit. "It could have been anybody," he would admit in later years.

Meanwhile, director Jack Arnold was scouting suitable locations for the underwater sequences and ended up at a water-amusement park called Wakulla Springs, near Tallahassee, Florida. His guide for the day was a personable twenty-one-year-old ex–Air Force swimmer named Ricou Browning, who had appeared in a lot of newsreels featuring divers and swimmers. Arnold pressed Browning into service, asking him to swim in front of the camera so he could check the perspective. Two weeks later, he was hired to play the creature in the underwater sequences. As a result, there were actually two actors playing the Gill Man, both uncredited, but in later years, when *Creature* became a cult film, it was Browning who attended fan conventions and signed autographs. Chapman happened to see a publicity photograph from the movie that had been signed by Browning, and he became enraged, because he remembered the picture and knew it was himself in the suit. So after thirty-five years, he set about letting the world know that he was the real creature, because he appeared in all the land sequences, which make up the bulk of the movie. "Sign your own picture," he told Browning, "don't sign mine."

In reality, it doesn't much matter who played the Gill Man, because the costume itself has one of the most inexpressive monster faces ever created. (There's only so much acting you can do with your eyes.) Arnold put ten-pound weights in the feet of the costume so that Chapman would be forced to walk slowly and ponderously, as though he's not quite comfortable on land, and the original underwater suit was so clumsy that Browning had to insist on several design changes just so he could propel himself through the water. It's true that all the surviving publicity photos have Chapman inside the rubber suit, but it's also true that Browning's expert swimming is what gives the movie its poignancy. The suit had no oxygen tank, so Browning had to hold his breath for up to five minutes at a time to get the major swimming shots. Just as the creature looks like an ungainly monster on the surface, he looks like a graceful, awe-inspiring part of nature when he's in his underwater element.

IN LATER YEARS, *CREATURE FROM THE BLACK Lagoon* would be lampooned mercilessly, with its fish-head gill creature being "borrowed" for horror parodies, and it's still reviled today by special-effects men who have turned "rubber suit" into a term of contempt. But it's not quite fair to condemn a creature for being ill-formed when it was intended to be half-human in the first place. By fifties standards, it was certainly real enough. The more ridiculous choices involve the early scenes, where we see only the creature's scaly hand, always reinforced by the three-note "Gill Man Scary Theme." (Several Universal composers contributed sequences to the film, including Henry Mancini, and they were all required to incorporate the three-note theme.) The very first scene, in which an identical hand is dug out of a fossil site, is downright goofy, and the ensuing conference of scientists—a staple of fifties movies, which still believed in "explaining" the science—has the hand displayed on an examination table like a piece of flea-market sculpture. (They could have at least removed a couple of fingers to make it seem more likely to have survived for 150 million years.) With everyone staring at the silly gill hand, one of the scientists pronounces, in true fifties style, "We can be sure of one thing: Whatever it was, it was very powerful!"

As if to reinforce this rather doubtful scientific conclusion, the next scene shows a hapless extra, left to guard the archeology camp, getting beaten to death by the creature, which is still revealed only by some closeup shots of its hand and arm. This murder seems unmotivated, although you could say that the archeologists had disturbed the creature's ancient burial ground, I suppose. But by making the creature's first act a senseless killing, the movie loses the moral ambiguity of *King Kong*, in which the creature becomes violent only when provoked by man. When the expedition arrives a short time later, the ponderous native captain makes a speech about this jungle, where everything has been unchanged since time began, and where centipedes are a foot long, rats are as big as sheep, and nine-foot-long catfish dine on humans. "Like everything in this jungle," says the captain, "all

THE MONSTER MAY OR MAY NOT
BE FALLING IN LOVE ...
BUT THE FOURTEEN-YEAR-OLD BOYS IN THE AUDIENCE DEFINITELY ARE.

killers." Shortly thereafter, Julia Adams bounces around the camp in lust-inspiring short shorts long enough for the now clichéd claw to come within inches of her leg. It's only a matter of time, the movie seems to be telling us, until the creature will kill again.

With that, the expedition ventures forward on the creaky barge *Rita* toward the mysterious Black Lagoon, where no one has ever come out alive, to find out if the rest of the fossilized creature could have washed downriver. The fishing expedition is overlaid with a love triangle between Carlson, the dedicated scientist in love with Adams, and the publicity-hungry killer capitalist funding the trip, played by Richard Denning. Denning and Adams have an ill-defined history implying that, as his former assistant, she has often rebuffed his sexual harassment, and now Denning tends to fondle his spear gun every time he sees the loving couple embrace or make sappy moon faces at each other. (Critics looking for symbolism could certainly say that Denning loves his spear gun entirely too much. He grabs it at every opportunity and uses it to solve every problem.)

Underwater photography is usually the most boring, slow-moving part of any movie, but Arnold's direction of the diving sequences as these two men venture down to search the lagoon are always crisp, fast-moving, and easy to follow. As soon as the creature appears, of course, Denning wants to kill it and take it home as a trophy while Carlson wants to preserve it for science. After the Gill Man is wounded by Denning's spear gun, the creature has

no alternative but to systematically eliminate the supporting players and protect his turf. But the creature's violence actually begins earlier, after a spent cigarette is absentmindedly tossed onto the surface of the pristine lagoon. This one image has led to a lot of claims that the movie is actually an ecology tract in which the monster is nature itself revolting against the depredations of man. But ecology, everyone agrees, was not on Jack Arnold's mind in 1954, and if anything, it was just another way to ruffle the lagoon water and create suspense.

It's easier just to assume that painfully wounding a Gill Man with a spear gun will make the Gill Man turn nasty. And he does, taking his revenge on crew members and eventually—after he's shot, drugged, beaten, netted, caged, and set on fire—building a crude dam at the entrance to the lagoon so the interlopers can't escape. But does he do it out of love or anger? When he finally gets his hands on Julia Adams—we knew it was inevitable—he takes her to his secret grotto and lays her body on some kind of rock altar. Carlson arrives in time to save her—Denning has, of course, gone on to his just rewards—but is armed only with a knife, and it's left for two supporting players who appear out of nowhere to pelt the creature with gunfire until he staggers into the water and swims away. What's odd about the last scene is that there's no moment in which we see what the monster's intentions are. He doesn't brush her hair away from her face or do anything except steal her, carry her, and dump her on a rock. (During filming, Chapman actually bashed Adams's head so hard that she missed several days

Ben Chapman, as the Gill Man, carrying an unconscious Julia Adams.

with a concussion.) In other words, we don't know any more about him than we did when he killed the guy in the camp in his first big scene. Then again, maybe a fourteen-year-old boy who suddenly had Julia Adams in his arms wouldn't have known what to do either.

Though they couldn't have known it at the time, *Creature from the Black Lagoon* would be the most enduring film of almost everyone who worked on it. Ricou Browning, the uncredited swimmer, was the sole exception. After becoming an underwater director on the hit series *Sea Hunt*, he co-authored a screenplay about a pet dolphin with his brother-in-law, and that project eventually became *Flipper*. After two *Flipper* features and a four-year *Flipper* TV series, he tried to score again with *Salty*, a feature about a sea lion, but lightning didn't strike twice. Meanwhile, he became a respected television director, especially on projects involving water and animals, and is still pitching concepts today.

Richard Carlson scored the lead in a series called *I Led Three Lives* and eventually became a director himself while continuing to take guest-starring roles on television. His last film as a director was *Kid Rodeo* in 1965, and his last acting appearance was on an episode of *Cannon* in 1973. He died in 1977 at the age of sixty-five.

Jack Arnold would continue to churn out B classics in the fifties, and was called "one of the most beloved B-movie directors in the history of Hollywood" by critic Bruce Elder. He nevertheless had long periods of not being able to find a job, so he filled in with episodic TV work, directing episodes of *Rawhide*, *Perry Mason*, *Wonder Woman*, *The Bionic Woman* and *It Takes a Thief*. His greatest achievement in TV, though, came when he briefly served as an executive at CBS, where he rescued a troubled show called *Gilligan's Island* from oblivion, became its producer, and directed most of the episodes. It's the only thing he did that's more famous than *Creature from the Black Lagoon*.

The movie itself would go in and out of fashion over the years, with critics uncertain whether to call it a camp classic or a genuine work of imaginative science fiction. It was licensed as one of the most popular pinball machines ever sold. Its poster—"Not since the beginning of time has the world beheld terror like this!"—became a prized collector's item. There were two sequels, but neither was as popular as the original. And Julia Adams's swimsuit and short shorts continued to be the means by which millions of boys were initiated into sexuality. But even that was not entirely what it seemed. The famous underwater sequence features brief footage of Julia Adams doing the backstroke, but as soon as the point of view switches to the creature, all the swimming is performed by stunt double Ginger Stanley. No wonder the monster was confused.

FOR FURTHER DISTURBANCE

The sequels to *Creature from the Black Lagoon* didn't really measure up to the original. REVENGE OF THE CREATURE (1955), also directed by Jack Arnold, is set in a Marineworld-style Florida amusement park where John Agar is an animal behaviorist studying the Gill Man. Lori Nelson replaces Julia Adams as his ichthyologist assistant and love interest. The creature escapes, of course, killing aquarium workers and kidnapping Nelson, resulting in a wild chase through Florida rivers, the creature's abduction of Nelson, and a finale in which the Gill Man is once again shot and apparently killed—but somehow he manages to stagger into the water again and dive deep. It's best-known for featuring Clint Eastwood as the idiot lab assistant. Ricou Browning reprised his role as the swimming creature, but Tom Hennesy played the Gill Man on land, notably in the scene in which he's chained to the floor and gouged with cattle prods, and another in which the creature flips a car.

In the final installment, THE CREATURE WALKS AMONG US (1956), Jeff Morrow plays a surgeon who leads an expedition to capture the Gill Man. Rex Reason plays the scientist, Gregg Palmer the diving expert, and Leigh Snowden the creature bait as Morrow's beautiful wife. After having drugs shot into his body, the Gill Man is pulled aboard the expedition yacht, but his scales and gills have been destroyed by kerosene flames. Morrow saves his life with an emergency tracheotomy that allows him to breathe on land, but the Gill Man is not too happy about it. While the beast is penned up in a stockade surrounded by an electrical fence, Morrow and Reason get into a love-triangle fight over Snowden, and the jealous Morrow ends up pistol-whipping Reason until he's dead. He drags the body to the creature's quarters, shoots a bullet into the Gill Man, and cries for help, trying to make it look like the monster has killed Reason. Wounded and furious, the creature tears down the fence, goes after Morrow, kills him, then disappears into the Pacific. Directed by John Sherwood, this lamest of the three movies used Ricou Browning as the Gill Man in some of the scenes, but Browning quit after filming started and was replaced by Don Megowan, who's a different size.

Jack Arnold was one of the most prolific directors of the forties and fifties, having started in film as an actor in 1937 with WE'RE ON THE JURY. *Creature* was his breakthrough film, but among his other notable features were IT CAME FROM OUTER SPACE (1953), THIS ISLAND EARTH (1955), THE INCREDIBLE SHRINKING MAN (1957), the classic teen exploitation film HIGH SCHOOL CONFIDENTIAL (1958) with Mamie Van Doren, and THE MOUSE THAT ROARED (1959), a British satirical comedy with Peter Sellers. He became Bob Hope's director of choice in the early sixties, notably in BACHELOR IN PARADISE (1961) and A GLOBAL

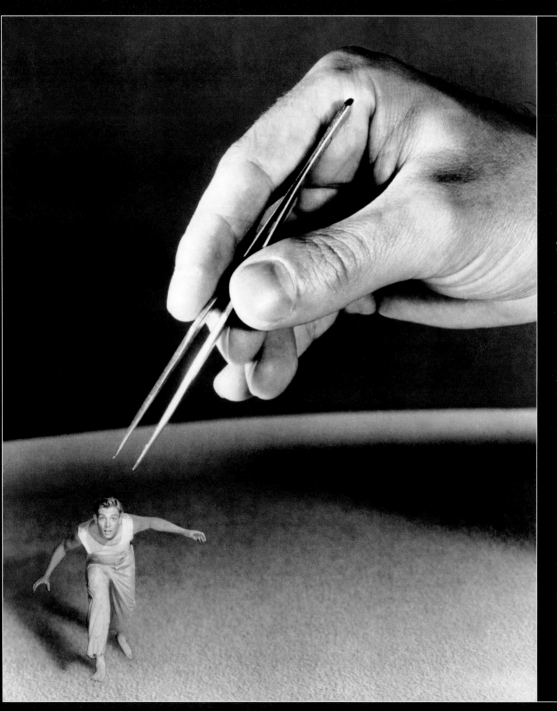

Grant Williams in Jack Arnold's *The Incredible Shrinking Man*.

AFFAIR (1964). In the seventies he detoured into black exploitation, making the under-appreciated BOSS NIGGER (1975) among others. He can be glimpsed in cameos in John Landis's INTO THE NIGHT (1985) and in THE FAVOUR, THE WATCH, AND THE VERY BIG FISH (1991). He wrote but did not direct THE MONOLITH MONSTERS (1957).

Milicent Patrick, who designed the Gill Man, was something of a fifties monster specialist, and her work can also be seen in IT CAME FROM OUTER SPACE (1953) in 3-D, SIGN OF THE PAGAN (1954), and THIS ISLAND EARTH (1955).

The cast of *Creature* was made up entirely of journeyman contract players who could hardly have known that this would be their most memorable appearance. Richard Carlson, who also starred in IT CAME FROM OUTER SPACE, may be the only actor to star in three 3-D movies. (The third one is 1953's THE MAZE.) Carlson had small roles in NO, NO, NANETTE (1940) and THE LITTLE FOXES (1941), but the only distinguished role among his later work is in TORMENTED (1960). He also directed films, but his work both as an actor and director is mediocre.

Julia Adams would never make another movie as famous as *Creature*, and in fact was consigned to a string of inconsequential programmers. Best among them are FRANCIS JOINS THE WACS (1954) with buxom B queen Mamie Van Doren, and SLAUGHTER ON TENTH AVENUE (1957) with mus-cleman Mickey Hargitay. THE LOOTERS (1955) is interesting as it's the film where she met costar Ray Danton, whom she would marry. After her semiretirement in the sixties to raise a family, she came back in Dennis Hopper's underrated THE LAST MOVIE (1971). Danton directed her in the 1975 horror film PSYCHIC KILLER.

The original FLIPPER (1963) was inspired by Ricou Browning after he got SEA HUNT producer Ivan Tors interested. It led to a sequel, FLIPPER'S NEW ADVENTURE (1964), followed by a network TV series that lasted for four years. Browning also wrote and directed SALTY, a better-than-average TV series about a pet sea lion, which ran one season, in 1973, before bombing as a 1975 feature film starring Clint Howard.

Creature owes many plot debts to the original monster classic KING KONG (1933), as well as both the book and movie versions of THE LOST WORLD (book 1918, movie 1925), and Edgar Rice Bur-roughs's LAND THAT TIME FORGOT trilogy from 1924. *Creature*, in turn, influenced all the other rub-ber-suit classics of the fifties and was still being borrowed from as late as 1975, when Steven Spiel-berg made JAWS. A Gill Man knockoff appears in MONSTER SQUAD (1987), but by that time the rub-ber suit was considered hackneyed, if not down-right ridiculous.

WRITTEN & DIRECTED BY

ROGER VADIM

STARRING

BRIGITTE BARDOT

"...AND GOD CREATED WOMAN" STARRING BRIGITTE BARDOT · CURD JÜRGENS · JEAN-LOUIS TRINTIGNANT · JANE MARKEN · JEAN TISS
LEOPOLDO FRANCÉS · JEAN TOSCANO · MARIE GLORY · GEORGES POUJOULY · CHRISTIAN MARQUAND · ROGER VADIM · RAOUL LÉ

"...AND GOD CREATED WOMAN"

...BUT THE DEVIL INVENTED BRIGITTE BARDOT!

ABELLE COREY · JACQUELINE VENTURA · JACQUES CIRON · PAUL FAIVRE · JANY MOUREY · PHILIPPE GRENIER · JEAN LEFEBVRE

NAL MUSIC BY PAUL MISRAKI   WRITTEN BY ROGER VADIM · RAOUL LÉVY   PRODUCED BY CLAUDE GANZ · RAOUL LÉVY   DIRECTED BY ROGER VADIM

IF IT WEREN'T FOR ONE MOVIE, RELEASED AT THE PERFECT TIME, BRIGITTE BARDOT MIGHT HAVE GONE BACK TO DANCING ON CRUISE SHIPS OR WORKING IN HER MOTHER'S PARIS BOUTIQUE.

T WAS HER SEVENTEENTH MOVIE—ALTHOUGH most people think it was her first—and she hadn't distinguished herself as an actress in any way. Her voice was coarse, her manner cold, her face a blank slate. She still had baby fat and a duck walk. Her butt was like a boy's—not a good thing in the era of Marilyn Monroe. To the gossipy press of Paris, she was the Pia Zadora of her day, a dumpling of a starlet who was all cheesecake and no class, constantly pushed forward by her Rasputin of a husband, Roger Vadim. She'd made a splash at the 1953 Cannes Film Festival by showing up uninvited, crashing a party on the USS Midway, and—with 3,500 American servicemen looking on—slipping off her raincoat to upstage Olivia de Havilland, Lana Turner, Esther Williams, and Yvonne de Carlo. Before *And God Created Woman*, she was a brunette. It was Vadim who changed her hair color, just as he changed the way she walked, the way she ate, the way she sat down and got up from chairs,

the way she arranged her décolletage, the way she spoke, and, perhaps most important, the way she pouted. And it was Vadim, a brash young screenwriter, journalist, and man-about-Paris, who alone thought she was the most beautiful woman in the world. "Physically as well as psychologically," he would say later, "she was the first star to be truly half masculine and half feminine." Once she had shuffled and mumbled haughtily through *And God Created Woman* in 1956, movies would never be the same—but, even more remarkably, womanhood would never be the same.

"The Vadim-Bardot alloy," wrote Bardot biographer Peter Evans in 1973, "was to change the very shape, look, consciousness, the resolve, and the animus of women in the second half of the twentieth century."

And it all started with the fact that both Bardot and her movie character, Juliette, loved sex. Juliette is the town slut. Vadim's screenplay makes no mistake about that, even though, with the French censor board looking over his shoulder, he had to imply more than he showed. And yet she's such a winsome slut. Before the movie is thirty seconds old, we see her entire naked body, stretching from one side of the Cinemascope screen to the other—and it was a long, long screen. The film was made at the maximum ratio of 2.35 to 1, meaning it's almost two and a half times longer than it is tall, and all of that celluloid is taken up by Bardot, her boyish butt included, as she reclines lazily on her stomach, soaking up the surreally bright Mediterranean sun and absent-mindedly kicking her feet. We're outside a modest cottage near Saint-Tropez, where the town's wealthiest man, played by the urbane, greying Curt Jurgens, has just driven up in his sporty Lancia convertible and spotted her feet dangling beyond the edge of the clothesline sheet that alone protects her from the eyes of the world.

"You have the feet of a queen," he says by way of introduction.

"Mr. Carradine," she says, recognizing his voice, "you have the devil of a nerve."

He tells her he's brought "the apple," and she rises up, wondering if he's truly gotten her the car he had promised. He's brought a car—but it's merely a toy convertible.

"You got me," she says, laughing.

"Not yet," he says. "But with that mouth you can have anything you want."

Teasingly, she sings "I'm a gold digger . . ."

And as he stands peering over the sheet at her voluptuous breasts—we can tell they're voluptuous

but we can't see them quite the way Curt Jurgens can—the whole framework of the movie is already established. Is she the seduced or the seducer? Is he a corrupter or a man about to be eaten alive? Whatever happens next, we know that it will all emanate from inside this enigmatic blonde who is both innocent and very, very nasty at the same time. Everything about her is too much—too much mouth, too much hair, too many curves, too much woman.

ROGER VADIM HAD SEEN ALL THIS WHEN SHE was a fifteen-year-old virgin studying to be a ballerina and occasionally posing for fashion magazines. He was six years older, and when he arranged a screen test for her—inviting her mother to come along, of course—he was the personification of everything a middle-class mom from the sixteenth Arrondissement did not want for her shy daughter. He had a devil-may-care scruffiness about him, long before that was fashionable, disdaining neckties and socks, wearing his hair long and unkempt, and even worse, he hung out with jazz musicians and other artistes who sat up all night drinking and smoking in the bohemian St. Germain des Pres neighborhood. It was Vadim, in fact, who invented the word discotheque. All the people playing records and dancing all night reminded him of a museum in Munich called the Pinakothek, so he coined the phrase, and it was picked up by his journalist friends.

The screen test was a disaster. Mama Bardot quarrelled with Vadim's friend and producer Marc

Allégret, and Brigitte was so nervous that she broke out in a skin rash. "Her voice sounds like she's wearing her mother's dentures," Allegret told Vadim, "and I hate the way she laughs." And those were the most polite things he said. In later years, Bardot had only vague memories of the meeting, but her first sight of Vadim never faded: "In my life I'd never met a man so handsome, so relaxed, so informal."

And they were soon, of course, in love. For Brigitte it was the love of a repressed young girl from the suburbs for an older man who moved in the exotic world of the city. For Vadim it was more complex. He became her father as well as her lover, and he relished the role. She did, too, clinging to her "Vava" like life itself. When they asked permission to be married, though, her devout Catholic parents firmly refused and said, furthermore, that she was forbidden to see him. They had secret afternoon trysts at a studio apartment off the Champs Elysées owned by Vadim's friend Christian Marquand, but Brigitte had to always be on alert, suspicious that her sister was spying for the parents. At one point, her father threatened Vadim with a gun. After one particularly bitter fight over Vadim, the family left for an outing and Brigitte stayed home alone. They

returned early to find her resting with her head in the lit gas oven with candles burning in the room. Fifteen minutes later, and her suicide would have worked. After that they compromised, saying that she could marry when she reached age eighteen, but hoping she would outgrow him.

Three months after her eighteenth birthday, on December 20, 1952, they were married at Notre Dame de Grace—Vadim was half Russian and had to convert from Russian Orthodoxy—and moved into a third-floor walk-up flat on rue Chardon-Lagache. Bardot was never the domestic type. "I despise cooking," she once said. "I'd rather not eat than confront a stove." But Vadim didn't want a conventional marriage, because even before they were wed he had started grooming his protégée for the screen. She never cared much for acting, was frankly bored by the tedious filming process, and gave up her dancing career only because it's what her husband wanted. He acted as her publicist, her coach, her manager, and the master of her every move. He cajoled directors and producers into using her in films, mostly in walk-on parts or small exploitation roles as a temptress. He got her into acting classes with the esteemed Rene Simon, but

MILLIONS OF MEN WERE IN LOVE WITH BARDOT, AND THE PRESS CREATED A NEW WORD FOR IT: "BARDOLATRY."

after a few months she dropped out. He introduced her to one of the hottest agents in Paris, Olga Horstig-Primuz, who would remain her only agent throughout her career, always referred to affectionately as "Mama Olga." As a way to get people to take her more seriously, Mama Olga placed Bardot in the Jean Anouilh play *Ring Around the Moon*. It would be her first and last time on stage. Even though Anouilh was thrilled with her work, she was bored after the first week—and the play ran for 100 performances.

By the time she was twenty-two, the marriage was starting to bog down, with Vadim missing his freedom and Bardot constantly creating drama to make him pay more attention to her. "Brigitte needs such intense passion every moment of her life," wrote Vadim in his memoirs, "and I just couldn't fulfill that any longer." They had shouting matches and physical confrontations, and once she locked him out of the apartment and left him on the street in his pajamas. He broke down the door, chased her through the house and spanked her—and then, of course, they made passionate love. It was that kind of relationship, perhaps too overheated to last, and after a time she would act outrageously with other men—while making a film in England she had a meaningless affair, even as she pronounced English men "boring"—and Vadim would infuriate her further by refusing to get angry about it. By 1956, when he wrote the scenario for *Et Dieu . . . créa la femme*, he felt a kind of desperation to make good on all his hard work and turn her into a movie star before their time ran out. "I'd liberated Brigitte and shown her

how to be truly herself," Vadim would write. "That was the beginning of the end of our marriage. From that moment, our marriage went downhill."

THE STORY IDEA CAME STRAIGHT OUT OF THE newspaper—three brothers in a village, all in love with the same woman, and a crime that results—and Vadim used it for the "scaffolding" of the script he eventually showed to his friend, producer Raoul Lévy. Lévy was a father figure for Vadim—his real father had died suddenly of a heart attack when Vadim was eight—and Lévy exuded worldliness with his seven-berth yacht, modern-art collection, and book matches etched with his profile. He thought Vadim's script was bad and told him so. He also doubted that his financial backers would ever accept Bardot in the lead. As a way to save money, Vadim suggested directing the film himself, and Lévy went along, even though most French directors at the time were in their fifties or sixties and the twenty-eight-year-old Vadim had never directed before. As Vadim refined the script, his vision of the project expanded to include widescreen projection and color, which were both very expensive. But he was trying to create a larger-than-life role for his wife; she was, after all, twenty-two years old, and his five years of trying had failed to create a breakthrough. Lévy sympathized and agreed to sell the film, but he was having bad luck with his own career and wasn't sure how to carry it off.

Late one night, Vadim got an excited phone call from Lévy, ordering him to meet him at the train station, where he would explain later. Vadim

"I THINK LIKE NAPOLEON...
WHEN IN LOVE,
THE ONLY VICTORY
IS ESCAPE, NO?"

hurriedly dressed and the two of them took a midnight train to Munich. Lévy's plan: "We're going to convince Curt Jurgens to be in our movie." Lévy's backers at Columbia Pictures Europe said they wanted a star's name above the title before they would put up the money, and Lévy had decided that Jurgens was their man. Jurgens had been a romantic lead in German films before the war. After being imprisoned by Goebbels, he made a slow comeback and had just scored a major hit with *The Devil's General*, in 1956. Now in his mid-forties, he was once again a major European box-office name.

The only problem was, Lévy and Vadim didn't know Jurgens, had never met him, and there was no part for him in the script. Lévy wanted him to play the role of the oldest brother, but Vadim pointed out that he was at least ten years older than the oldest brother's mother and that he spoke with a German accent. "Then you'll write a part for him when we get to the hotel," Lévy told Vadim. And that's what he did. While Lévy set up the meeting with Jurgens, Vadim bunkered down in a hotel room and wrote sixty new pages in three days. To keep him motivated, Lévy sent smoked salmon to the room, as well as caviar, vodka, and a hooker named Maria.

When Vadim told the hooker what he was doing, she offered to be his typist, even contributing character traits for his portrayal of Juliette. By the time they drove out to Curt Jurgens's country house to meet him, the role of businessman Eric Carradine had become almost bigger than the oldest brother. And Jurgens amiably agreed to do it, in part because it would be filmed in his favorite part of Europe, the South of France. A few days later, Columbia approved the script, the casting, and a $600,000 budget—enough for Technicolor filmstock and Cinemascope. The project was a go.

The movie was filmed in May and June of 1956 in Saint-Tropez, with interiors at the Victorine Studios in Nice. Vadim's longtime friend Christian Marquand was given the role of the cruel older brother Antoine. For the crucial part of Michel, the weak, nervous middle brother whom Juliette marries as a way to avoid being sent back to the orphanage, he chose a young actor named Jean-Louis Trintignant, who did, in fact, have a weak and nervous nature. Unlike the other men on the set, he was shy, inexperienced, came from provincial Nimes, and was the odd man out among the worldly, yacht-loving sophisticates who were making the film. After Bardot met him, she demanded a meeting and went into a screaming fit with Lévy and Vadim. "How do you expect me to play a love scene with him?" she demanded. "He's too small. He's ugly. And in any case he's not my type." Five weeks after the start of filming, she had fallen in love with him.

CRITICS HAVE ALWAYS DISMISSED *AND GOD Created Woman* as a lightweight melodrama, but I disagree. It's a compact story with witty, rapid-fire dialogue, and it has an emotional honesty about the relationships between men and women that was remarkable for its time. Men may have flooded into theaters to lust after Bardot, but I suspect it's the young females in the audience who appreciated it more. Juliette is a passionate child-woman, entirely ruled by her emotions, who desperately needs understanding and love but refuses to bargain away her freedom in order to get it. There are four men simultaneously in lust with her—the three Tardieu brothers and Eric Carradine—but each understands only a part of her. Antoine gives her passion but nothing else. Carradine understands the cynical libertine in her but dismisses her innocent idealism or thinks it's something she'll outgrow. Michel, whom she marries on the rebound, gives her patience and security but can't rouse himself to the kind of raw sexuality she craves. And Christian, the youngest brother, still a child himself, is the only one who listens to her without judgment and with 100 percent understanding. Together the four

men would make her perfect lover and husband. Individually they drive her toward desperation.

As the film progresses, Bardot becomes increasingly disheveled. That famous blonde hair becomes luxuriantly unkempt. She stops wearing shoes. She wears clothes that seem picked up off the floor and thrown over her shoulders—simple smocks, wraparounds and men's robes (thirty years before it was fashionable to do so). She's the focal point of every scene. Even when she's not seen on camera, the men are gazing up stairways, or staring at the ocean, or watching her through windows, and we know that their every thought is of Juliette. And even when she has no lines, she can steal the whole scene by the way she leans against a wall, curls up on a divan, or sprawls in a chair. Yet she's not acting so much as just *existing* on the screen. Vadim wrote the script to perfectly conform to her real-life nature, and that nature was essentially tough and unemotional. She lets the men come to her. She broods, but she always accepts what is. She loves animals, children, sun, sea, and the cha-cha-cha more than she loves any man. She never weeps or whines. Each time she's betrayed—when she overhears Antoine in the restroom saying that "girls like Juliette are good for one night, then you forget them," when he leaves her standing by the road, when Michel refuses to kiss her, when she throws herself at Antoine and is left alone under a broken tree as he walks coldly away—her face is granite. We have to search for the emotion. If the part had been played by a passionate actress—someone like Anna Magnani—we probably would have had a

Following pages: Juliette ignores her lover Michel.

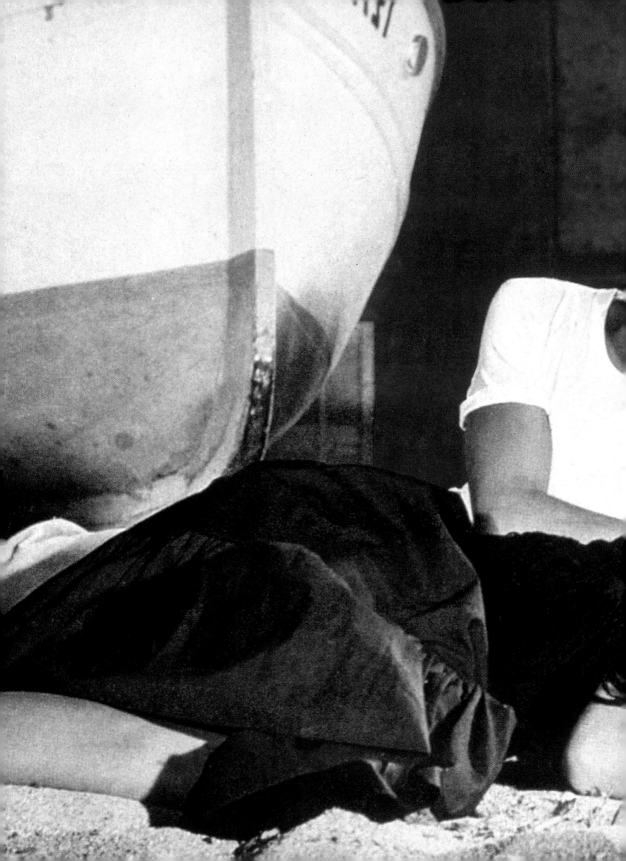

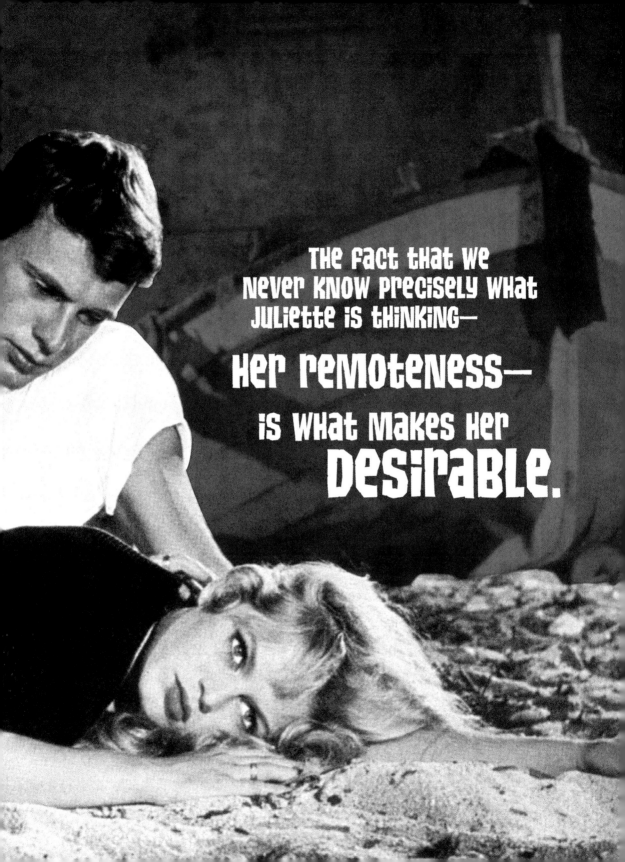

THE FACT THAT WE NEVER KNOW PRECISELY WHAT JULIETTE IS THINKING—

HER REMOTENESS—

IS WHAT MAKES HER DESIRABLE.

better movie, but it wouldn't have fascinated the world. The fact that we never know precisely what Juliette is thinking—her remoteness—is what makes her desirable.

Juliette was the first movie heroine to do whatever the hell she wanted, whenever the hell she wanted, without suffering for it in the end. She's like the goddess Diana, a regal and deadly creature of the woods, and because she's partly immortal, she's always alone, even when in the company of a man. The film is full of unforgettable iconic images: When Antoine, exhausted on the beach from saving Juliette's life, has his head pressed down by her bare foot; when her blonde mane whips around her head as she stares down the empty road; when she rises nude from her wedding bed, shielded by the translucent sail of a model boat; when she slinks downstairs in her groom's robe and ransacks the wedding table, wordlessly gathering food and wine for her wounded husband as the scandalized guests stare; and, of course, when she dances her wild mambo with the black calypso band in the basement of the town's most notorious bar. In all of these scenes she's the woman apart, the force of nature that will show us only part of her immortal spark but will never be controlled or won. No wonder women started dressing like her, acting like her, and making her into the Madonna of her era.

Even as Vadim was creating the only screen goddess who could compete with Marilyn Monroe for the world's attention, he was watching her give in to the seduction of Trintignant. At first Bardot encouraged the shy young actor simply as a way to make Vadim jealous, but toward the end of the shoot it was a full-blown love affair. The crew was frankly amazed that Vadim could continue to direct her love scenes with the very man she was cheating with, then return each night to live with her at the Hotel Negresco in Nice. Raoul Lévy loved the scenes that Vadim was turning in, but he felt he was witnessing a train wreck. "He gets so carried away," Lévy told friends, "that he is practically becoming an accomplice in his wife's adultery." If anything, the tension drove Vadim to work even harder, because he realized that he might never get another chance to use her as his canvas. With Gallic sophistication, he calmly discussed the situation with her, and they agreed to continue to live together until the film was finished. But Trintignant turned out not to be nearly so classy. He showed up at the hotel demanding that Bardot either come with him or never see him again. He ranted and raved like the jealous possessive lover that he was and threatened Vadim—and eventually Vadim gave Trintignant what he wanted. "She was my wife," he would explain later. "In a way, she was also my daughter. I did not wish to take on the role her parents had always played. I told her she could leave."

Of course, Vadim's reminiscences in later life may not be as accurate as the impressions of those on the outside at the time. Lévy, for one, thought that Vadim was devastated by the loss. When the film wrapped, he said, "The director won. The husband lost." Vadim's main regret, at least publicly, was that the press implied he had pimped his own wife to get the movie made. It was much more complicated, he always insisted, and the marriage was doomed before she ever met Trintignant. But when he went on to marry and love the most beautiful women in the world—Annette Stroyberg, Jane Fonda, Catherine Deneuve—while using all of them in his films the same way he used Bardot, the image of him as a hedonistic gigolo would stick. "Without a care in the world," Vadim said, "I put my foot in a trap that I have been stuck in since. Portraying my wife in love with another man, playing with her emotions and, above all, showing her naked in the arms of her lover—I was really doing the newspapermen's jobs for them."

THE FILM PREMIERED—AFTER SEVERAL CUTS demanded by the French censors—on December 4, 1956, at the Normandie Theatre on the Champs Elysées. Two days later, Vadim and Bardot filed for divorce. It was a low point for both of them, because the film was all but ignored by the French public and the critics were vicious. "The best thing about this film," said one reviewer, "is that it will forever end the career of that annoying little starlet." Bardot was devastated by the reviews that called her "vulgar," and Vadim was dismissed as a hack. This was the era of great French directors like Truffaut, Godard, and Rivette, and Vadim would never be considered worthy of the same attention. Truffaut himself wrote a review of the film, calling it "simultaneously amoral (rejecting the current moral system but proposing no other) and puritanical (conscious of its amorality and disturbed by it)."

It's actually the story of two people who learn to love each other. Michel learns that his marriage will have no chance unless he becomes strong and assertive. When he slaps Juliette across the face, four times hard, her expression goes from shock to the beginning of tears to what is almost a smile. We see life in her face, at that moment, for the only time in the film. It's a film about the courage it takes, sometimes acting against your own nature, to save a marriage. But France, for some reason, didn't get it right away. The first-run Paris take was only $125,000, or 21 percent of the film's budget. Desperate to save his film, Lévy flew to New York and offered distributors all North American rights for a flat $200,000—but there were no takers.

And then the film opened in London. The Fleet Street press had been entranced by Bardot ever since she had come there to make a silly Dirk Bogarde comedy called *Doctor at Sea* and had wowed everyone at a press conference with her broken English. (Typical question: "What was the best day of your life?" Bardot's answer: "It was a night.") They had invented the phrase "sex kitten" to describe her, and Kenneth Green, the director of publicity at Pinewood Studios, had dubbed her "the girl with the Pekinese profile." Now they welcomed the film that was driving British censors batty even before it arrived. The title was deemed blasphemous, so when it opened on March 13, 1957, it had been changed to *And Woman . . . Was Created*. It sold out the first day and went into general release throughout the rest of the country.

JULIETTE WAS THE FIRST MOVIE HEROINE TO DO WHATEVER THE HELL SHE WANTED, WHENEVER THE HELL SHE WANTED, WITHOUT SUFFERING FOR IT IN THE END.

But by that time the box office receipts were pouring in from the rest of the world as well. It was a hit in Tokyo, Hong Kong, the Middle East, and Scandinavia. In Germany, there was a riot at one of the theaters. Millions of men were in love with Bardot, and the press created a new word for it: "Bardolatry."

In America, where it didn't open until November, it became the first real "art film," and for years that term would be code for scandalous European films that are full of sex. By this time it had been condemned by the Vatican, which obviously helped the box office, and the American distributor came up with a great tagline for the poster: ". . . But the devil invented Brigitte Bardot!" It broke records everywhere and ran for a year. In Lake Placid, New York, the local priest offered the theater owner $350 if he would withdraw the film and substitute a more decorous title. When he refused, the theater itself was banned by the church for six months. The Jehovah's Witnesses proclaimed Bardot's eternal damnation. ("I've been condemned from more pulpits than Satan," she once said.) In Philadelphia the film was confiscated by the police. In Dallas the police chief forbade blacks from seeing it, on the theory that it would cause mischief in black neighborhoods. And the American press was just as adoring as the British, with *Look* magazine calling Bardot "the female James Dean" and *Life* proclaiming, "Since the Statue of Liberty, no French girl has ever shone quite as much light on the United States." It quickly became the most successful foreign film ever to play in the United States, beating out homegrown epics like *The Ten Commandments* and *Around the World in 80 Days.* Eight million Americans saw it, despite constant censorship and attacks by women's leagues. It earned $4 million in the U.S. alone, and distributors went crazy buying up all of Bardot's earlier films and releasing dubbed versions with titles like *The Light across the Street, Please! Mr. Balzac,* and *The Bride Is Much Too Beautiful.*

BARDOT'S SALARY FOR *AND GOD CREATED Woman* had only been $11,400. (Vadim's was even worse: $2,850.) But the international success would make her a celebrity for the rest of her life. Raoul Lévy immediately signed her for four more films at $25,000 per movie plus a percentage of the take. Mama Olga landed her a lucrative Hollywood contract, but at the last minute she decided not to take it. Her English was not that good, and she was terrified of leaving France. It may have been the smartest decision she ever made.

She would make more than forty films, including eight more for Vadim, and work with some of the greatest directors of the French New Wave. It's a wildly uneven body of work—her best performance was probably in Godard's *Contempt*, in 1963—but she was already one of those stars whose reputation can survive any failure. When she appeared on screen, she was always Bardot, and the public wouldn't have let her be anything else.

BB, as she would become known in the press, measured 35-23-35 and stood five-foot-seven, as every lovesick boy knew. She posed for *Playboy* twice, in June 1964 and April 1969, and was number four on that magazine's "100 Sexiest Stars of the Century," despite having been out of the business twenty-seven years when the list came out. She was so popular in the sixties that she had a thriving singing career, with stage shows, rock-video-type films, and several European hits, including "Bubblegum" in 1960 and "Bonnie & Clyde" and "Harley Davidson" in 1967. When she told her songwriter Serge Gainsbourg that she wanted to record the most beautiful love song in the world, he wrote "Je T'aime . . . Moi Non Plus" (I Love You . . . Me Neither). She recorded it complete with moaning orgasmic sounds, and her husband at the time, German businessman Gunter Sachs, was so enraged that he wouldn't allow it to be pressed. Her recording career lasted almost twenty years, from 1963 to 1982, and included five breathy albums that seethed with sex.

But it was her film career—or rather, the affairs and scandals surrounding her film career—

that made her a familiar name all over the world. "I play myself," she said frankly. "I'm not good enough to play somebody else. That's why I like simple, wild, sexy parts." And wild, sexy parts were what she got, taking advantage of her natural sultry insolence and the deliberately provocative way she moved. In every role, the subtext was, "I don't care." She may never have learned to act, but she learned how to work the camera. "All I can say," said Stephen Boyd, her costar in *The Night Heaven Fell*, "is that when I'm trying to play serious love scenes with her, she's positioning her bottom for the best angle shots."

In 1973, she did one last film for Vadim and then retired from the screen. *L'Histoire Tres Bonne et Tres Joyeuse de Colinot Trousse-Chemise* was poorly received, like most of her films, but by that time her love life had become more dramatic than any story she ever starred in. It's as though, in learning from Vadim how to be Juliette, she had established a pattern she would return to the rest of her life. There were always dozens of men in love with her, and she coolly picked and chose the ones that appealed to her—and had wild, passionate marriages that lasted about three years at a time. Between marriages, she had love affairs with the rich, the famous, and the merely attractive. "I live my whole life around my man—work, play, dreams, everything," she once said. "My lover is the center of my existence. When I am alone, I am lost. I can find myself only with a lover. . . . Outside a relationship, I am in space."

Her friends worried about her ability to keep it up. "When a man attracts her," said French novelist

Marguerite Duras, "Bardot goes straight to him. Nothing stops her. It does not matter if she is in a café, at home . . . she goes off with him on the spot without a glance at the man she is leaving. In the evening, perhaps she will come back, perhaps not."

The affair with Trintignant hadn't even lasted a year. For one thing, Trintignant was already married to a young actress named Stephane Audran, and she refused to grant him a divorce. When he was called up for military service, everyone knew it was over, because Bardot couldn't stand to be without a man, even for a day. She would marry three more times, first to the actor Jacques Charrier, who impregnated her a few months before their marriage in 1959. When her son, Nicolas, was born in 1960, the press swarmed around her hospital bed to photograph the famous infant, but to the question as to whether she would have more children, her immediate answer was "No! Never again!" The marriage was doomed, because Charrier couldn't deal with the constant attention of press and public. He had several nervous collapses and one total breakdown. When she starred in a film called *The Truth*, she had an affair with her costar Sami Frey, and Charrier tried to commit suicide twice, then brutally attacked the new lover. When the film wrapped, Bardot attempted suicide herself, by taking barbiturates and slitting her wrists. Toward the end of the three-year marriage, she took Nicolas to Charrier's parents and washed her hands of him. "I am no mother and I won't be one," she said.

"It is better to be unfaithful," she once said in an interview, "than to be faithful without wanting

to be." She was in the center of the go-go sixties—in fact, she was one of its inventors—and she was linked at various times to every jet-setting playboy of the day, including Marlon Brando, Warren Beatty, Mick Jagger, Sean Connery, Jean-Paul Belmondo, and many others—yet through it all she remained close friends with Vadim. Her third marriage, in a Vegas wedding, was to German playboy Gunter Sachs, and, like Charrier, he lasted three years, from 1966 to 1969. She wouldn't marry again until the nineties, when she linked up with politician Bernard d'Ormale, but in the meantime the intense relationships consumed her. "I think like Napoleon," she said. "When in love, the only victory is to escape, no?" And yet Vadim would defend her to the end. "Though she had a gift for infidelity," he would say, "she always suffered if she had an affair with more than one man at a time."

In 1976, she founded the Brigitte Bardot Foundation for the Protection of Distressed Animals, and the few public appearances she's made since then are to support animal-rights causes around the world. Oddly enough, given the mess she made of her personal life, she invested all of her money carefully and wisely. With holdings in oil, sugar, real estate, Nestlé, and the Printemps stores, she had no reason to work anymore. And as she became more and more reclusive, she chose Saint-Tropez, the site of her original fame, for her permanent home.

Vadim, on the other hand, was never loved by the public or the press. Yet he was a good director and a meticulous one. *And God Created Woman* is not only told well but is richly cinematic, bathed in a brilliant light, with dazzling aquamarine waters and rich crimsons for Bardot's famous dress. He would make other, more ambitious films about women—like *The Night Heaven Fell* with Bardot, *Les Liaisons Dangereuses* with his then-wife Annette Stroyberg, and *The Game Is Over* with his then-wife Jane Fonda—that deserved better treatment than they received. He remained true to his friends, including Raoul Lévy, who, after a love affair, tragically shot himself dead in 1967 outside a young model's apartment in Saint-Tropez. Meanwhile, Vadim became a devoted family man with four children after his fifth and final marriage, to the actress Marie-Christine Barrault, which lasted fifteen years. But when he died February 11, 2000, at the age of seventy-two, he was remembered in the press for two things—his beautiful wives and lovers and his colossal flops, like *Barbarella*, a sci-fi sex comedy with Fonda that bombed in 1968, *If Don Juan Were a Woman*, his 1973 lesbian fantasy that ended Bardot's career, and his disastrous late-eighties American remake of *And God Created Woman* with Rebecca De Mornay. There was a feeling that he had "lost it" somehow, or had never been talented to begin with, but it would have been more gracious to say that he was a daring experimenter whose experiments sometimes misfired. The few tributes to Vadim included backhanded compliments, such as Charles Taylor's description of him as "the classiest exploitation filmmaker who ever lived."

But someone should have at least made the point that when Vadim first saw Bardot on the cover of *Elle* magazine in 1949 and asked her mother to bring her to a screen test, something extraordinary happened. It took him seven years, but the inspiration of that day finally emerged on the screen and influenced hundreds of movies since then. "When I met Brigitte for the first time," he recalled, "I was immediately struck by her posture, her bearing, and her curved waist. She held her head like a queen." It's very similar to what Eric Carradine would say about Juliette at the beginning of *And God Created Woman*. But by the end of that movie, Eric Carradine has sacrificed his own desires so that Juliette can have a chance at real love with a young, foolish boy who may someday know how to take care of her. "That girl is made to destroy men," he says—an eerie prophecy. And yet this destroyer of men, this creation of Vadim, was also the liberator of actresses. Within a few years, Elizabeth Taylor, Shirley Jones, Melina Mercouri, and Marilyn Monroe would all play free-spirited women of easy virtue on the screen. Actresses were no longer hemmed in by middle-class ideas of rectitude. And it all happened because of something Vadim saw in Bardot that no one else could.

Some critics were so unkind as to say that without Bardot there would have been no Vadim. But Bardot, on the day after his death, said it was the other way around. "Vadim was seduction itself," she said. And the other men she married? "They were only husbands."

FOR FURTHER DISTURBANCE

Roger Vadim would continue to use Bardot as his leading lady during the years of her greatest fame, but none of their collaborations would ever attain the international success of *And God Created Woman*. The best of the lot are THE NIGHT HEAVEN FELL (1958), CIRCLE OF LOVE (1964), and THE GAME IS OVER (1966).

Bardot's early work is hard to find. Her first movie was a comedy called LE TROU NORMAND (CRAZY FOR LOVE) in 1952. Her revealing nude scenes that same year in THE GIRL IN THE BIKINI (1952) apparently haven't survived, although it was rereleased in an English version after she became famous, along with the two movies made just prior to her 1956 breakthrough, PLEASE! MR. BALZAC (written by Vadim) and THE BRIDE IS MUCH TOO BEAUTIFUL. In this early "ripe ingenue" period, she appeared in LES DENTS LONGUES (THE LONG TEETH) in 1952, LE PORTRAIT DE SON PÈRE (THE IMAGE OF HIS FATHER) in 1953, LA LUMIÉRE D'EN FACE (THE LIGHT ACROSS THE STREET), and a Vadim-written project called CETTE SACRÉE GAMINE (NAUGHTY GIRL) in 1956, but the only early role that required real acting was as the ambitious starlet Sophie in 1955's FUTURES VEDETTES (FUTURE STARS), directed by Marc Allegret and written by Vadim, and released in the states in later years as *Joy of Loving*. Easier to find are Robert Wise's HELEN OF TROY (1955), Rene Clair's THE GRAND MANEUVERS (1955), Anatole Litvak's ACT OF LOVE (1953), with Kirk Douglas, in which she has only one line of dialogue, and IF VERSAILLES COULD TALK (1954), with Sacha Guitry, Jean Marais, Claudette Colbert, and Orson Welles, which was released in the U.S. as *Fabulous Versailles*. Other roles for Bardot completists include TRADITA (CONCERT OF INTRIGUE) in 1954, LE FILS DE CAROLINE CHERIE (THE SON OF DEAR CAROLINE) in 1955, and one of her few English films, a Dirk Bogarde comedy called DOCTOR AT SEA (1955). Her famous milk-bath scene occurs in the 1956 Italian film MIO FIGLIO NERONE (NERO'S BIG WEEKEND), with Alberto Sordi, Vittorio de Sica, and Gloria Swanson.

Both Bardot and Vadim made their best films for other people. After *And God . . .* , Bardot was cast in classy pictures for the first time, notably in the 1958 melodrama EN CAS DE MALHEUR (LOVE IS MY PROFESSION), with Jean Gabin, based on a Georges Simenon novel about a trollop who corrupts and destroys a lawyer. Perhaps Bardot's crowning performance was for Jean-Luc Godard. As Camille Javal in CONTEMPT (1963), Bardot played a version of her sex-tigress self again, but it marked the first time the French public grudgingly admitted that she possibly had real acting talent beyond the pouts and the posturing. Godard would use her again in MASCULINE-FEMININE (1966).

Vadim made LES LIAISONS DANGEREUSES (1959), a modern retelling of Choderlos De Laclos's epistolary novel, with Jeanne Moreau as a calculating temptress and Gérard Philipe as her husband, and—continuing Vadim's lifelong interest in jazz—a score by Thelonious Monk and Art Blakey's Jazz Messengers. One of Vadim's best films is BLOOD AND ROSES (1961), a lyrical modern Gothic based on the Sheridan Le Fanu vampire tale *Carmilla* and shot on the grounds of Emperor Hadrian's villa, starring Elsa Martinelli and Mel Ferrer, with Vadim's wife Annette Stroyberg as the vampire.

Vadim's most famous film in America is BARBARELLA (1968), starring his then-wife, Jane Fonda, in a sci-fi sex comedy based on a French comic strip that was supposed to be "the sexual *Alice in Wonderland*" but was shot on a sterile sound stage and is full of off-putting imagery such as mutant dolls with razor-sharp teeth that rend Fonda's flesh.

Bardot's schlock output in the sixties is legendary—THE TRUTH (1960), which she considers her favorite film, even though she had a hot affair with costar Sami Frey that caused husband Jacques Charrier to attempt suicide; Louis Malle's critically panned A VERY PRIVATE AFFAIR (1961), featuring experiences from her real life; DEAR BRIGITTE (1965), an English-language Jimmy Stewart comedy in which she has a single scene at the end; Louis Malle's VIVA MARIA! (1965); an Edgar Allan Poe anthology called TALES OF MYSTERY AND IMAGINATION (1968); and the Sean Connery western SHALAKO (1968).

Bardot's final film with Vadim was DON JUAN 1973, also called *Don Juan*, or *If Don Juan Were a Woman* (1973), a ludicrous farce indicating

that Vadim didn't learn his lesson from *Barbarella*.

Bardot's final movie before retiring was L'HISTOIRE TRÈS BONNE ET TRÈS JOYEUSE DE COLINOT TROUSSE-CHEMISE (1973), although she did a documentary about her life in 1983.

Vadim remade *And God Created Woman* in either 1984, 1986, 1987, or 1988—it was apparently re-edited several times—and it is a God-awful rock-and-roll musical comedy starring Rebecca De Mornay as a New Mexico pop singer, with Frank Langella and Vincent Spano in supporting roles.

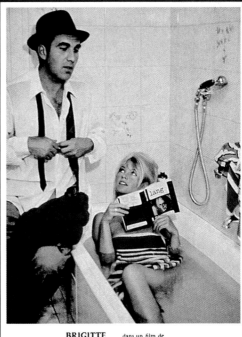

BRIGITTE
BARDOT
dans un film de
JEAN LUC GODARD

LE MÉPRIS

d'après le roman d'ALBERTO MORAVIA

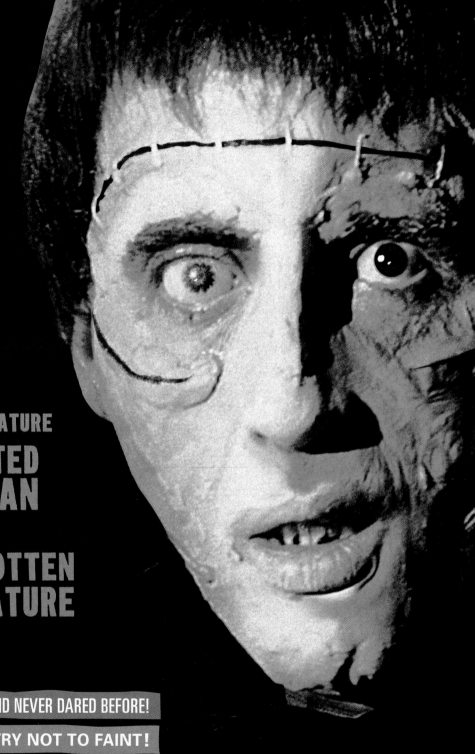

THE CREATURE
CREATED BY MAN & FORGOTTEN BY NATURE

ALL NEW AND NEVER DARED BEFORE!

PLEASE TRY NOT TO FAINT!

THE CURSE OF FRANKENSTEIN

...will haunt you forever!

a

HAMMER FILMS
production

PETER CUSHING ⚡ CHRISTOPHER LEE ⚡ HAZEL COURT ⚡ ROBERT URQUHART

written by JIMMY SANGSTER   produced by ANTHONY HINDS and MAX ROSENBERG   executive producer MICHAEL CARRERAS   directed by TERENCE FISHER

Everything about "The Curse of Frankenstein" seemed destined for colossal failure, beginning with the name. There's no real "curse" in the movie— unless you consider Frankenstein's ruthless personality a curse on himself...

AND THE TITLE WAS ACTUALLY INVENTED AS A legal strategem to avoid being sued by Universal Pictures, owner of the 1931 classic. The script was written by a glorified office boy who had previously written one less-than-successful cheapie after begging producer Anthony Hinds to let him break into screenwriting. By 1957, when the film was released, there hadn't been a Frankenstein movie for nine years, and the last one—the ludicrous *Abbott and Costello Meet Frankenstein*—seemed to have finished off the genre for all time. Horror films in general were passé, having given way to the science-fiction craze. The star of *Curse* was a forty-four-year-old journeyman actor who had failed to make it in Hollywood and needed a job—any job. The cast spoke with upper-class British accents at a time when Marlon Brando and James Dean had all but eliminated theatrical speech from the screen. It was a costume drama full of high-collared aristocrats in frock coats and equestrian gear, a period piece set in the Swiss Alps around 1880, and it featured a monster whose makeup had to be carefully designed so as to not use a single feature of the square-headed Frankenstein makeup of Boris Karloff, which was patented by Universal. The production company, Hammer Films, was a struggling little studio facing extinction. Its B-movie crime mysteries were no longer in demand from a British film industry that was being whittled away by television, and its one bona fide hit—*The Quatermass Xperiment*—had been recycled so many times that there was very little left to do with it. There was no money—the budget was £65,000—and there was basically only one set: the house and grounds of Down Place, a ramshackle manor house at Water Oakley, Windsor, that had recently been grandly rechristened as Bray Studios.

So of course the movie was an overwhelming overnight success. Britain's first color horror film opened at the Warner Theater in Leicester Square, where the lobby had been outfitted as Baron Frankenstein's lab, complete with a bandaged headless torso floating in a glass tank, and you couldn't beg, borrow, or steal a ticket. Curse would end up earning $80 million, more than seventy times its production cost. It would make Peter Cushing a star. And it would transform Hammer Films into one of the greatest horror factories in history.

Watching it today, it's hard to conceive of the impact it had. The dialogue is stilted, the plot predictable, the ending anticlimactic. But it had two things going for it. It was drenched in color that could only be called lurid. Garish blood red was the dominant color, but the whole film was steeped in rich primary hues that looked like they were painted onto the film stock by a psychopathic Belgian impressionist. And it had, for the first time on any screen, graphic gore.

The most famous shock moment occurs when the creature, his head swathed in bandages like the Invisible Man, unwraps the gauze to reveal a one-eyed visage that is scarred and blistered and burned like one of those accident victims in highway-safety films. But it was just one of several full-bore Grand Guignol details. This was the first film to show preserved eyeballs, brains in glass jars, and the slow unwrapping of a pair of disembodied hands. Another image, of a head floating in a jar with its skin peeling off, didn't make it past the censor, but for the prickly United Kingdom public, even the tamer stuff was revolutionary. Who knew that the splatter film would have its first incarnation in a proper suburb of London?

The critics shredded it to bits, of course, using words like "disgusting," "degrading," and "horren-dous"—although "horrendous" is a strange word to use in condemning a horror film. "The atmosphere of butchery pervades all," crowed one critic—thereby, of course, insuring that the run would be extended. With understated British acerbity, Paul Dehn wrote: "Philip Harben, preparing 'Tête de Veau Vinaigrette' from a live calf on TV, could hardly be more explicit." Christopher Lee, the then-unknown actor who played the monster, was vilified by critic Denis Gifford as "Jerry Lewis with acne." He had been hired for his talent as a mime, but the bowl haircut and ossified putty makeup made it impossible for him to show any real emotion. They called Cushing's portrayal of Baron Frankenstein one-dimensional, and said the script was full of gratuitous and unmotivated violence. (They were especially offended by the reanimation scene, in which the creature attacks and tries to strangle Cushing for no apparent reason—and yet the brain is, after all, badly damaged, and he is, after all, seeing his killer for the first time.)

Hammer took advantage of all the bad publicity, using a twenty-second TV commercial showing the scene in which Lee rips off his bandages to reveal the road-kill face. They immediately announced a sequel, using the same creative team, to be called *The Blood of Frankenstein*. (By the time it came out, a year later, it had been changed to *The Revenge of Frankenstein*.) Universal, alarmed that an upstart B-movie company had ripped off its franchise, filed suit in New York to prevent the movie from being registered in the states. But Hammer had been so careful with the script, makeup, and

Following pages: Frankenstein (Peter Cushing) monitors his monster.

Hinds pressed young Jimmy Sangster into service,
giving him instructions to
"Make Frankenstein a shit."

character names that they could successfully argue that it was based on Mary Shelley's original 1818 novel (not really true—it's almost the exact opposite of her story), and within six months it was selling out at the Paramount Theater in Times Square.

THE TIMING COULDN'T HAVE BEEN BETTER FOR Hammer Productions Ltd., a company formed in 1934 and named after the vaudeville team of Hammer and Smith. The Will Hammer half of that team was a music-hall roustabout whose real name was William Hinds. As vaudeville started to die, he managed to finagle his way into music publishing, showbiz promotion, hotel management, and theater management in Surrey, East Anglia, and other provincial outposts. When Hammer was formed, Hinds had four partners, the most important being Enrique Carreras, a Spaniard who had opened up the first multiplex theater in the world, the 2,000-seat Blue Halls in London, which had become a successful chain by the late 1920s.

Hammer made its first film in 1935—a parody of *The Private Life of Henry the Eighth* called *The Public Life of Henry the Ninth*—but mostly the company limited itself to short subjects and one-hour crime dramas, sold for a flat fee to theater owners who needed a second feature to fill out a program. It wasn't until after World War II—when Col. James Carreras and Anthony Hinds, sons of the founders, were brought into the business—that the first true Hammer film was released. In 1948, they made *Dr. Morelle: The Case of the Missing Heiress*, which was inspired by a BBC radio melodrama and was filmed

entirely at a house in Cookham. Over the next nine years, they would repeat the formula—acquiring proven radio properties from the BBC (most of them involving adulterous love affairs), casting them with fading American stars, then filming them on the cheap at various country houses and selling them as second, or "B," features. Actors and directors worked on deferred salaries, generally sharing 5 percent of the film, and the atmosphere was that of a relaxed and collegial stock company. At the start of each filming day, whoever arrived first was expected to brew the coffee.

Carreras handled the money and the deals. Hinds handled the production. And as they built their motley crew at Bray Studios, in-house stars emerged. Terence Fisher became the house director, mostly because he could shoot quickly and still carry off a little style. What would come to be known as "the Hammer look" was born out of sheer necessity, dictated largely by the available sets and the scripts that went further than what was generally allowed at the time. When they discovered just how sexy and shocking Technicolor film stock could be, they created a formula that would be copied for decades—first by Roger Corman with his Edgar Allan Poe films of the early sixties, and later by Francis Ford Coppola and Clive Barker.

But in 1955 they were struggling for survival. *The Quatermass Xperiment*, budgeted at £42,000, saved them for a time. It was Hammer's forty-third feature, and it became the most successful British sci-fi film of the fifties (which is kind of like saying the best Mexican wine). It was actually the earliest version of what British director Ridley Scott would realize fully twenty-four years later with *Alien* (1979). The story of a manned rocket ship that becomes infested with a cosmic virus, turning an astronaut into a mutant capable of ingesting entire populations (in the best you'll-never-believe-this tradition, he becomes fused at one point with a cactus), it was released in the United States as *The Creeping Unknown*, but didn't catch on with Americans since they weren't familiar with the original TV version. It was just successful enough in Britain, though, for Hammer to attempt a sequel. *Quatermass 2* (*Enemy from Space* in the States) was adapted from existing material, the original teleplay for *Quatermass* by Nigel Kneale. Around the same time Hammer released *X The Unknown* to cash in on its success with the first *Quatermass*. Its title took advantage of the notoriety of the first film's having received an X rating. Although *Quatermass 2* included what is generally regarded as Hammer's most horrific image of all time—the famous melting head—the box office was not that good.

CASTING ABOUT FOR SOMETHING THAT WOULD rescue the company from the onset of television, Cinema-scope, and big-budget Hollywood imports, the company turned to a script that had been submitted by two New York businessmen, Milton Subotsky and Max J. Rosenberg, who wanted Hammer to help them make a new version of the Frankenstein story. Hammer contacted Boris Karloff to see if he was available to play the monster,

but Universal got wind of the idea and wrote threatening legal letters, specifically mentioning the Frankenstein makeup that was created by Jack Pierce. Hammer abandoned the idea of using Karloff, but they also decided they couldn't use Subotsky's script either. It was too close to Universal's version.

Instead, Anthony Hinds pressed young Jimmy Sangster into service, giving him instructions to change the time period, base it on the Mary Shelley novel (which was in the public domain), and, most important of all, "Make Frankenstein a shit." Three weeks later, Sangster turned in a shooting script. The fifty-two-year-old Fisher was chosen to direct, partly because he had never seen the original Universal movie and never read the novel.

But Sangster had made so many changes to the Shelley novel that it was almost unrecognizable. He added a framing device through which Baron Frankenstein, awaiting execution, tells his story from prison. The human side of the creature—his gentle soul in a grotesque body, his groaning, frustrated attempt to understand himself—was eliminated entirely. In Sangster's version he's a vicious animal, incapable of pity or understanding, and his brain is damaged three times, making him into little more than a tormented rabid dog and thereby avoiding the psychological irony of the original work. Instead of being a young student, Victor Frankenstein was made into an idle rich forty-year-old amateur scientist—mostly to accommodate Cushing. Instead of being a man tortured by his conscience, he is a cold, ruthless killer on the verge of madness. It has been suggested by one critic that he was a "Faustian Oppenheimer" and that the subtext of the movie is horror at what the atomic-bomb scientists had created. But it's hard to believe that Sangster had anything so subtle in mind. If anything, the scene where Frankenstein makes the creature go through his "tricks"—"stand up," "walk," "sit"—makes it play as an animal-rights tract.

Women were not Sangster's strong point—he would be castigated in future years for being a misogynist—and so the love story suffered as well. Thirty-year-old redhead Hazel Court, trying for a comeback after failing to become a star at both Gainsborough and Rank studios, is a cipher in the role of Frankenstein's clueless wife. (She would be used to much better effect in Roger Corman's movies.) Valerie Gaunt, as the slutty maid who becomes a nuisance to Frankenstein, is much more interesting, but ends up as little more than a plot device to show just how evil the baron is. The only real conscience in the movie is provided by Robert Urquhart in the thankless role of Paul Krempe, Frankenstein's tutor and collaborator, who ultimately turns against his pupil.

Christopher Lee ended up hating the movie, and refused to play the role in any of the sequels. A year later, though, Hammer would give him the lead in *Horror of Dracula*, with Cushing as Van Helsing, and for the next fifteen years Lee and Cushing would alternate leads, often appearing in the same film, as Bray Studios flourished and the ramshackle manor house was used to create European villages, London mansions, and Spanish plazas. Universal did an abrupt about-face and announced that it would partner with Hammer, turning over its entire horror catalog for remakes, to avoid the embarrassment of its whole franchise being released by Warner Bros. Lee played the Mummy (with Cushing as the archeologist). He also appeared in a Sherlock Holmes movie, in Fu Manchu movies, and as Scaramanga in the James Bond film *The Man with the Golden Gun*. Cushing reprised Frankenstein five more times, as well as Sherlock Holmes and Doctor Who. Ironically, he would end up being better known for his Van Helsing than for his Frankenstein.

Part of the reason for this was that Hammer had discovered that, while the Frankenstein story was limited, the Dracula story could be spun off in infinite directions. They would release fifteen more vampire movies, all the later ones with lesbian subplots, until the trend ran out of steam in 1975 and the company was forced into bankruptcy. Michael Carreras didn't give up right away and tried to get several other features off the ground, including a Loch Ness monster project, but the fashion had passed. Peter Cushing, the house star, was sixty-three by that time, and he had never emotionally recovered from his wife's death in 1971. *Curse* had saved the company from an almost certain death in 1957, but it had also condemned it to a formula that would eventually have to run out. Despite several attempts to revive Hammer—the latest by advertising mogul Charles Saatchi in 1997—the idea seemed to be cursed. The meaning of the title was apparent at last.

FOR FURTHER DISTURBANCE

The Curse of Frankenstein reinvigorated Hammer Films and resulted a year later in the studio's unearthing of the other famous Universal franchise in **HORROR OF DRACULA** (1958), with Christopher Lee as the count and Peter Cushing as Van Helsing. Later, Hammer would also revive **THE MUMMY** (1959), with Lee as the mummy and Cushing as the archeologist. In the meantime, they churned out Frankenstein sequels, all but one directed by Terence Fisher, with mixed results—the perfectly adequate **REVENGE OF FRANKENSTEIN** (1958); followed by the atrocious **THE EVIL OF FRANKENSTEIN** (1964) directed by Freddie Francis; then the kinder, gentler **FRANKENSTEIN CREATED WOMAN** (1967), with *Playboy* Playmate Susan Denberg as the girl-friend whose brain is preserved; followed by **FRANKENSTEIN MUST BE DESTROYED!** (1969), which Fisher intended to be the final installment. Alas, they revived the franchise for **THE HORROR OF FRANKENSTEIN** (1970), a black-comedy version regarded as Hammer's biggest mistake ever, featuring David Prowse as the monster in white cycling shorts and Ralph Bates as a psychopathic Frankenstein. The final sequel, **FRANKENSTEIN AND THE MONSTER FROM HELL** (1974), was Terence Fisher's last film and the last appearance of Cushing as

Frankenstein, his hair now white, his hands turned to stumps, assisted by a mute girl and a young doctor who help him create a creature from the bodies of inmates. The monster (David Prowse) has an intelligent artistic personality at first, but gives in to the murderous instincts of his criminal's body. Frankenstein wants to mate the monster to his female assistant, but in the end the creature is ripped apart by angry inmates. Technically the final film is one of the best, with very gory details, including open brain surgery and mutilated bodies.

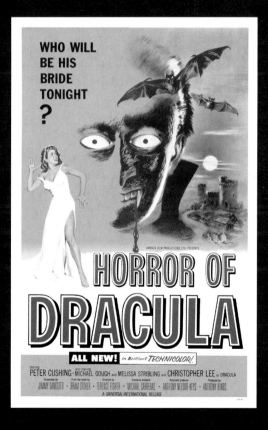

The success of all these films resulted in Hammer going after every available gothic horror story in the public domain, including Sherlock Holmes in THE HOUND OF THE BASKERVILLES (1959), THE TWO FACES OF DR. JEKYLL (1960), THE PHANTOM OF THE OPERA (1962), and the especially well-done THE CURSE OF THE WEREWOLF (1961), which launched the career of Oliver Reed. Ultimately the *Dracula* films, and vampire films in general, turned out to be the most lucrative releases for the company, and Hammer continued to make them right up until the time of its bankruptcy in 1976. Other notable Hammer films include PLAGUE OF THE ZOMBIES (1966), which predated George Romero's NIGHT OF THE LIVING DEAD by two years, and a feminist version of Jekyll and Hyde called DR. JEKYLL AND SISTER HYDE (1972).

The last big Hollywood treatment of the Frankenstein story had been ABBOTT AND COSTELLO MEET FRANKENSTEIN (1948), which combined real horror with slapstick comedy, influencing Quentin Tarantino, who saw the film at age five and began to develop a lifelong love of mixed-genre movies.

For the ancient history of Hammer Productions, the key titles are THE PUBLIC LIFE OF HENRY THE NINTH (1935), their first release, THE MYSTERY OF THE MARIE CELESTE (1936) with Bela Lugosi, and DR. MORELLE (1948), regarded as the first "true" Hammer film. Their breakthrough film was the proto-*Alien* thriller THE QUATERMASS XPERIMENT (1956), with Richard Wordsworth as the monster, released in America as *The Creeping Unknown*. Other notable titles from this developing period are WOMEN WITHOUT MEN (1955) and the Quatermass sequel X THE UNKNOWN (1957).

Peter Cushing would be best known for Van Helsing, not Frankenstein, but he also appeared frequently in non-Hammer films over the next three decades, including, most notably, as Grand Moff Tarkin in STAR WARS (1977).

Christopher Lee would never play the monster again, but he would reprise the role of Dracula for a decade, beginning with DRACULA, PRINCE OF DARKNESS, in 1966. His most acclaimed role was

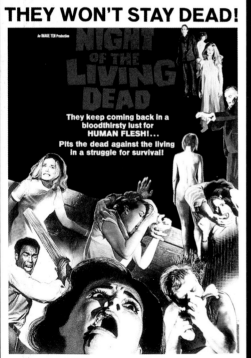

THEY WON'T STAY DEAD!

An IMAGE TEN Production

NIGHT OF THE LIVING DEAD

They keep coming back in a bloodthirsty lust for HUMAN FLESH!... Pits the dead against the living in a struggle for survival!

Starring JUDITH O'DEA · DUANE JONES · MARILYN EASTMAN · KARL HARDMAN · JUDITH RIDLEY · KEITH WAYNE

as the star of RASPUTIN, THE MAD MONK (1966), but he also played Sherlock Holmes, Scaramanga and especially Fu Manchu in a long-running series that included THE FACE OF FU MANCHU (1965), THE BRIDES OF FU MANCHU (1966), THE VENGEANCE OF FU MANCHU (1967), THE BLOOD OF FU MANCHU (1968), and FU MANCHU'S CASTLE (1969). He was also one of the most memorable James Bond villains, in THE MAN WITH THE GOLDEN GUN (1974).

The success of *Curse of Frankenstein* unleashed a virtual avalanche of variations on the Frankenstein theme among low-budget Hollywood studios, including some of the worst movies ever made. In TEENAGE ZOMBIES (1958), Chuck Niles based his zombie on Christopher Lee's Frankenstein performance. The biggest financial success was American-International Pictures' I WAS A TEENAGE FRANKENSTEIN (1957), followed by Allied Artists' FRANKENSTEIN 1970 (1958) and Astor Pictures' FRANKENSTEIN'S DAUGHTER (1959). For cult value alone, you might want to watch FRANKENSTEIN MEETS THE SPACE MONSTER (1965), JESSE JAMES MEETS FRANKENSTEIN'S DAUGHTER (1966), or EROTIC RITES OF FRANKENSTEIN (1972). The genre reaches its nadir with the excruciating BLACKENSTEIN (1973), starring John Hart as a doctor who transplants arms and legs onto a Vietnam quadruple amputee, turning him into a serial killer.

The final Hammer sequel, *Frankenstein and the Monster from Hell.*

BLOOD FEAST

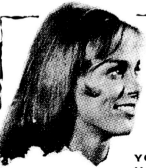

Introducing
CONNIE MASON

YOU READ ABOUT
HER IN PLAYBOY

AN ADMONITION
If You are the Parent or Guardian
of an impressionable adolescent
**DO NOT BRING HIM or PERMIT
HIM TO SEE THIS MOTION PICTURE**

MORE GRISLY THAN

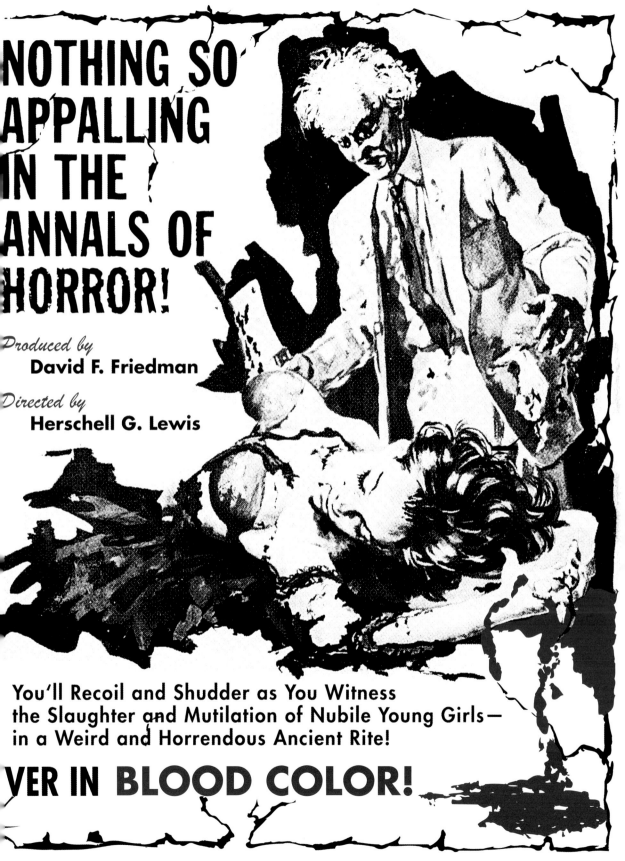

One of the most famous stories
in exploitation history occurred
at the Bellevue Drive-In in Peoria, Illinois,
on July 19, 1963, four months before
the JFK assassination supposedly made
America a more violent place.

STANFORD KOHLBERG, A P. T. BARNUM TYPE who tried everything from pony rides to hot-air balloons to fireworks shows to popularize his chain of drive-ins, had financed a film so graphically violent that he wanted to see if it was even possible to get other theaters to play it. The film was the brainchild of two Chicago showmen, producer David F. Friedman and director Herschell Gordon Lewis, both of whom would become legendary as the creators of some of the cheapest and most disgusting films ever made. Kohlberg had put up the money for this new kind of film, which didn't have much going for it in the way of acting, plot, or production value, but did have one new element: blood. Not just a little squib on the shirt when someone died, but gouts of blood—gallons of it—spurting and gurgling out of bodies in extreme closeup as a maniac Egyptian caterer named Fuad Ramses slaughtered young virginal girls and prepared a cannibalistic feast from their body parts. As the advertising poster put it: "Nothing so Appalling in the Annals Of Horror! You'll Recoil and Shudder as You Witness the Slaughter and Mutilation of Nubile Young Girls—in a Weird and Horrendous Ancient Rite! An admonition: If you are the parent or guardian of an impressionable adolescent, do not bring him or permit him to see this motion picture. Introducing Connie Mason: You read about her in *Playboy*. More grisly than ever, in blood color!"

The movie was, of course, *Blood Feast*, and on the day of its premiere, Friedman and Lewis were still wondering whether they had created something that would be banned by law, shunned by theater owners, or, worst of all, ignored altogether. Sweating it out in their downtown Chicago offices, they suddenly became so curious about what they had wrought that they decided to drive down for the unspooling. They hopped into Lewis's Chrysler Imperial, stopped to pick up their wives (who despised the film), and skedaddled down the highway. But about a mile from the theater, somewhere on Plank Road, a few miles west of town, they ran into a traffic jam. At first they thought there was an accident ahead, but then it slowly dawned on them: All the cars were lined up to see *Blood Feast*. By the time they got to the entrance, the police were turning people away because the drive-in could only hold 1,500 cars. A legend was born.

What's interesting about the story is that the movie was obviously a success before anyone had actually seen it for the first time. The crowds had thronged the theater on the basis of the lurid ad campaign alone. It did continue to make money—$17,000 for the one week it played Peoria, followed by bookings over the next fifteen years that earned an estimated $7 million. That's a terrific return on a movie that only cost $24,500 to make, but it's no blockbuster, even by the standards of the sixties. *Blood Feast* was impressive primarily for its sheer longevity, moving around the country one week at a time, living and dying on its ad campaign, so that as late as 1980 it was still turning up in Texas drive-ins, sometimes on a double bill with Tom Laughlin's *Born Losers*. Unlike most cult movies, though, you're not likely to find many film buffs who saw it during its first release. It wasn't that kind of movie. In cities, *Blood Feast* played grind houses as an occasional respite from their steady diet of soft-core porn. In less populous areas, it played drive-ins, often as a late second or third feature when presumably the "family audience" had already gone home. In both cases, it had an almost entirely male clientele, the "raincoat crowd," as they were once called: bored and lonely seekers of cheap thrills. Not the kind of guys who write cult-film memoirs.

BUT THEN, AROUND **1980**, AFTER IT WAS finally played out, the reputation of the film underwent a miraculous seachange that would make it all but immortal in underground film circles. *Blood Feast* became the first real find of what I call pop-culture archeology. And for that to happen, there had to be nothing less than a revolution in the way these films were watched. For the first time there were young devotees who regarded the exploitation film not as pure entertainment, but as a cultural artifact that was celebrated because it was forbidden, antisocial, sleazy, and bizarre. Not to get too philosophical about it, but in a way it's like watching yourself watching the film. Part of the experience is being sophisticated enough to appreciate the film on two levels—as an assault on the senses that outrages the middle class and as part of a subculture that only initiates know about. It's no accident that punk rock and the first generation of underground film critics arose at the same time. In fact, quite a few metal bands named themselves after gore films, and others recorded songs in tribute to famous gore scenes. (The group 10,000 Maniacs was intended as a tribute to Lewis and Friedman's follow-up film, *Two Thousand Maniacs*, but the band members got the name wrong.) *Blood Feast* became hip with a young generation that was highly educated, media-saturated, and rebelling against everything in the culture that was plain vanilla or beloved by the masses. As low culture became high camp, *Blood Feast* was loved because it was despised.

This was the first movie in which people died with their eyes open, the first movie to show limbs hacked off on camera, the first movie to show brains and intestines and gaping wounds. The turning point in the movie—the point at which people would either get sick, leave, groan, or cheer—comes when the killer reaches into a woman's mouth and rips her tongue out. It was actually a sheep's tongue, dressed with special stage blood, minced cranberries, and Kaopectate to make everything congeal realistically, and to this day, it's probably the main reason *Blood Feast* will never be seen on television.

But there were three people in particular who popularized the movie and launched the age of "camp gore," a movement which continues to this day in the form of hundreds of annual video releases that attempt to out-gore Lewis, the "Wizard of Gore" himself. The first critic to understand the appeal of *Blood Feast* was Baltimore's John Waters, a fan of sleaze whose *Pink Flamingos* broke ground by being an exploitation film that was self-consciously tongue-in-cheek. (It's not that *Blood Feast* and other films of its era didn't have humor, both intentional and unintentional, but Waters was the first to play every scene with a wink and a nudge, letting the audience in on the joke.) Waters interviewed Herschell Gordon Lewis for his book *Shock Value*, giving the first real celebrity treatment to the man who directed what Waters called "the Citizen Kane of gore." "His films are impossible to defend," Waters wrote, "thus he automatically becomes one of the great directors in film history." You could almost treat this as the credo of the whole punk-film backlash I'm describing.

But then, in the summer of 1980, two revolutionary fanzines appeared at almost precisely the same moment. One was *Sleazoid Express*, a cut-and-paste job put out by a B-movie fanatic named Bill Landis who spent all his spare time trolling "the Deuce"—New York's 42nd Street near Times Square—where he wrote droll tributes to movies like *Shriek of the Mutilated* and *Bloodsucking Freaks* that at the time were considered part of the dregs of society, even lower than pornography. Landis was a total-immersion sort of critic in these pre-video days, venturing into murky rundown theaters where he described the "Popeyes" (plastic-bag-toting regulars wearing ill-fitting stained clothes and two or three tattered coats) and the "Blockheads" (sweaty, thick-necked musclemen in tight shirts) who were as much a part of the show as the film itself. Although Landis had a master's degree in finance, he preferred working as a projectionist in porno theaters and hanging out at gay cruise dives, like a cinematic Jack Kerouac. He said that his life changed at the age of nine, when he saw an ad for *Guttertrash* by the inimitable Andy Milligan. Landis idolized Lewis. "The whole point of Lewis's movies," he said, "is that he hates people."

That same summer, a second fanzine appeared, this one a hand-lettered weekly guide to weird movies on TV, called *Psychotronic*. This was the brainchild of Cleveland native Michael Weldon, another habitué of the Deuce who had moved to

New York specifically to experience the dark side. Weldon lived over a witch supply store on the Lower East Side and was into drugs and punk music as well, but he was actually more of a media-friendly popularizer than Landis. When his *Psychotronic Encyclopedia* came out in the early eighties, describing hundreds of movies that had never been reviewed in the mainstream, illustrated with tasteless one-sheets rescued from 42nd Street dumpsters, Weldon became the unofficial caretaker of the weird, twisted, and bizarre treasures rescued from the trash heap of film history.

After that, the retro rush was on. Fanzines sprang up everywhere—*Trashola* out of San Francisco, the *Gore Gazette* in New Jersey, *Confessions of a Trash Fiend* in New Jersey, *The Splatter Times* out of Tennessee, *Scareaphanalia* in New York, *Chicago Shivers* in Chicago, and the eventual keeper of the flame, the slick, four-color *Fangoria* magazine, which continues to publish after all these years, inspiring two more generations of horror fans, special-effects makeup artists, and would-be directors. Before the advent of the Internet, there were perhaps 200 underground publications devoted to hard-core cult movies, with hundreds of others that included gore movies as part of their coverage of punk rock, horror fiction, grunge, Goth, or death metal. And every one of them would have killed for an interview with Herschell Gordon Lewis, widely regarded as the man who started it all with Blood Feast.

By the time he became famous, though, Lewis was long-retired from filmmaking, settled comfort-ably into a luxury condo in Plantation, Florida, and making a small fortune as one of the world's leading authorities on direct-mail marketing, better known as junk mail. He wrote books on the subject, conducted seminars around the world, and hired himself out at $10,000 per letter if you wanted him to write your direct-mail piece. When I interviewed him in the late eighties, he spoke fondly of his old films, but seemed not quite aware that they were famous. Lewis's partner David Friedman was also semiretired by that time, writing his entertaining memoirs from his hometown of Anniston, Alabama. The two men had split up in 1964 after making their "gore trilogy"—*Blood Feast, Two Thousand Maniacs,* and *Color Me Blood Red*—but would be reunited thirty-eight years later as the producer (Friedman) and director (Lewis) of *Blood Feast 2: All U Can Eat* (2002), which was financed by an obsessed New Orleans fan of the original named Jacky Lee Morgan.

LEWIS AND **F**RIEDMAN WERE ODD PARTNERS FROM the beginning. Lewis was an urbane intellectual who spoke a perfect King's English. He has, in fact, an MA in journalism and a Ph.D. in psychology, credentials that landed him a position teaching English and humanities at Mississippi State University before he decided he'd rather make money. In the fifties he took jobs at radio stations in Pennsylvania and Wisconsin, became a producer at WKY-TV in Oklahoma City, and eventually joined a Chicago advertising agency. He was ready to go out on his own when

he met Friedman, and together they formed Mid-Continent Films.

Friedman was a southerner who had grown up on the carnival grounds, traveling the circuit with his carnie uncle, and he was a born huckster. (Those over-the-top posters and ad campaigns were his specialty, even though Lewis was the professional ad man.) Friedman had forced himself to get an electrical engineering degree at Cornell, and served with a filmmaking unit of the U.S. Army Signal Corps in World War II, but he ended up working as a craps croupier in notorious Phenix City, Alabama, after the war. In 1946, he sold a pair of army-surplus searchlights to Kroger Babb, the famous road-show king (see pages 24–41), and his life was changed forever. He would work briefly as a publicity agent for Paramount, but the corporate life didn't agree with him, and he became a professional road-show manager, traveling the country for Babb with an Italian-made version of *Uncle Tom's Cabin* then eventually producing his own projects.

Lewis was the artist, and Friedman was the ballyhoo man. Together they made some of the cheapest yet most profitable movies in history. They hit their stride when they discovered the money to be made in "nudie-cuties," the almost unbearably boring genre that flourished from 1960 to 1963. (A series of court decisions allowed nudity on the screen for the first time, but only if the film took place entirely within a nudist camp.) But after shooting *Boin-n-g!* in 1962 (yes, the title means what you think it means), they noticed that the grosses for nudist-camp films were declining and

went in search of new genres. That fall, they shot *Scum of the Earth*, about a gang of pornographers who lure young college girls into posing for dirty pictures. During the Christmas holidays, Friedman attended a carnival convention, where he ran into an old friend named Eli Jackson.

Jackson owned a burlesque theater in Cincinnati and was married to a stripper named Virginia "Ding Dong" Bell (measurements: 48-24-36) who was so well known nationally that she made a queenly $1,500 a week. Burlesque had been dying for years, but now it was truly doomed because the nudie-cuties had destroyed its only real marketing tool. Why go see strippers wearing pasties when you could see unlimited breast nudity in a film? In fact, many of the burlesque houses had started running nudie films between shows, then limiting the number of shows, and were now on the verge of getting rid of live entertainment altogether. The first "adults only" theaters in America were converted burlesque houses.

Jackson had a proposition for Friedman. He wanted to put up the money for a nudie film starring his wife, and furthermore he had already written the script. (He was so fearful that his blockbuster story would be stolen before he could get it produced that he refused to let anyone see it until the first day of shooting.) Always ready to deal, Friedman quickly called Lewis in Chicago, and they made an agreement to shoot the film as hired guns. They would produce, direct, create a trailer, poster, and pressbook, then deliver a finished print to Jackson for a set fee. The only problem was, Virginia

The seminal tongue-ripping scene.

Bell was pregnant, so they had to shoot within sixty days.

The forgettable film would be called *Bell, Bare and Beautiful* (the title was a parody of the hit film *Bell, Book and Candle*), and it was mostly an excuse for Friedman and Lewis to put together a cast and crew with someone else's money and then use the extra time to make their own film. They brainstormed together, searching for new genres, and came up with one word: gore. Something that had never been done before. One day they walked over to the office of their favorite financier, theater-chain owner Stanford Kohlberg, and outlined the plot. The mother of an Egyptology student hires an exotic Egyptian caterer to furnish her daughter's wedding, and the caterer turns out to be a maniac who cooks a cannibalistic feast. Kohlberg said, "How much do you need?" and quickly wrote a check for $24,500.

On February 2, 1963, Friedman and Lewis checked into the Suez Motel on Collins Avenue in Miami Beach, where they were greeted by Jackson and his partner Leroy Griffith, the owner of a Miami burlesque house. The filming of the forty-page script began that very night with a cast of strippers and carnival workers, and three-and-a-half days later they were finished, despite Virginia Bell's strange policy of not allowing anyone else to be in a scene with her when she exposed her famous breasts.

The guerrilla filmmakers quickly moved on to their own project, with Lewis searching for the perfect stage blood and Friedman—a barfly and ladies' man—trolling the local night clubs to find the five nubile young "virgins" they would need for Fuad's victims. Miami Beach was in its heyday, with famous hotels like the Eden Roc and the Fountainebleau attracting beach girls from all over America, so it wasn't difficult to line up the needed cheesecake. Several hires were made by Friedman during drinking sessions at the Playboy Club, including the star, Connie Mason, who would become a Playboy Playmate of the Year the following January. Meanwhile, Lewis had discovered a company called Barfred Cosmetics in Coral Gables that manufactured stage blood, but he didn't like the consistency of it. It was too thin and unrealistic. He made several suggestions about how to thicken and darken the recipe and eventually bought eight gallons of the new improved version. The company still sells the *Blood Feast* blood to this day.

After five days of preproduction, they started filming. Lewis directed and operated the camera. Friedman produced and recorded the sound. Bill Kerwin, who had appeared in several Lewis-Friedman films under various pseudonyms (to avoid trouble with the actors union), starred as the homicide inspector, delivering lines like "This time he took the brains—now what kind of creature would do that?" and "Frank, if I'm right, these are the leftovers." Lyn Bolton was hired from the Miami Little Theater to play the outrageously hatted mother who is instantly hypnotized by Fuad. Sandy Sinclair, a pretty blonde they had used in *Scum of the Earth*, was hired for the shocking pretitle sequence, in which she gets her eye plucked out and her leg hacked off in the bathtub. An old carnie pitchman named Scott Hall was cast as the chief detective. (The Smithsonian Institution would later ask Hall to record his standard sideshow "pitch" for posterity.) Another of Friedman's carnie friends, Al Golden, played the lecturer on ancient Egyptian religous cults. Ashlyn Martin, a friend of Connie Mason's, played the young lover on the beach whose head gets sliced open with a machete. (The owner of the Suez Motel asked if his guests could watch this scene the night it was shot on the beach outside. Lewis and Friedman said sure, and Fuad Ramses had an audience for one of his most vomitous moments.) One of Friedman's drinking buddies, Jerry Eden, played the Egyptian priest who removes a gooey, pulsating heart from a human sacrifice victim in a flashback scene.

The night before the classic tongue-ripping scene, though, the victim still hadn't been cast. Lewis told Friedman he needed a good-looking girl with a huge mouth—and quickly. The huge sheep's tongue had been waiting in the refrigerator for three days, and it was getting rancid. Friedman headed for the Playboy Club again, and as it turned out, his waitress was a blonde Scandinavian named Astrid Olsen, who, he instantly noticed, had a big mouth. She agreed to do the job, and the next night she showed up on the set with her "Neanderthal" boyfriend, recalled Friedman. "He thought this was gonna be a big starring part in a big Paramount picture, and it was one day's work!" Still, she performed like a trouper, holding the sheep's tongue, stage blood, and God knows what else in her mouth

until Fuad could properly rip it out and make movie history. She and the boyfriend then tentatively inquired about when they would be needed for the rest of her role—but that was the role.

BLOOD FEAST IS ONE OF THOSE MOVIES THAT'S more fun to talk about than to actually watch. It came straight out of the traditions of the carnival, which means it was all icing and very little cake. The two key performers were Connie Mason, who was so lifeless and unprepared that she drove Lewis insane ("She never knew a single line, not one, ever") and Mal Arnold as Fuad Ramses. Arnold was a local actor who had seemed OK during his interview—he had his film debut as an extra in a nudie-cutie called *Goldilocks and the Three Bares*—but when the camera rolled, he insisted on using the world's worst Bela Lugosi accent, bugging out his Groucho Marx eyebrows, and exaggerating a hokey limp. A great deal of the movie's cult value is created by the yin-yang effect of the beautiful Connie Mason's deadpan nonacting with the slimy-haired Mal Arnold's delirious overacting. ("Nearly ready!" he announces to no one in particular as he stirs his grisly body-part stew. "The ancient formula needed for rebirth!") In one scene, Mason is obviously reading her lines from a table lamp, and in another Arnold seems to be in a trance as he wields a barbed whip on a female victim clad in tattered, bloody panties, chained to a blood-smeared wall. "Stop your sniveling!" he barks at her. But all the hideously goofy elements come together in the climactic scene, when Arnold asks Mason to lie on his kitchen counter, arms straight up in the air, so that he can complete the 5,000-year-old feast. "Hey, you wouldn't sacrifice me on an altar, would you?" asks Mason, who then gets the giggles, interrupting Fuad's incantation to Ishtar. When the virginal bride is rescued, the mom adds, "Oh, dear, I guess we'll have to eat hamburgers."

Fortunately, the facade of the Suez Motel featured a garishly painted plastic replica of the sphinx, which, shot from below at dusk, could almost be made to look like the real thing. Creating Fuad Ramses's shrine to the goddess Ishtar ("I am your slave, my lady of the dark moon!") would prove more daunting. A department-store mannequin was painted yellow and dressed in vaguely Arabian attire, but it looked neither menacing nor interesting. Friedman solved the problem by driving to the Miami Serpentorium and purchasing a seven-foot-long Colombian boa constrictor for $30. They draped it over the mannequin—it still doesn't look that creepy—and used the snake in a couple of other scenes for no particular reason except ambience. Add in a gratuitous swimming pool scene—featuring another local cutie named Toni Calvert as the girl who eventually gets whipped to death—and a final chase sequence in which Fuad Ramses is ground up by the sanitation trucks of the City of North Miami, and that's pretty much the movie. Scott Hall, as the chief detective, has the best line in the film: "He died a fitting death, like the garbage he was." Unfortunately, Lewis's script fails to observe the first rule of horror—when the monster is dead, the movie is over—and subjects us to a long explanation of just how Kerwin solved the murders. (All the victims, it turned out, belonged to the same book club.) "Who knows if the spell of this monstrous goddess," says Kerwin in one last burst of ominous foreboding, "has possessed anyone else?" (So Lewis did set up the sequel that would be made thirty-nine years later!)

Friedman and Lewis had shot two complete features in sixteen days. The editing, scoring and mixing on both took another two months, and by June *Blood Feast* had killed 'em in Peoria. From the opening titles, in which letters dissolve into rivers of gooey blood (courtesy of a plastic ketchup squeeze bottle) to the ponderous, somewhat annoying organ-and-timpani soundtrack to the leaden acting and jump-cut editing (the result of shooting too little coverage for editor Bob Sinise—father of Gary Sinise—back in Chicago), *Blood Feast* was a seventy-minute patchwork morality tale that had one thing going for it: It was grisly beyond belief. Since no movie of this kind had ever been seen before, it was even noticed by the mainstream press, which used words like "inept," "crude," "unprofessional," and "fiasco." "*Blood Feast*," wrote Kevin Thomas of the *Los Angeles Times*, "is a blot on the American film industry. In production, exhibition, and promotion it is an example of the independently made exploitation film at its very worst. It is an insult to the intelligence of all but readers of horror comic books."

By that time it didn't matter, though. Among theater owners, Friedman and Lewis were now kings of this particular molehill. Harry Kerr, the drive-in king of the Carolinas, played the picture in all 350 of his drive-ins. Friedman printed up "vomit bags" inscribed "You May Need This When You See BLOOD FEAST," and even though a half-million were passed out at screenings, today they're quite valuable collector's items. There were protests against the film in San Diego and Tampa, but given the subject matter, *Blood Feast* attracted very little negative attention of the type these movies usually thrive on. Friedman did his best to make people believe that perhaps those death scenes were real, but no one got very outraged. (Thirteen years later, the film *Snuff* would carry off the illusion of actual on-screen death, but with far less explicit gore effects than the ones used in Blood Feast.) Things were so slow in Sarasota that Friedman tried to stir things up by swearing out an injunction against his own film, alleging that it violated local obscenity laws. He expected to get two days publicity out of the stunt, but the presiding judge surprised him by granting the injunction. He had to actually fight in court to get it lifted.

Kohlberg was so happy with the movie that he gave them the money for two more gore films, both of which turned out better than *Blood Feast* but neither of which became as famous. *Two Thousand*

Maniacs was a gore version of *Brigadoon*, about a southern town where a Civil War massacre took place and, once every hundred years, the dead martyrs rise from their graves to take revenge on Yankee tourists. *Color Me Blood Red* was one of the many versions of *A Bucket of Blood*, the Roger Corman classic from 1959 about an artist who has to kill in order to make his works lifelike.

BUT SUCCESS BROUGHT CONFLICTS BETWEEN Lewis and Friedman. They disagreed first about the direction of Mid-Continent Films. Friedman wanted to spend more money and make pictures with better production values so they could compete with slicker exploitation filmmakers like Russ Meyer. (Lewis thought paying for professional actors, for example, was a waste of money. "I see filmmaking as a business," he once said, "and pity anyone who regards it as an art form and spends money based on that immature philosophy.") They also argued over how to deal with Stanford Kohlberg. Kohlberg attempted to renegotiate their profit-sharing deal after the first films started making money. Lewis wanted to sue, but Friedman went the way of all carnies and settled with him quietly, selling his shares in

"I see filmmaking as a business . . . and pity anyone who regards it as an art form and spends money based on that immature philosophy."

all three films and infuriating Lewis in the process. Friedman would move to Los Angeles and partner with exploitation pioneer Dan Sonney, while Lewis would go back to his advertising business and continue to make films when he could. But neither man would have the impact alone that they'd had as a team.

Even by the standards of the weird exploitation world, Lewis had a strange career. He ended up directing thirty-eight films, using a variety of pseudonyms: Lewis H. Gordon, Sheldon Seymour, Georges Parades, Armand Parys, R.L. Smith. He would make any kind of film for a price. He even made children's films as a hired gun. He made films about the sexual revolution, went through a cornpone phase with moonshine epics, and made the first all-female motorcycle-gang movie. Yet he always returned to gore—partly because he was fascinated by the magician's challenge of creating new realistic effects that had never been seen before. If *Blood Feast* was the *Citizen Kane* of gore, then *The Wizard of Gore*, in 1972, was Lewis's *A Midsummer Night's Dream*. It was to be his final experiment in gory special effects, his swan song. Later that same year, he moved to Florida and got out of the exploitation business.

After moving to California, Friedman's career flourished. First he made *The Defilers*, a "roughie" about two punks who kidnap and rape a girl who's just arrived in Hollywood. By the early seventies, Friedman had a fairly standard formula, with most of his pictures featuring female masturbation, heterosexual sex, lesbians, and sadomasochism, even

though they would be considered mild fare by the standards of *Deep Throat*, the movie that changed everything, in 1972. Friedman also made the classic *Ilsa, She-Wolf of the SS*, but later disavowed it and had his name taken off after a dispute with the Canadian producers.

Friedman also became an exhibitor when he and his partner Dan Sonney bought a theater at Fifth and Hill in downtown Los Angeles that would become the flagship of the famous Pussycat Theaters chain. In 1960 there had been only twenty adult theaters in the whole country, most of them retrofitted burlesque houses, but by 1970 there were 750, and a good many of them sported the Pussycat trademark, promising a haven for the nervous male clientele that would sometimes study the one-sheets outside for hours before being brave enough to go inside. The theaters were notorious for being places where you didn't really want to know what your neighbor was doing, and if he wanted to know what you were doing, it was probably in order to make a sexual proposition. The Pussycat in downtown Los Angeles had so many problems of this type that eventually Friedman and Sonney simply ripped out every other seat so no one could sit next to anyone else! Friedman, although a staunch Republican, became the first president of the Adult Film Association of America, an anticensorship trade organization formed in 1969.

The world of adults-only film was changing, though, especially after *Deep Throat* made hardcore sex legal almost everywhere. To compete, Friedman started spending more money on production.

The Erotic Adventures of Zorro cost $76,000, and his most expensive picture ever was a *Billy Jack* ripoff called *Firecloud* in 1975. By that time, the age of the nudie, the roughie, the ghoulie, the gore film, and the softcore lesbian pictures Friedman was fond of had all passed. The adult theaters had all switched over to hard-core pornography, and Friedman didn't have much interest in it. He did produce a few X-rated films—*Seven into Snowy*, *The Budding of Brie*, *Matinee Idol*—but by the mid-eighties he was bored with the business and returned to Alabama and his first love, the carnival circuit.

No one in the cast or crew of *Blood Feast* had much of a career. Mal Arnold was never seen again. Connie Mason was hired by Friedman for *Two Thousand Maniacs*, over Lewis's strenuous objections, but that turned out to be her final film. She posed for a Scandinavian Airlines newspaper ad and did a television commercial for shampoo, then got married to an executive at *Playboy* and vanished from public view—not a moment too soon for Lewis. "I've often felt that if one took the key out of Connie's back," he said, "she'd simply stand in place. Acting was simply not one of her talents."

In later years, after *Blood Feast* had become a cult legend, much was made of its being the first slasher film, but in fact it had little in common with *Halloween*, or *Friday the 13th*, or *The Texas Chain Saw Massacre*, all of which used much less gore anyway. Its importance had little to do with technical innovations—when the sequel was made, thirty-eight years later, Lewis used basically the same effects in the same crude way—but much to do

with the fact that it created a new commercial market for Grand Guignol filmmaking. "A typical audience member," Lewis said of those days, "would live south of the Mason–Dixon line, would be between twenty-five and forty-five, would live in rural rather than urban circumstances, would probably be male, would not be highly educated, and would have a terrific number of prejudices." In other words, rednecks—the opposite of the over-educated computer nerds who would later love his films.

Friedman was even more brutally honest. "I've exploited the basest human emotions," he said, speaking of his films as a whole. "But the one I exploited most was loneliness. That's who was paying my way, a lot of very lonely men."

The word used most often to describe *Blood Feast* is "groundbreaking," and that it was. It loosened up the dirt so that other, better financed, more talented filmmakers—like John Waters, Rob Zombie, Tim Burton, John Carpenter, and Tobe Hooper—could mold it into clay. "*Blood Feast* is an accident of history," said Lewis, offering the most realistic and accurate assessment of the film. "We didn't deliberately set out to establish a new genre of motion picture. Rather, we were escaping from an old one. *Blood Feast* is like a Walt Whitman poem. It's no good, but it's the first of its type, and therefore it deserves a certain position."

FOR FURTHER DISTURBANCE

Herschell Gordon Lewis made almost all of his films in the sixties, retired in 1972, and made a one-shot comeback in 2002. Some of his oddities have vanished without a trace, but the surviving films are readily available on video and consist of basically three types: nudie-cuties, gore, and what we'll call social realism.

The first two films Lewis made with his partner David Friedman were sort of proto-nudies: LIVING VENUS (1960), a thinly disguised behind-the-scenes exposé of *Playboy* starring Harvey Korman, and THE PRIME TIME (1960), starring "seven of the ugliest girls ever to appear in a film," according to Lewis (although one of them was Karen Black in her movie debut).

If you've seen one nudist camp film, you've pretty much seen all of them—pasty, pudgy nekkid people playing volleyball and posing behind strategically positioned bushes—but the first one made by Lewis and Friedman was THE ADVENTURES OF LUCKY PIERRE (1961), a painful, pun-filled comedy starring a burlesque comedian and filled with voyeuristic vignettes featuring nude girls. *Adventures* earned $175,000 on an investment of $7,500. The last surviving nudie made by Lewis and Friedman is BOIN-N-G! (1963), which may well be the zenith of the genre. Other Friedman-Lewis nudie-cuties include DAUGHTER OF THE SUN (1962), and NATURE'S PLAYMATES (1962), both made in Florida, as well as GOLDILOCKS AND THE THREE BARES (1963). But, unless you enjoy ugly people playing volleyball in the nude, don't bother to find them. Also of historical interest is GARDEN OF EDEN, the first nudist camp film in modern times, released in 1954 and declared legal by the New York Court of Appeals, thereby opening the floodgates to the genre. Lewis would return to the nudie genre in 1969 with one of his strangest films, on a résumé full of strangeness—LINDA AND ABILENE, a lesbian western shot at the Spahn Movie Ranch around the time the Manson family was there.

After the success of *Blood Feast*, Lewis and Friedman made two more gore films, TWO THOUSAND MANIACS (1964) and COLOR ME BLOOD RED (1965). Of the three, *Two Thousand Maniacs* is probably the most successful and the one adopted by punk rockers in the seventies. Lewis continued to make gore films on his own, including his favorite, A TASTE OF BLOOD (1967), and the goofy THE GRUESOME TWOSOME (1967). His most entertaining gore effort is THE GORE-GORE GIRLS (1972), featuring Henny Youngman and several startling effects, including the French-frying of a girl's head and a scene in which a woman's nipples are cut off and milk spurts into champagne glasses. His final venture into gore was THE WIZARD OF GORE (1972), about a Grand Guignol magician who turns out to be actually killing people onstage.

Others would go further with the gore genre,

notably MAKE THEM DIE SLOWLY (1981), an Italian cannibalism classic that played for years at grind houses and drive-ins. Lesser gore classics include SNUFF (1976), a fake snuff film promoted as the real thing, SHRIEK OF THE MUTILATED (1974), and BLOODSUCKING FREAKS (1976).

In the social realism genre, Friedman and Lewis made SCUM OF THE EARTH (1962), about a gang of pornographers who lure young girls into posing for dirty pictures. After the partners broke up, Lewis made what may be the best film of his entire career: SUBURBAN ROULETTE (1967), about married couples who swap partners, featuring *Playboy* superstar June Wilkinson. Also notable is the first all-girl biker film, a cult classic called SHE-DEVILS ON WHEELS (1968), which is one of his most watchable efforts. He also made BLAST-OFF GIRLS (1967), about a go-go girl rock band; THE GIRL, THE BODY & THE PILL (1967), about the birth-control revolution; MISS NYMPHET'S ZAP-IN (1970), about the drug-and-sex-crazed sixties; the ultimate hooliganism movie and one of the most brutal films about juvenile delinquency, JUST FOR THE HELL OF IT (1968); and a couple of hillbilly movies—THIS STUFF'LL KILL YA (1971), about a moonshine ring run by a fake evangelist, and YEAR OF THE YAHOO! (1972), a precursor of THE CANDIDATE (1974) and BOB ROBERTS (1992), about a country singer who runs for the U.S. Senate.

Lewis also worked as a director for hire, but his efforts in that area—including JIMMY THE BOY WONDER (1966) and THE MAGIC LAND OF MOTHER GOOSE (1967)—are mostly lost.

After Friedman parted with Lewis and went to California, he made THE DEFILERS (1965), a "roughie" about two punks who kidnap a girl who's just arrived in Hollywood and rape her. Working with budgets of about $25,000, he continued with a string of movies that tended increasingly toward lesbianism and sadomasochism—THE NOTORIOUS DAUGHTER OF FANNY HILL (shot in 1966 by the then-unknown Laszlo Kovacs), A SMELL OF HONEY, A SWALLOW OF BRINE (1966); SHE-FREAK (1967), a remake of *Freaks* that Friedman calls his favorite film; HEADMISTRESS (1968); BRAND OF SHAME (1968); THE LUSTFUL TURK (1968); STARLET (1969); THAR SHE BLOWS (1969); TRADER HORNEE (1970), which became a goofy cult favorite; THE LONG SWIFT SWORD OF SIEGFRIED (1971); THE EROTIC ADVENTURES OF ZORRO (1972); and his most expensive picture, FIRECLOUD (1975), which attempted to take advantage of the *Billy Jack* (1971) craze. Friedman produced ILSA, SHE-WOLF OF THE SS (1974) covered on pages 166–185. He also dabbled briefly in hard-core, making SEVEN INTO SNOWY (1977), THE BUDDING OF BRIE (1980) and MATINEE IDOL (1984), before retiring from film and returning to the carnival circuit.

Lewis and Friedman were reunited in 2002 for BLOOD FEAST 2: ALL U CAN EAT, which continued the Egyptian catering saga, this time in New Orleans. The effects are eerily similar to the ones in the original film, but almost forty years later, they seem dated.

Unchanged men in a changing land.
Out of step, out of place and desperately out of time.

THE WILD

STARRING
WILLIAM
HOLDE[N]

ALSO STARRING EMILIO
CHANO URUETA ·
YOLANDA PONCE ·
MARGARITO LUN[A]

BUNCH

ERNEST ORGNINE · **ROBERT RYAN** · **EDMOND O'BRIEN** · **WARREN OATES** · **JAIME SANCHEZ** · **BEN JOHNSON**

Z · STROTHER MARTIN · L.Q. JONES · ALBERT DEKKER · BO HOPKINS · DUB TAYLOR · PAUL HARPER · JORGE RUSSEK · ALFONSO ARAU
ENAS · BILL HART · RAYFORD BARNES · STEPHEN FERRY · SONIA AMELIO · AURORA CLAVEL · ENRIQUE LUCERO · ELIZABETH DUPEYRÓN
EYRÓN · PEDRO GALVÁN · GRACIELA DORING · MAJOR PEREZ · FERNANDO WAGNER · JORGE RADO · IVAN SCOTT · SEÑORA MADERO
GONZÁLEZ · LILIA CASTILLO SCREENPLAY BY WALON GREEN · SAM PECKINPAH PRODUCED BY PHIL FELDMAN DIRECTED BY SAM PECKINPAH

THE FIRST TIME "THE WILD BUNCH" WAS SHOWN TO AN AUDIENCE, AT A TEST SCREENING IN KANSAS CITY ABOUT THIRTY PEOPLE WALKED OUT WITHIN THE FIRST TEN MINUTES, AND AT LEAST ONE OF THEM PROCEEDED TO THROW UP IN THE ALLEY OUTSIDE THE THEATER.

BAD-BOY DIRECTOR SAM PECKINPAH WENT back to the editing room and cut the 190-minute film down to 143. The next place it was shown was at a special film festival sponsored by Warner Bros. in the Bahamas. The high-toned crowd in evening dress booed the film and shouted at the screen. Peckinpah's reaction was to stand up in the theater and yell back at the sons of bitches, lacing his speech with the profanity he spent a lifetime perfecting. By the time the film was released, in the summer of 1969, it already had a reputation as the bloodiest, most violent, and most sickening display of carnage ever made. Normally that kind of buzz would translate into a box office hit, but the film was disturbing on so many levels that word of mouth was bad on it. It was depressing, people said. It was not a fun movie. It was exhausting. And yet some people were mesmerized by it. Ron Shelton, a minor-league baseball player for the Arkansas Travelers, saw the film on opening day in Little Rock and returned every day for two weeks, watching it again and again, sometimes twice in the same day, so much so that he was late to the ball park and in danger of losing his job. Years later, after Shelton had become famous for directing movies like *Bull Durham*, *White Men Can't Jump*, and *Blaze*, he said that as soon as he saw it, he didn't want to play baseball anymore. He wanted to be a director. He wanted to someday create something as breathtakingly beautiful as *The Wild Bunch*.

The Wild Bunch is like that. It was despised and it was loved. Even those who worship it have to admit that they're made intensely uncomfortable by it. It's not an easy movie, and it has so many layers of text, subtext, countertext, subliminal imagery, and perverse undercutting of its main characters that it can be watched over and over again with new levels of understanding, if not exactly appreciation. In my opinion, it's the American *Hamlet*. Hamlet was not an especially lovable guy, and neither is Pike Bishop, the broken-down guilt-ridden boss of the gang of desperadoes trudging wearily toward their doom in a wicked little Mexican town. Pike Bishop is not a man of many words, so he doesn't make a "To be or not to be" speech. In the final sequence he says simply, "Let's go." And one of his men replies, "Why not?" You can make an argument, as some have, that at that moment this unholy gang of killers has decided to fight for honor and duty: They have to save their captured comrade. But their last act before retrieving their rifles and taking the death walk is to bicker with some whores over how much they owe. A few moments later, Pike himself, the ostensible hero of the story, uses a woman as a human shield—she's blown to ribbons in his arms—so he can get to a machine gun and spray gunfire all over a Mexican village, destroying innocents and bad guys alike. Of the many bullet hits Pike takes before he dies, the two most deadly are fired by a woman and a grinning child. This is a literal bloodbath in which everyone is damned. As in *Hamlet*, there is death on top of death on top of death, and the few survivors seem smaller in stature than the ones who have perished. No wonder critics called Peckinpah a nihilist. No wonder audiences found him depressing.

W**ARNER BROS. COULDN'T DO MUCH WITH** the movie. Right before it opened, producer Phil Feldman waited until Peckinpah was vacationing in Hawaii and then cut an additional ten minutes to get it closer to two hours. That temporarily appeased theater owners but threw Peckinpah into one of his trademark violent rages as he threatened a lawsuit and further cemented his reputation as the most difficult director in Hollywood. The shorter version still didn't perform in theaters, partly because it was the same summer that *Butch Cassidy and the Sundance Kid* was released. Now there were some outlaws people could identify with. Although the overall theme of the two movies is the same—criminals trying to hold on as the Wild West is dying—one swept the Academy Awards and the other was merely nominated in two categories and then consigned to history. There's still an institute and a film festival called Sundance, but there will never be a Peckinpah Academy of Film. *The Wild Bunch* is mostly discussed in film classes and at out-of-the-way repertory theaters. It was not even seen in its original form until 1995, when a restored director's cut was released in theaters, and all those many years later it was still controversial. The MPAA Ratings Board tried to change its rating from the R it had received in 1969 to an NC-17, which would have made it impossible to release. Only intense lobbying by Warner Bros. and petition campaigns by writers and directors forced the MPAA to relent and leave the R alone. To this day, *Butch Cassidy* is by far the more popular film, but *The Wild Bunch* is the more influential. The reason is that Sam Peckinpah, God bless him, refused to Hollywoodize his story. Can you imagine Peckinpah using a three-minute bicycle-riding montage backed by B.J. Thomas singing "Raindrops Keep Falling on My Head"? I rest my case.

For those seeing *The Wild Bunch* for the first time, it might be difficult to understand why there was such editorial outrage over its violence. Peckinpah wasn't the first director to use blood squibs. Those little explosive red packets that simulate a bullet wound had been used in *Bonnie and Clyde* two years earlier. But Peckinpah was the first to use this many thousands of them. "I don't think he set out to demonstrate a bucket of red paint," said his lifelong friend Warren Oates, who played the jittery redneck Lyle Gorch in the film. "He set out to do something else. But on the set he'd say 'I want more,' and the prop man, or the makeup man, would throw him more: more blood, more guts. Some of the scenes were ghastly." Likewise, Peckinpah wasn't the first director to use slowmotion in the middle of a massively violent scene—Akira Kurosawa had pioneered that technique—but he was the first one to choreograph it so minutely that it became a ballet of death. He spent a full year in the editing room, making 3,643 cuts, the record for a Technicolor film. Many of the cuts are as short as three frames, or one-eighth of a second, so they can't even be seen with the naked eye. The final battle scene, which unfolds with the same visual chaos you would experience if you were there, has 339 cuts in only seven minutes of film.

But Peckinpah was an easy target. He was a profane, hard-drinking, brawling, gambling, whoring lone wolf who made enemies everywhere he went. So he took the brunt of the critical attack against explicit on-screen violence, especially for his slow-motion massacre scenes. And yet, as we now know from thousands of eyewitnesses, people who have endured shootings, car crashes, plunges from cliffs, earthquakes, tornados, fires—they all say the same thing, that it happened in slow motion. There is something that occurs psychologically when death threatens; the brain seems to slow down time. Peckinpah was the first to put that on film, and since then it's been copied by much less sensitive directors in much less worthy action films—and now it's become a bit of a cliché. But *The Wild Bunch* made all those films possible. Without *The Wild Bunch*, directors like Martin Scorsese and John Woo and Oliver Stone would have been censored to death, especially early in their careers. Ironically, many of the directors most freqently battered by the MPAA in its crusade against violence are the ones who hate violence the most and take it the most seriously. "If I could, I would make the violence ten times worse than I'm allowed to," Scorsese once said. Like Peckinpah, Scorsese is a propagandist against violence. And yet movies like *Total Recall* and *Die Hard*, which keep their violence relatively clean, have much higher body counts and routinely get R ratings. The more serious artist makes a killing an important event, almost a religious moment, something you can't quickly forget. The MPAA tried to revise *The Wild Bunch* rating not because it's more violent, but because it doesn't apologize for the violence or make sure that enough of the unrighteous are killed and the righteous spared. *The Wild Bunch* is dangerous because, at its most intense moments, its violence is unnervingly savage and beautiful at the same time.

When Peckinpah made the film, he was already an outcast in Hollywood. He had been blacklisted for three years after making *Major*

Dundee in northern Mexico, where there was brawling on the set, fifteen crew members were fired, the budget got out of control, and Charlton Heston became so enraged that he reportedly charged Peckinpah on his horse and tried to run him through with a saber. Nevertheless, when Columbia threatened to pull the plug, it was Heston who put up $600,000 of his own money to finish the film. It didn't help, though, because the picture came in at 161 minutes and Columbia chopped 55 more out of it without Peckinpah's approval. Shortly thereafter, Peckinpah was fired after working only three days on *The Cincinnati Kid*, and his Hollywood fate seemed to be sealed. He was an unemployable, undisciplined loose cannon who changed scripts on the set and went through money like water. He knocked around doing TV jobs for a while—he had written and produced *The Rifleman* early in his career—and got a job adapting *Noon Wine* as a TV movie. It won some awards, and Phil Feldman at Warner Bros. decided to give him another chance, even though the studio begged him not to.

But by that time there weren't many actors around who wanted the lead in a Peckinpah movie, especially this lead—an aging outlaw, getting so weak he can barely mount his horse anymore; who has killed and robbed his way through life and is now so hardened that he can use a temperance parade full of women and children to shield himself from gunfire; or coldly put a bullet through the head of a wounded comrade who has grown too weak to ride, or raise his hat in laughing triumph as he watches a dozen men on horseback go to their deaths on the bridge he's just blown up. And he was the good guy in the film. The lead role was turned down by Lee Marvin, Burt Lancaster, James Stewart, Charlton Heston, Gregory Peck, Sterling Hayden, Richard Boone and Robert Mitchum. The actor who finally got it was William Holden, who, appropriately enough, had his own reputation as a mean, nasty drunk, a brawler, and a womanizer. He had been acting in films for thirty years and lived in Switzerland to avoid paying taxes. He was Peckinpah's perfect leading man.

But there are actually two leading men in *The Wild Bunch*, and the relationship between them forms the arc of the story. The other one is Deke Thornton, played by Robert Ryan, who was nine years older than Holden but otherwise had a parallel career. Early in the movie we learn that Thornton and Pike once rode together, but Thornton got captured and tortured in Yuma Prison. Now he's been liberated by a steely-eyed railroad baron, played by Albert Dekker, because he's the only man who has any real chance of catching Pike's gang. The railroad man gives Thornton a crew of ghoulish hired gunmen who like to strip booty off dead bodies,

THE MORE SERIOUS ARTIST MAKES A KILLING AN IMPORTANT EVENT,
ALMOST A RELIGIOUS MOMENT,
SOMETHING YOU CAN'T QUICKLY FORGET.

then puts a bounty on Thornton's head so he can't run. Pike and Thornton share the same code—you don't kill the man you ride with—so the whole movie is an extended chase that sets up the question "Will Thornton be able to kill Pike?" The movie begins with a massacre, during which Thornton and Pike lock eyes but intentionally shoot away from each other, and it ends with a massacre. But the final confrontation never occurs. Peckinpah violates the cardinal rule of screenwriting—the two antagonists must always face each other, one on one—and at some point does an amazing and beautiful thing. The two men become one. One dies and the other dies with him. One lives and the other lives through him. The reason this movie rises above its violent context and affects us so strongly is that, miraculously, it might just be a love story.

IN THE FILM'S VERY FIRST IMAGE, CHILDREN ARE playing and laughing beside the railroad tracks as Pike and his men, disguised as World War I soldiers, ride into San Rafael, Texas, to carry out a bank robbery. Peckinpah shows us what's making the children laugh: They're slowly torturing scorpions to death by poking them around in a bed of red ants. Later they'll set fire to the ants and scorpions amid ecstatic cries of childhood delight. In other words, they're killers. Everyone in the movie is a killer. The whole universe is full of killers. The movie takes place in the land of the damned, where the only houses are burned and broken and the only people who could be called leaders are vicious opportunists who have the best weapons and the most men. The young, the old, the infirm are all mired in the muck. When we see the town of Agua Verde for the first time, the opening image is a baby suckling at a woman's breast, and across that breast is a bandolier. The only idealist in the movie is Angel, played by Jaime Sanchez, who rides with Pike and his gang so that one day he can liberate his village and his people. And yet Angel, too, is a killer, putting a bullet through the heart of his unfaithful woman and almost getting the whole gang killed.

Once you accept this universe—a godless world where killing is not only necessary, it's essential—then Pike does become a somewhat honorable man. When the old coot Sykes loses control of the horses on some sand dunes and almost gets everybody killed, the hot-headed Gorch brothers want to kill him. Sykes, played by the legendary Edmond O'Brien, has become dead weight and dangerous. And that's when Pike makes his only real "speech." "When you side with a man," he yells at the gang, "you stay with him. And if you can't do that, you're like some animal. You're finished. We're finished." It's the only sign that these wild remorseless men have some degree of honor. But they cling to it precariously. It's not their natural instinct. They believe it because, in their narrow world of guns, whores, and loot, it's all they have. As they're riding to a train robbery, Pike says, "I'd like to make just one last big score and then back off." Dutch, his sidekick and conscience, played by Ernest Borgnine in one of the greatest roles of his career, says, "Back off to what?"

Ernest Borgnine as Dutch (right) and William Holden as Pike.

EVERYONE IN THE MOVIE IS A KILLER.
THE WHOLE UNIVERSE
IS FULL OF KILLERS.

IT'S NOT POSSIBLE HERE TO GO OVER THE dozens of different readings of the film, which include claims that it was a statement about the Vietnam War; that it's an affront to women (if anything, it's an affront to humanity); or that it has a homosexual subtext (a claim made about almost all buddy movies). What I can say is that it is one of the few genuine American epics, and it's no accident that Peckinpah used some of the most beloved character faces from Hollywood to populate his world of killers. William Holden, Ernest Borgnine, Robert Ryan, and Edmond O'Brien look and talk and sound the same as they did in a dozen other westerns, but their American bravado has been turned on its head and they've become terrorists without even knowing when the change took place. It's also no accident that Peckinpah used Emilio Fernandez, the most famous actor and director in the history of the Mexican film industry, to play the loathesome General Mapache. Fernandez was the most famous actor on the set in the Mexico that Peckinpah loved. Half Indian, he had been born in northern Mexico and actually participated, as a boy, in the Mexican Revolution of 1910–17. And most telling of all, Peckinpah cast Ben Johnson, the sidekick of John Wayne himself, as Tector

Gorch. What kind of world are you living in when you see Ben Johnson naked in a wooden tub, fondling the breast of a hooker?

Peckinpah would no doubt say that it's the world we all live in. Critics have called *The Wild Bunch* the last great American western. (Clint Eastwood's *Unforgiven* in 1992 is sometimes compared to *The Wild Bunch*, but there's really no comparison. It lacked the perversity and unflinching realism of Peckinpah and had a feminist subtext besides.) Peckinpah's achievements wouldn't really be celebrated until after he died, in 1984. The only positive thing that came out of *The Wild Bunch* is that it was sufficiently admired to earn him a remarkably productive ten years of filmmaking. By the time he made *Convoy*, in 1978, he was once again in chaos, as a set burned down, he ran three weeks late, equipment was stolen, he had no written ending for the movie, and he was constantly feuding with the studio. It would be five more years before his final film, *The Osterman Weekend*, which was released a year before his death.

The Wild Bunch was his masterpiece, though, and it was one of those films that changed the lives of everyone involved, even though most of those lives didn't have much longer to run. It was Robert Ryan's last great role; he would succumb to

"I DON'T THINK SAM IS A HORRIBLE MANIAC ... IT'S JUST THAT HE INJURES YOUR INNOCENCE, AND YOU GET PISSED OFF ABOUT IT."

cancer four years later. The movie revived William Holden's career, and he would score again in *Network* before falling on a rug while drunk and fatally gashing his head on a table in 1981. Warren Oates died of a sudden heart attack in 1982, shortly after he and Peckinpah had gone in together on a Montana ranch. Edmond O'Brien would never again have a role as good, and died in 1985 at the age of seventy. Emilio Fernandez was convicted of manslaughter in 1976 for shooting a farm laborer but served his term and died at home in 1986. Ben Johnson would finally win an Oscar, for *The Last Picture Show*, in 1971, and died in 1996 at the age of seventy-six. Strangest of all, Albert Dekker never even saw the film. He died during editing. He was found naked in his Hollywood apartment, locked in the bathroom, his wrists handcuffed, leather ropes tied around his ankles, waist, chest, and neck, with hypodermic punctures on his arms and buttocks and profane words written all over his body in lipstick. The police suspected an autoerotic suicide, but the coroner ruled the death an accident.

Of the original gang, only Ernest Borgnine and Bo Hopkins, who dies in the opening massacre, lived to see the millennium. By that time Peckinpah had become shrouded in a mythology so thick that everyone in the business wanted to somehow connect with him. When I worked on the movie *Casino*, in 1995, there were stars and celebrities coming and going every day on the set, but none of them inspired more reverence than the day L.Q. Jones, who played one of the goofball bounty hunters in *The Wild Bunch*, showed up. David

Warner, one of Sam Peckinpah's favorite actors, once said, "Sam's greatest tragedy was that *The Wild Bunch* was so good." Or as Burt Young, another great character actor, once put it, "Sam's a pain in the ass, but we all want to be part of his gang. He's a genius, the bastard."

In the nineties there was finally something of a Peckinpah revival, beginning with Paul Seydor's documentary *The Wild Bunch: An Album in Montage*, which used seventy-two minutes of black-and-white footage that had been shot over three days on location and then filed away by Warner Bros. The 1995 rerelease introduced the film to a whole new generation—but maybe that wasn't even necessary. Another film that came out in '95, the Macedonian Academy Award nominee *Before the Rain*, opens with an image of children in a circle, torturing and burning alive small creatures for their amusement. Filmmakers halfway around the world didn't need to be reminded that *The Wild Bunch* was one of the greatest movies ever made. "I don't think Sam is a horrible maniac," his friend Warren Oates once said of him. "It's just that he injures your innocence, and you get pissed off about it."

FOR FURTHER DISTURBANCE

The Wild Bunch is available in three versions, but the only one approved by director Sam Peckinpah was the 145-minute European version, which includes a flashback showing how Thornton was captured, a flashback showing how Pike's lover Aurora was killed, a scene in the desert establishing that Crazy Lee is Sykes's grandson and that Pike deliberately abandoned him, a raid by Pancho Villa on Mapache as he awaits a telegram, the aftermath of Villa's raid in Agua Verde, and one minute of festivities at night in Angel's village. The 1995 restoration does not include the intermission that occurred immediately after a scene in which Pike and Dutch are riding together, and Pike says, "This is our last go-round, Dutch. This time we do it right."

Before Sam Peckinpah broke out of episodic TV in the sixties he was briefly picked to direct the western ONE-EYED JACKS (1961), and made additions to the original screenplay. But when Marlon Brando took over as director, Peckinpah received no screen credit. His directorial debut was THE DEADLY COMPANIONS (1961) with Brian Keith, followed by RIDE THE HIGH COUNTRY (1962), which many consider his best work. He followed up *The Wild Bunch* with the equally violent and explicit STRAW DOGS (1971). His own favorite film was JUNIOR BONNER (1972), which was released the same year as his biggest commercial hit, THE GETAWAY (1972). His other work includes MAJOR DUNDEE (1965), starring Charlton Heston in the film that got Peckinpah blacklisted for three years; THE BALLAD OF CABLE HOGUE (1969); PAT GARRETT AND BILLY THE KID (1973); the cult favorite BRING ME THE HEAD OF ALFREDO GARCIA (1974); THE KILLER ELITE (1975); CROSS OF IRON (1977), and the ultimate CB trucker film, CONVOY (1978). His final film was the thriller THE OSTERMAN WEEKEND (1983), based on the Robert Ludlum novel.

William Holden's first lead role was in GOLDEN BOY (1939), based on the Clifford Odets play about the boxing business. His breakthrough to stardom came in Billy Wilder's SUNSET BOULEVARD (1950) as Gloria Swanson's boytoy. He won the Academy

The Peckinpah cult hit *Bring Me the Head of Alfredo Garcia.*

Award for STALAG 17 (1953) and won the hearts of millions of women as the rough suitor of Kim Novak in PICNIC (1955). He had a late-life triumph in the hit NETWORK (1976). His last film was Blake Edwards's S.O.B. (1981).

Robert Ryan was an undistinguished contract player before breaking through in THE WOMAN ON THE BEACH (1947) as Joan Bennett's illicit lover. He would play film-noir heavies for most of his career—as an anti-Semitic murderer in CROSSFIRE (1947), the villain in ACT OF VIOLENCE (1949), the suspicious husband of Barbara Bel Geddes in CAUGHT (1949), an over-the-hill boxer in THE SET-UP (1949), and a cynical lover in CLASH BY NIGHT (1952). Other notable roles include BAD DAY AT BLACK ROCK (1955), GOD'S LITTLE ACRE (1958) and BILLY BUDD (1962).

Ernest Borgnine debuted in CHINA CORSAIR (1951), but his breakthrough role was as the ruthless sergeant in FROM HERE TO ETERNITY (1953). He was memorable as the heavy in *Bad Day at Black Rock*, but then won the Oscar for MARTY (1955) as a lonely middle-aged mama's boy looking for love. His other notable work includes THE DIRTY DOZEN (1967) and THE POSEIDON ADVENTURE (1972).

Ben Johnson, known for most of his career as John Wayne's sidekick, broke into the business as Henry Fonda's riding double in FORT APACHE (1948), then worked steadily for John Ford and other western directors in SHE WORE A YELLOW RIBBON (1949), RIO GRANDE (1950), WAGON-MASTER (1950), SHANE (1953), and THE LAST PICTURE SHOW (1971), among others.

Warren Oates was a close friend of Peckinpah's and appeared in almost all of his movies. His breakthrough role was in Peckinpah's RIDE THE HIGH COUNTRY (1962). *The Wild Bunch* is considered the best role of Oates's career, but he became known in later years for his work in the Monte Hellman movies TWO-LANE BLACKTOP (1971), COCKFIGHTER (1973), and CHINA 9, LIBERTY 37 (1978). His last film was TOUGH ENOUGH (1983).

Veteran heavy Albert Dekker starred in DR. CYCLOPS (1940) as the scientist who shrinks people to the size of dolls and was known for off-beat character roles. Among his memorable performances were THE KILLERS (1946), GENTLEMAN'S AGREEMENT (1947), EAST OF EDEN (1955), KISS ME DEADLY (1955), SUDDENLY LAST SUMMER (1959) and THE SOUND AND THE FURY (1959).

Edmond O'Brien won the Oscar as the sweaty press agent in THE BAREFOOT CONTESSA (1954), then was nominated again for SEVEN DAYS IN MAY (1964). Bo Hopkins made his film debut in *The Wild Bunch*, but would give his most memorable performance in AMERICAN GRAFFITI (1973) as the drawling hot-rodding kid from the wrong side of town. Emilio Fernandez, the most famous actor and director in Mexico, is best known for his direction of two films, FLOR SILVESTRE (1943) and MARÍA CANDELARIA (1943). Strother Martin's most famous role was in COOL HAND LUKE (1967).

THE WILD BUNCH: AN ALBUM IN MONTAGE (1996) is Paul Seydor's documentary on the making of the movie, with Ed Harris portraying the voice of Sam Peckinpah, and it's part of the DVD release.

Wanna see Shaft? Better ask yo

RICHARD ROUNDTREE
is

SHAF

The mob wanted Harlem back. They got Shaft . . . up to here.

"SHAFT" STARRING RICHARD ROUNDTREE · MOSES GUNN · CHARLES CIOFFI · CHRISTOPHER ST. JOHN · LAWRENCE PRESSMA
ARNOLD JOHNSON · DOMINIC BARTO · GEORGE STRUS · EDMUND HASHIM · DREW BUNDINI BROWN · TOMMY LANE · AL KIF
CASTING BY JUDITH LAMB   ART DIRECTION BY EMANUEL GERARD   SET DECORATION BY ROBERT DRUMHELLER   COSTUME DESIGN BY JOSEPH G. AULISI   MAKEUP

mamma!

T

NN MITCHELL · VICTOR ARNOLD · SHERRI BREWER · REX ROBBINS · CAMILLE YARBROUGH · MARGARET WARNCKE · JOSEPH LEON
EN RUSKIN   ORIGINAL MUSIC BY ISAAC HAYES · J. J. JOHNSON   CINEMATOGRAPHY BY URS FURRER   FILM EDITING BY HUGH A. ROBERTSON
N BELL   PRODUCER JOEL FREEMAN   ASSOCIATE PRODUCER DAVID GOLDEN   DIRECTED BY GORDON PARKS   WRITTEN BY ERNEST TIDYMAN · JOHN D. F. BLACK

"SHAFT" IS FAMOUS FOR MANY THINGS—
THE BOOM IN "BLAXPLOITATION" FILMS,
THE INVENTION OF BADASS BLACK ATTITUDE,
THE ULTIMATE WAH-WAH RHYTHM-AND-BLUES SCORE,
THE DEPICTION OF NEW YORK AS A DARWINIAN CESSPOOL—
BUT THERE'S ONE I'VE NEVER SEEN MENTIONED.
"SHAFT" ALSO INVENTED
PEDESTRIAN TERRORISM.

FROM THE OPENING SHOT, WHEN PRIVATE detective John Shaft emerges from the subway at Broadway and 42nd Street in his trademark black leather trenchcoat and beige cashmere turtleneck, he strides across Manhattan like a man who owns the place, never being so uncool as to actually pay attention to traffic. The cars can just bloody well adapt to him, and death to the motorist who doesn't. In fact, this was such an important stylistic detail to director Gordon Parks that he told Richard Roundtree, his star, never to look to the side when he crossed a street. Roundtree was understandably made a little nervous by this instruction—he was raised in the suburbs and not really that comfortable on the streets—and so he actually went out every day and practiced, checking his peripheral vision to see how much he could know about the cars without looking and how

aggressive he could be without getting run down. For that famous opening shot, backed by Isaac Hayes's classic "Theme from Shaft," Parks put the camera on top of a Times Square building and shot without closing the street. When Shaft almost gets hit by a cab, that's Richard Roundtree almost getting hit by a cab! Fortunately he stays in character and glares at the driver. He really does own this town.

After *Shaft* was released, in 1971, the streets of New York would never be the same. Every black adolescent and wannabe badass adopted the walk, the style, the swagger, the indifference to traffic, and the rather stilted lingo (added over writer Ernest Tidyman's objections) of that baaaaad mother—shut yo mouth!—I'm talkin' 'bout Shaft, we can dig it. If ever a single movie transformed a whole culture, *Shaft* was that movie. This was no black-pride wussy boy trucked in for the high school assembly. Shaft was a tough loner who dealt with the world on his own terms, and if that meant he occasionally had to knock somebody through a window or bust up some Italian goombahs in the Village, then that's what he'd do. Women loved him, of course, both gorgeous, purring black women and the freaky white women he picked up whenever he felt like it. Shaft was a force of nature, a lover of money, sex, and action—probably in that order.

SHAFT WAS NOT THE FIRST BLAXPLOITATION movie, although most people think it was. The term was invented by *Variety* after *Shaft* broke open the floodgates, but in fact the trend toward all-black, all-the-time cinema had been building for some time. In 1971 the only bona fide black mainstream star was Sidney Poitier, but he was too elegant to be an action hero, and besides, his audience was 70 percent white. Blaxploitation would reverse that ratio—for the first time movies could be successful on black box office alone—and Richard Roundtree would become the first action hero (actually antihero) who belonged entirely to the African-American community.

Roundtree was a total unknown when he landed the lead in *Shaft*. Director Gordon Parks, known for his thoughtful 1969 film *The Learning Tree*, about racism in a small Kansas town, wanted a new face, so he avoided the few "names" that would have been the more obvious choices. The first black action star had been Jim Brown, the former Cleveland Browns running back, who debuted

as a cavalry sergeant in *Rio Conchos* in 1964 but didn't get national attention until *The Dirty Dozen* in 1967. By 1970 he had made eleven films in three years and should have been the first choice to play Shaft, but by then he had a reputation for being difficult to work with. The other possibility was a much more polished actor named Raymond St. Jacques, who had broken ground for black actors in 1964 when he landed a role on *Rawhide*. He subsequently turned in many memorable roles—as the brutal Haitian police captain in *The Comedians* (1967), as the black man falsely convicted of raping and murdering a white woman in *If He Hollers Let Him Go* (1968), and as a wisecracking detective in *Cotton Comes to Harlem* (1970), considered by some to be the first blaxploitation film.

Richard Roundtree, on the other hand, was a college dropout and a bit player known mostly for being a pretty boy. He had grown up in New Rochelle, New York—home of Rob and Laura Petrie, for God's sake!—and been voted Most Popular, Most Handsome, and Best Dressed at New Rochelle High. He went to Southern Illinois University on a football scholarship, migrated toward the drama department ("because that's where the pretty girls were"), then left school entirely to go on the road with the Ebony Magazine Fashion Fair, touring seventy-nine cities as a model. He eventually joined the Negro Ensemble Company in New York, and when the audition came for *Shaft*, he was in Philadelphia, touring with the road company of *The Great White Hope*. He was all of twenty-nine years old.

The character of John Shaft—tough, sinewy private eye who doesn't take guff from white cops, black revolutionaries, Harlem bosses, or Mafia dons—was the creation of Ernest Tidyman, a hard-drinking white journalist who just decided one day that it was time for a black detective novel. The slim novel—which the movie follows pretty closely—had already been sold to MGM by the time it came out, in early 1971. (The studio was looking for black properties after the success of *Cotton Comes to Harlem*, which had grossed $20 million on a $2 million investment, especially since all its megareleases were flopping.) Tidyman, the son of a Cleveland crime reporter, was forty-three years old and the sort of old-school street journalist that doesn't exist anymore. He had only a seventh-grade education—it was the era when most reporters didn't go to college—and had learned to write while working for the *Cleveland News*, the *New York Post*, and the *New York Times*, which he joined in 1960, serving as editor of the *New York Times Magazine* from 1966 to 1969 before quitting to write novels. In later years, he would often tell the story of pitching the idea of a black private-eye series to his publisher. "What's the detective's name?" he was asked. Tidyman hadn't thought of a name yet, so he looked out the window of the office and saw a sign that said "Fire Shaft." "Shaft!" he said.

I find the story hard to accept at face value, since the name is so perfect for the character Tidyman created: His whole life is about shafting and getting shafted, and, of course, he has an amazing shaft. The novel version of Shaft didn't really break any new literary ground. It's written with the short, punchy street vernacular of a hundred books before it, and Tidyman's similes tend to be funny but lack the punch of a Raymond Chandler. ("Shaft felt like a ninety-year-old woman who had tried to hitch a ride on the back of a bus in wet sneakers, lost her footing, and fallen in the path of at least two cabs.") What the book did have was uncompromising sexuality and violence. Shaft is angry much of the time, and he has the street instincts of a wildcat and the sexual stamina of a bull. His closest literary predecessor is probably Mike Hammer. (Shaft was not the first black private eye, by the way. Ed Lacy had written a series of novels about a black shamus named Toussaint Moore.)

BUT THE NOVEL PULLS ITS PUNCHES WHEN IT comes to Shaft really taking on Whitey. Shaft has no civil-rights views at all; he dislikes black people as much as white ones. He doesn't actually take on the Establishment—he takes on the safer white institution of the Mafia. And it's not even an accurate depiction of the Mafia; it's a special superracist Mafia that kidnaps the daughter of a Harlem crime kingpin. (Three things wrong with this picture. The Mafia wasn't into kidnapping. They didn't harm women. And at the time of the novel and the movie, Joey Gallo had formed an alliance between his Brooklyn mob and the black Harlem mob.) Shaft gets involved with a black revolutionary group, but only because its leader is his childhood friend and he wants to save his lame ass. Shaft doesn't live in Harlem, even though his cases take him there; his home base is a bachelor pad in Greenwich Village, which agrees with his bohemian nature, and his office is in Times Square. Throughout the story, he has a love-hate relationship with a white police detective who constantly enables Shaft to do things like withhold evidence and kill people and then walk free—because supposedly the NYPD needs Shaft on the streets, where he can go places they can't. (The same cop-private eye relationship would be stolen for *The Rockford Files*, with James Garner as the ex-con renegade gumshoe constantly refusing to cooperate with a frustrated LAPD lieutenant.) Later blaxploitation films would get much darker in their treatment of the white system, and yet Shaft was perceived as being very ahead of its time on civil rights. In one of the movie's most famous scenes, Shaft sits at a table in Cafe Reggio, on the home turf of the Mafia, where a flashily dressed mob soldier walks over, stares him in the eye, and says, "I'm looking for a nigger named Shaft." Without missing a beat, Shaft says, "You found him. Wop." Early audiences would erupt in cheers at that moment, providing some needed juice to a plot that had become confusing while at the same time remaining thin as a pancake. (Oddly enough, TV versions of *Shaft* have this famous scene altered, so that the mob guy says, "I'm looking for Shaft," and Shaft answers, "You found him"—pretty much losing the whole black-Italian tension.)

What's ironic about *Shaft*, in retrospect, is that the movie that put black actors and directors into the mainstream was frequently regarded by the black community as an embarrassment. It was panned by critics, both black and white, and the blacks involved in making it didn't even defend it that aggressively. Clayton Riley, a black *New York Times* critic, called *Shaft* "an extended lie, a distortion that simply grows larger and more unbelievable with each frame." Junius Griffin of the NAACP, lumping it with all blaxploitation films, called it "a ripoff." Roy Innes, the then-national director of the Congress of Racial Equality (CORE), said that "the present black movie phenomenon . . . in its ultimate destruction of the minds of black youth, is potentially far more dangerous than Stepin Fetchit and his lot." And Black Panther leader Huey Newton didn't like the way blaxploitation movies, including Shaft, treated black revolutionaries. "They leave revolution out," he said, "or if it's in, they make it look stupid and naive. I think it's part of a conspiracy."

Actually, *Shaft* is such a conventional Hollywood movie that you could have made the main character white—or Chinese, for that matter—with very few alterations. It's full of private eye clichés— the mysterious client who lies to him; the beautiful woman who has to be rescued; the ambiguous relationship with the law; the decaying mean streets that the detective understands but is not really a part of. Perhaps this is why, when Gordon Parks got Ernest Tidyman's script, he insisted on hiring a second screenwriter to "blacken it up." The assignment went to a former *Star Trek* writer with the highly appropriate name of John D. F. Black, who added all the "cats," "right ons," high-fives, and some of

Following pages: Shaft interrogates an uninvited visitor.

SHAFT HAS NO CIVIL-RIGHTS VIEWS AT ALL;

HE DISLIKES BLACK PEOPLE
AS MUCH AS WHITE ONES.

"HE HATED THE IDEA THAT PEOPLE WOULD HEAR ALL THAT PHONY BLACK DIALECT."

the famous one-liners. ("I got two problems, baby—I was born black and I was born poor.") Tidyman was mortified by the changes—because he knew he would get blamed for them. As his son Nathaniel Rayle later recalled, "He hated the idea that people would hear all that phony black dialect and think 'What did you expect from a white screenwriter?'" Tidyman had problems with other aspects of the production, too. He thought Roundtree was "too pretty" to be a badass, and he thought the Isaac Hayes proto-rap voiceover on the theme song was hokey. Tidyman took to doing an imitation of Hayes at bars that was apparently pretty hysterical. "Who dat Shaft! Who dat man!" he would sing for his bibulous audience.

As it turned out, Tidyman didn't have to worry. He soon became one of the few white recipients of the NAACP Image Award in the history of that organization—although there were raised eyebrows when the clueless audience cheered at his introduction and then were startled to see he was a white man. The prolific Tidyman would go on to write seven more *Shaft* novels over the next three years, finally killing off the character in 1975 in *The Last Shaft* as blaxploitation petered out. But by that time he'd moved on to even bigger projects, winning an Oscar for *The French Connection* (1971) and adapting his novel *High Plains Drifter* for

Clint Eastwood. Even though two *Shaft* sequels were made—*Shaft's Big Score*, based on Tidyman's novel, and *Shaft in Africa*, which Tidyman had nothing to do with—the book that Tidyman fans consider the best of the lot, *Shaft Among the Jews*, was never filmed.

TIDYMAN NEVER TRIED TO CLAIM *SHAFT* WAS anything more than it appeared to be—an escapist detective yarn—but the other creative people were upset by their icy critical reception. "I hate that term, blaxploitation," said director Gordon Parks. "*Shaft* has nothing to do with exploitation. I don't know where they got that. What *Shaft* was about was providing work for black people that they never had before, letting them get into films. That's not exploitation. *Shaft* was the type of film that Hollywood made with white actors. Cagney could have been in *Shaft*. But I didn't notice that they called those kind of movies white exploitation."

Actually, they did. "Exploitation" was a venerated term among Hollywood moguls, used simply as a synonym for marketing, and the Cagney gangster films were highly controversial. But everyone involved in *Shaft*, including Isaac Hayes and Richard Roundtree, seemed to think "blaxploitation" was a slur—partly because black intellectuals were hammering away at the trend. "The blaxploitation films are a phenomenon of self-hate," said Tony Brown, the dean of Howard University's school of communications. "Look at the image of *Super Fly*. Going to see yourself as a drug dealer when you're oppressed is sick. Not only are blacks identifying with him, they're paying for the identification. It's sort of like a Jew paying to get into Auschwitz."

Unfortunately, most people didn't distinguish between *Shaft* and the later, more cynical blaxploitation films, and it didn't help that the most controversial of them all, *Super Fly* (1972), was directed by Gordon Parks Jr., the son of the Shaft director. *Super Fly* came out a year after *Shaft* and tells the story of Youngblood Priest, a cocaine dealer ("fly" is the ghetto name for coke) looking to make his last big sale before retirement while battling corrupt white cops who try to steal his stash. Priest spends the movie sniffing coke himself, beating up black competitors and white cops, enjoying sex with his black mistress and an eager white girl, then driving off into the sunset in his Rolls Royce, rich and happy.

It was the kind of movie that Gordon Parks Sr. never could have made. Parks was, in fact, such a poster boy for self-made black intellectuals that he no doubt had to burn a few bridges just to work for Hollywood at all. Born in 1912, the youngest of fifteen children raised in Fort Scott, Kansas, he had been forced to seek work at sixteen, when his mother died, scrambling around as a dishwasher, a flophouse janitor, a piano player in a whorehouse, a hotel busboy, a musician with bandleader Larry Duncan's orchestra, a Civilian Conservation Corps

day laborer, and a railroad dining car waiter on the Northern Pacific. His life changed when, as a young man, he bought a $12 camera in Chicago and started doing fashion shoots for department stores and supplementing his income with portrait work. This led to a job with the Office of War Information during World War II—training ground for many great photographers and directors—followed by a stint with Standard Oil of New Jersey shooting industrial layouts. His big break came in 1948, when he submitted a photo essay on a Harlem gang leader to *Life* magazine. In the coming years, he would work for many magazines—alternating between high fashion shoots in Paris and New York and social realism photography in the slums of Harlem, Mississippi, and Brazil—but he was most closely associated with *Life*. He was friends with Ingrid Bergman, Gloria Vanderbilt, Malcolm X, Muhammad Ali, Stokely Carmichael, and the Black Panthers, among others, and his photos of the Jim Crow South were among the most influential catalysts for change as civil-rights laws were finally passed in the sixties.

Though he had always been interested in making films—directing short documentaries in Brazil and elsewhere—he didn't get the chance to make a feature until he was fifty-six years old. John Cassavetes, the guru of independent filmmakers, was a fan of Parks's 1963 autobiographical novel, *The Learning Tree*, and he sought out Parks to tell him he wanted help bringing down the color bar in Hollywood. Parks gave him permission to pitch the movie version of *The Learning Tree*, and twenty-four hours later Cassavetes called, telling Parks to take the next plane to the coast, where Cassavetes would be waiting for him in the office of Warner Bros. executive Kenny Hyman. Hyman bought *The Learning Tree* on the spot and hired Parks to write and direct with a $3 million budget. Parks resigned from *Life* magazine after almost a quarter-century, and eventually he made the film, which opened in August 1969 to mixed reviews. (It was briefly retitled *Learn, Baby, Learn* and became more influential with time, so much so that at one point Jerry Falwell tried to get it banned from schools.) *The Learning Tree* was the first major Hollywood release directed by a black man, which is why MGM called on him two years later, when *Shaft* was in the works.

SHAFT IS ONE OF THOSE MOVIES THAT'S BETTER than its screenplay, and there are two reasons for that. One was Parks's photographic ability. The streets of New York have never looked so gloriously sinister and alive, almost as though the city itself is a character in the story. (Compare the 2000 remake, with its lifeless generic-urban cinematography.) The second reason for its success was the score of funkmaster Isaac Hayes, which was perfect for its time. Hayes was a writer-producer at Stax Records in Memphis who was known mostly for the hits he wrote for Sam and Dave ("Soul Man," "Hold On, I'm Coming"), but "Theme from Shaft" would make him a star in his own right while, oddly enough, launching his own film career as an actor. (How many film composers have become actors? I think the answer would be . . . one.)

"Theme from Shaft" became a monster number-one radio hit—despite being almost four minutes long—and at some point Hayes wrote down the entire lyrics to the song. Since I've never heard most of these words, I can only assume it was some kind of working text that was pared down before the final version was released, but they're worth preserving just for their value to future funk historians:

"Who's the black private dick that's the sex machine to all the chicks? If your answer is 'Shaft!,' then you're damn right. But I ask then, who is the man who would risk his neck for his brother man? If you again answer, 'Shaft!' can you dig it? Can I ask who's the cat that won't cop out when there's danger all about? Would that answer again be 'Shaft'? If so, right on. You know, they say this cat Shaft is a bad mother-(Shut your mouth.) I just talkin' 'bout Shaft here. (We can dig it.) From everything that I've ever read, the only thing that's for sure, is that he's a complicated man but no one understands him but his woman. (JOHN SHAFT!)"

The "We can dig its" were sung, of course, by the Bar-Kays, with Hayes himself doing the basso profundo lyric line that has been credited as the first rap song. The movie soundtrack won the Oscar and the Grammy and went platinum.

ALAS, BLAXPLOITATION LASTED A LITTLE LESS than three years and then vanished abruptly. It had been made possible by a combination of several things—the tail end of the "black is beautiful" trend that was part and parcel of the hippie era; the failure of big-event Hollywood movies as filmgoers abandoned downtown theaters (New York's first suburban multiplex opened the same week *Shaft* premiered); and the continuing youth movement in Hollywood that had been constantly in search of new niche markets ever since *Easy Rider* in 1969. Between 1971 and 1975 there were 200 blaxploitation movies released, most of them God-awful, 80 percent of them written and directed by white men, and in retrospect, *Shaft* is the least representative of them.

Shaft turned out to be the twelfth most successful film of the year, earning an initial domestic gross of $7 million on an investment of $1.5 million—and temporarily saving MGM from financial ruin. But it would be a tiny independent film called *Sweet Sweetback's Baad Assss Song*, released at virtually the same time, that would establish the more long-lasting blaxploitation formula. Unlike *Shaft*, *Sweet Sweetback* had a following that was virtually 100 percent black, and director Melvin Van Peebles said he made it to "get the Man's foot out of all our black asses" by telling the story of "a brother getting the Man's foot out of his ass." Van Peebles had been working in Europe, where he was the editor of the French edition of *Mad* magazine and an actor with the Dutch National Theatre. He had managed to get a director's permit from the French Film Center to shoot a short version of his novel *Story of a Three-Day Pass*, about a black GI stationed in France. That led to his getting hired to direct *Watermelon Man*, the underrated comedy starring Godfrey Cambridge as a white man who turns black overnight and loses his job, family, and house. But *Sweetback* was to be

Van Peebles's pièce de résistance, the first film where he had total control—and he succeeded in spite of terrible acting, low production values, a budget of only $500,000, and a plot that would strain the credulity of the most credulous. Van Peebles took the starring role himself as Sweetback, a professional live-sex-act performer whose boss is named Beetle the Pimp. When Sweetback happens to see a couple of cops whupping up on a black militant named Mu-Mu, Sweetback deals with them violently and flees into Harlem. For the rest of the movie, he's a ghetto hero and a cop killer, getting his way by offering his sexual favors to any woman who can help him. (Women even have sex with him while he's handcuffed.) He finally escapes to Mexico, and an end title card comes up: "Watch out! A baad assss nigger is coming back to collect some dues."

ODDLY ENOUGH, THIS CARTOONISH FILM— in which a stud black hero fornicates his way to freedom—has all the elements that would be unfairly attributed to *Shaft* in later years. And because it made money, it would be copied in endless variations throughout the blaxploitation cycle in a sort of cynical white-man's version of what the black audience really wants: a sexually potent black man, constantly oppressed by white guys who he has to beat up and kill, fighting for gangster respect and material wealth. Of course, Charles Bronson in the *Death Wish* series and Clint Eastwood in the *Dirty Harry* series were white versions of the same myth, but they were always given higher motives for their vigilante violence. They never used women or did anything for money, for example, whereas the black antiheroes were sometimes celebrated for being pimps, armed robbers, and, in Melvin Van Peebles's original, oppressed live-sex-act performers.

No wonder the NAACP finally said "Enough." The blaxploitation films made after 1971 have been described by film historian Daniel J. Leab as among the most shallow and demeaning films ever made. They were, he writes, "filled with sadistic brutality, sleazy sex, venomous racial slurs, and the argot of the streets. Social commentary of any sort was kept to a minimum. Superspade was a violent man who lived a violent life in pursuit of black women, white sex, quick money, easy success, cheap 'pot,' and other pleasures. In these films white was synonymous with every conceivable kind of evil and villainy. Whites were moral lepers, most of whom were psychotically antiblack and whose vocabulary was laced with the rhetoric of bigotry." In other words, the films that were initially conceived as an antidote to racism became . . . racist.

As the blaxploitation trend started to peter out, the battlefield was littered with one-shot wonders who would never again get the chance to act, direct, or star. The only survivors were those who became independent producers themselves, like Fred Williamson, another retired football star who made some of the strongest titles of the blaxploitation years—*Hammer*, *Black Caesar*, *The Legend of Nigger Charley*—and then continued to work steadily for the next thirty years as a star in Europe; a supporting player in Hollywood; and as the director-producer-star of his own low-budget films, which wisely moved away from the blaxploitation formulas and followed the example of Shaft—an action hero who happens to be black. *Shaft* had opened up the door for black actors and directors, but it was a younger generation who would walk through that door. Between 1975 and 1985 there were only two mainstream black stars—first Richard Pryor, then Eddie Murphy—but by the late eighties there was more black work available in Hollywood than ever before, although there were still complaints by the NAACP that much of the work for black

IN OTHER WORDS,
THE FILMS THAT WERE INITIALLY CONCEIVED AS AN
ANTIDOTE TO RACISM
BECAME . . . RACIST.

actors involved disreputable character types. (The charge doesn't really hold up, since almost all acting work is a disreputable character type of one sort or another.)

UNFORTUNATELY, THE PEOPLE ASSOCIATED with *Shaft* didn't benefit that much from the smashing of the color bar. Typical was the career of Isaac Hayes, who parlayed his fame from the movie into a series of films in which he appeared in his recording-career persona of Black Moses, "a bald sex bomb in chain vests and tights." "I started with a chain necklace," he said, explaining his penchant for jewelry overkill. "Then a chain belt. Then I put a chain vest on, and women went crazy. So I said, why not give them a cheap thrill? I had the tights, chains, French rabbit-fur boots. All auctioned off now." Hayes's last starring role was at the tail end of the blaxploitation cycle, in *Truck Turner*, but he continued to make TV appearances as a supporting player on *The Rockford Files* and *The A Team*. By the time he went bankrupt, in the nineties— hence the auctioning off of his beloved chains and rabbit fur—he was one of the blaxploitation players who felt left behind by the whole trend.

"There were white writers," said Hayes, "and they wrote their interpretation of how they thought it should go. They didn't have a deep understanding. They didn't live there. And they just kept dishin' out the same kind of thing, and it was insulting that they had the audacity to do that. But again, the people in the hood were eating it up because they finally had their own people on the screen. So

that's what was wrong with it. I had some problems with blaxploitation. You had whitesploitation films, too: *Chained Heat*, *The Texas Chain Saw Massacre*, and all that junk. But they had other choices. We only had one. Now there's a whole different emergence of black filmmakers who have creative control. And it's almost tippytoeing, it's bordering on exploitation, when you talk about *Boyz N the Hood* and all that kind of stuff."

After his bankruptcy, Hayes followed the example of John Travolta and became a Scientologist. For much of the nineties he was a morning radio host in New York City, while occasionally going back to the recording studio and finding time to be crowned a king in Ghana. In 2002, he was inducted into the Rock and Roll Hall of Fame, along with the Ramones and the Talking Heads, and to this day he's one of the most recognizable presences on the streets of New York, much more so than Richard Roundtree or anyone else associated with blaxploitation, with the possible exception of Jim Brown.

Roundtree, who was paid only $12,500 for *Shaft*, was not so lucky. "I didn't know what I was doing when I made *Shaft*," he said. "I was scared, and Gordon held my hand throughout the filming." He starred in both *Shaft* sequels, and it wasn't until the last one that he realized he had become famous. He had also become typecast forever, a fate sealed by a series of lame CBS movies-of-the-week based on the Shaft character. There were seven of these ninety-minute movies, alternating Tuesday nights on a wheel with the show *Hawkins* and *Tuesday*

Night Movie. The series debuted with such high hopes that NBC felt compelled to match it with their own black detective (James McEachin in *Tenafly*), but it was a pale, sickly parody of the movie character. Shaft was emasculated, watered-down, and made to work within the system instead of being the fierce loner of the movie. Despite some high-powered supporting players—Robert Culp, Tony Curtis, and George Maharis as bad guys, Michael Ansara as a police sergeant, Jayne Kennedy and Cathy Lee Crosby as cheesecake—it was despised by public and critics alike. "*Shaft* on TV," wrote Cecil Smith of the *Los Angeles Times*, "makes Barnaby Jones look like Eldridge Cleaver." Or, as Ernest Tidyman might have put it, "Who dat man?"

By that time, Roundtree was associated with a dead genre. He was still popular enough to get second and third leads—for example, in *Diamonds* with Robert Shaw, a movie that performed so badly in 1975 that it was temporarily retitled *Diamond Shaft* in an effort to market it to the black community and squeeze extra profit out of it. After that, it was mostly TV guest shots on shows like *Dr. Quinn, Medicine Woman* and *Rescue 77* and the occasional low-budget action film, but he never stopped working. He got another shot at a series in 1997 with the critically acclaimed urban drama *413 Hope St.*, but it was canceled by Fox after one season. He played Booker T. Washington in the TV movie *Having Our Say* and was in Arnold Schwarzenegger's sole directing effort, *Christmas in Connecticut*. And from time to time he would resurface in the mainstream—*City Heat* with Clint Eastwood, *Seven* with Morgan Freeman and Brad Pitt, *George of the Jungle*, *Man Friday* with Peter O'Toole, and *Steel* with Shaquille O'Neal.

The biggest challenge of his life came in 1993, when he was diagnosed with breast cancer—although extremely rare in men, it does happen—and underwent a modified radical mastectomy and six months of chemotherapy. He was supporting a wife and three kids at the time, so he had to keep the disease a secret in order to continue working. Now in his sixties and in full remission, he talks to men about breast exams, since he's one of the few celebrities ever to have the disease.

SHAFT WOULD OUTLIVE ALL THE OTHER blaxploitation films, mainly because Ted Turner bought the MGM library in the early eighties and discovered that it was a perennial favorite on his TV networks, even in a heavily edited format. As a younger generation discovered the film, blaxploitation become popular all over again in the late eighties and nineties, with Keenen Ivory Wayans directing the ultimate blaxploitation sendup, *I'm Gonna Git You Sucka!*, using many of the original stars, and Quentin Tarantino using blaxploitation elements in all his films while pumping new life into the careers of Pam Grier, Fred Williamson, and other mean black dudes and dudettes from the seventies. Ernest Tidyman didn't live to see the renaissance, having died of kidney failure at age fifty-six after a lifetime of drinking. By that time, he had become known for writing big-event miniseries, such as *Guyana Tragedy: The*

Story of Jim Jones and *Alcatraz: The Whole Shocking Story*. But he always appreciated the fame that came late in life from *Shaft*.

For Parks, on the other hand, that fame was bittersweet. He had regarded *Shaft* as a lark, an interlude between more serious projects, but when Hollywood gave him the chance to make his dream movie—*Leadbelly*, the story of Texas bluesman Huddie Ledbetter—audiences didn't respond. By the end of the seventies, he was one more director that Hollywood had toyed with for a while then cast aside. Not that he didn't have plenty to do. He had always dabbled in music composing, writing an orchestral work for the Vienna Symphony and a concerto for cellist Yo-Yo Ma, and in the eighties he choreographed a ballet in honor of Martin Luther King. He eventually settled into the role of the patriarchal black intellectual, winning award after award, collecting twenty-four honorary doctorates, and being especially proud of the Gordon Parks Independent Film Award, a $10,000 prize given each year to a young African-American writer or director. In 1988, he received the National Medal of the Arts, and ten years later, pushing ninety but still active, he dedicated the Gordon Parks Academy in East Orange, New Jersey, a magnet school for students in radio, animation, film, and television.

Unfortunately, Parks did live to see the 2000 *Shaft* remake, starring Samuel L. Jackson in the Roundtree role. The new screenwriters—who had to be black, because Jackson refused to say words written by white men—changed Shaft to a cop (!) who quits the force halfway through the movie and

removed the "sex machine" aspect entirely, pretty much abandoning the gritty, lone-wolf aspect of his character. The result is yet one more shoot-'em-up action flick and nothing that could be said to affect the culture in one way or another.

Pop-culture enthusiasts have endlessly analyzed the popularity of *Shaft*, and most of them regard it (wrongly) as the first celebration of a black hero. He wasn't the first and he wasn't really a hero in any classic sense. He was just a tough guy with a great wardrobe who did what he wanted. "Before Roundtree," writes Jeff Siegel in *About... time* magazine, "black actors who wanted to be stars had to be like Sidney Poitier—safe enough for a white daughter to bring home for dinner. After Roundtree, black actors who wanted to be stars could look forward to having the white daughter for dessert." But this is too simplistic. It's hard to take *Shaft* seriously anymore when "Theme from Shaft" is being used to sell French fries for Burger King, with Mr. Potato Head playing Shaft, but to me the likeability of the character has to do with his flippancy about race relations. He really doesn't care. He's a truly free man. As the critic Maurice Peterson once wrote, this was "the first picture to show a black man who leads a life free of racial torment." Ernest Tidyman and Gordon Parks put a black character in the mainstream by refusing to treat him as a hero, role model, or victim, and by refusing to treat him as black.

FOR FURTHER DISTURBANCE

Everyone argues about which movie is the first true blaxploitation film, with most coming down on the side of either *Shaft*, the biggest moneymaker, or SWEET SWEETBACK'S BAAD ASSSSS SONG (1971), the Melvin Van Peebles cheapie about a live-sex-show performer who gets unjustly busted by the cops and then fornicates his way to freedom, beating up bigots along the way. Actually, better arguments could be made for two earlier films— COTTON COMES TO HARLEM (1970), the MGM film based on a novel by Chester Himes that made *Shaft* possible when it grossed $20 million (ten times its budget), and WATERMELON MAN (1970), Van Peebles's previous film, a comedy starring Godfrey Cambridge as a bigoted white insurance salesman who wakes up black and loses his family, job, and possessions as a result. (Cambridge actually stars in both movies. In *Cotton Comes to Harlem*, he plays jive-talking detective Gravedigger Jones. He and his partner, Coffin Ed Johnson, played by Raymond St. Jacques, are trying to figure out who robbed the Back to Africa rally.) The fact that both 1970 movies were comedies probably explains why they weren't considered as important as *Sweetback* and *Shaft*.

There were more than 200 blaxploitation movies made in the seventies, but the most impor-tant ones were Gordon Parks Jr.'s SUPER FLY (1972), which is the ultimate over-the-top pimp-lifestyle movie; COME BACK, CHARLESTON BLUE (1972), the sequel to *Cotton Comes to Harlem*; MELINDA (1972), starring Calvin Lockhart; COOL BREEZE (1972), starring Thalmus Rasulala, Judy Pace, Jim Watkins, and Pam Grier in one of her first roles; HAMMER (1972), the blaxploitation debut of Fred "the Hammer" Williamson; BLACULA (1972), with William Marshall and Vonetta McGee; the classic THE MACK (1973), starring Max Julien as an ex-con turned pimp, running hos with his main man Richard Pryor; Fred Williamson in Larry Cohen's BLACK CAESAR (1973); FOXY BROWN (1974), in which Pam Grier kicks all kinds of ass; WILLIE DYNAMITE (1974), with Roscoe Orman as the world's number-one superpimp, a mean mother hassled by cops, competing gangs, and social workers who want to take his hos away; Matt Cimber's sleazy THE CANDY TANGERINE MAN (1975), starring John Daniels as the baddest pimp on the Sunset Strip, filmed with actual hookers and hoods; BOGARD (1976), also called Black Fist, starring Richard Lawson, who is so tough he's known by the ghetto term for "Humphrey Bogart"; CAR WASH (1976), starring Franklin Ajaye, Bill Duke, George Carlin, Antonio Fargas, and Richard Pryor; and Jamaa Fanaka's PENITENTIARY (1979), starring Leon Isaac Kennedy, who has to do hard time in a cell with a homosexual psychopath, then boxes his way out of prison and avenges the death of a friend in a prison-gang war. *Penitentiary* was the last hit of the blaxploitation era and spawned two equally well-made sequels, PENITENTIARY II (1982) and PENITENTIARY III (1987).

There would be major competition for the title of worst blaxploitation film, mainly because they were all churned out on the cheap. BAD, BLACK & BEAUTIFUL (1974), starring Gwynn Barbee, is fairly excruciating, as are RUN, NIGGER, RUN (1974), starring Bobby Stevens, lead singer of the Checkmates Ltd., in his first and only performance as a dope-smuggling pimp, and SWEET JESUS PREACHER MAN (1973), which stars Roger E. Mosely as a Mafia hit man disguised as a ghetto

Never a dude like this one!
He's got a plan to stick it to The Man!

THE SIG SHORE PRODUCTION

Super Fly

See and hear CURTIS MAYFIELD play his Super Fly score!

The Sig Shore Production "SUPER FLY" starring RON O'NEAL · CARL LEE · JULIUS W. HARRIS · SHEILA FRAZIER · CHARLES McGREGOR · Music Composed and Arranged by CURTIS MAYFIELD · Screenplay by PHILLIP FENTY · Produced by SIG SHORE · Directed by GORDON PARKS, JR. · from Warner Bros., a Warner Communications company R

preacher who decides to help out the community by turning on his bosses. THE BLACK GODFATHER (1974) stars a wooden Rod Perry as a syndicate boss trying to get rid of an evil-whitey drug empire. NIGGER RICH (1974) has a similar plot, with Paul Harris as the godfather battling the wops with the help of a drag-queen hit man, played by Serena. Al Adamson's wacky DYNAMITE BROTHERS (1973) is a kung-fu *Death Wish* story starring Alan Tang and Timothy Brown. BROTHERHOOD OF DEATH (1976) is a talky assemble-the-squad flick about three soul brothers from Nam who cruise around in a school bus fighting the Ku Klux Klan. And THE $6000 NIGGER (1980) stars the "chitlin' circuit" comedian Wildman Steve as a wino given a serum that makes him bulletproof.

There are other blaxploitation oddities that defy classification. THE LEGEND OF NIGGER CHARLEY (1972) is a western starring Fred Williamson as a man who goes from slave to gunfighter, and it was ballyhooed for weeks with a giant banner in Times Square that said "Nigger Charley Is Coming." Although it was one of Paramount's best-performing pictures of the year, Williamson was peeved that studio executives wouldn't even mention the title in public. TRICK BABY (1973) is the only blaxploitation film starring a white man— a character named Johnny O'Brien, known in the ghetto as "White Folks" by his friends and "Trick Baby" by his enemies. Since he was fathered by a white john who impregnated his prostitute mother, he can pass for white. He and his partner, Mel Stuart, take on the mob after they unwittingly pull a con on a Mafia chieftain's uncle. In DOLEMITE (1975), Rudy Ray Moore establishes a category all his own, as a kung-fu pimp and stand-up comic who's released from prison on a temporary pardon so he can recruit an army of karate-kicking prostitutes and build a machine-gun-equipped pimpmobile to make war on the pimp who framed him. Dolemite returns in THE HUMAN TORNADO (1976), and this time he has to make all-out war on a redneck sheriff after selling his sexual services to the sheriff's wife. And special mention should be made of WELCOME HOME, BROTHER CHARLES (1975) for having one of the most original plots in film history: The star's penis takes on a life of its own, stretches to more than twenty feet long, and creeps across rooms to invade the bodies of sleeping women.

Gordon Parks Sr., *Shaft's* director, was already known as the first black director to make a Hollywood film, THE LEARNING TREE (1969), based on his 1963 autobiographical novel about growing up in Kansas in the twenties that was briefly retitled *Learn, Baby, Learn.* He would use the cachet of *Shaft* to land his dream project, LEADBELLY (1976), the story of Texas bluesman Huddie Ledbetter that, although critically acclaimed, didn't return its investment and effectively ended Parks's big-budget career.

Pulp novelist Ernest Tidyman, the creator of *Shaft,* would win the Academy Award a year later for his screenplay for THE FRENCH CONNECTION (1971). He also adapted his novel SHAFT'S BIG SCORE! (1972) for the screen and wrote HIGH PLAINS DRIFTER (1973) before becoming a TV-

miniseries specialist. Two of his TV projects are available on video: GUYANA TRAGEDY: THE STORY OF JIM JONES (1980) and ALCATRAZ: THE WHOLE SHOCKING STORY (1980). He had nothing to do with the second sequel, SHAFT IN AFRICA (1973), or the ill-fated *Shaft* TV series.

After the two sequels and the TV series, Richard Roundtree starred in a modest thriller called DIAMONDS (1975) opposite Robert Shaw, and it was rereleased later as *Diamond Shaft* to capitalize on his fame. *Shaft* was not his film debut. He had already appeared in WHAT DO YOU SAY TO A NAKED LADY? (1970). Other feature roles would include MAN FRIDAY (1975) with Peter O'Toole, GAME FOR VULTURES (1979) with Richard Harris, the South Korean epic INCHON! (1982) with Laurence Olivier, CITY HEAT (1984) with Clint Eastwood, SEVEN (1995) with Morgan Freeman and Brad Pitt, ONCE UPON A TIME . . . WHEN WE WERE COLORED (1996), GEORGE OF THE JUNGLE (1997), and STEEL (1997) with Shaquille O'Neal.

Isaac Hayes, known mostly as a songwriter and music producer prior to *Shaft,* parlayed his newfound fame into a full-fledged recording and acting career. For his album *Black Moses* (1972), he was billed as "a bald sex bomb in chain vests and tights," and shortly thereafter he made his film debut in Duccio Tessari's THREE TOUGH GUYS (1974) as an ex-cop trying to raise money to prove his innocence of the crime that got him kicked off the force. (Italian star Lino Ventura is the motorcycle-riding priest who helps him fight Fred Williamson's gang.) He also appeared in ESCAPE FROM NEW YORK (1981) as the Duke of New York, and in the Keenen Ivory Wayans send-up of blaxploitation **I'M GONNA GIT YOU SUCKA** (1988). One of the funniest scenes in the movie has badass black dudes strolling down the sidewalk to an Isaac Hayes funk theme, and then the camera pans back behind them to show Hayes himself, playing the theme as he walks.

You can't talk about black action stars without mentioning the first one, Jim Brown, who debuted in **RIO CONCHOS** (1964) as a cavalry sergeant and broke through in the World War II blockbuster

THE DIRTY DOZEN (1967). He was considered too difficult to approach as the lead in *Shaft*, but within a year had released his own blaxploitation movie, **SLAUGHTER** (1972).

A renaissance of interest in blaxploitation almost thirty years later resulted in a slick remake of **SHAFT** (2000) starring Samuel L. Jackson, but Tidyman's outsider character was softened, de-sexed, and legitimized, even to the point of making him a cop.

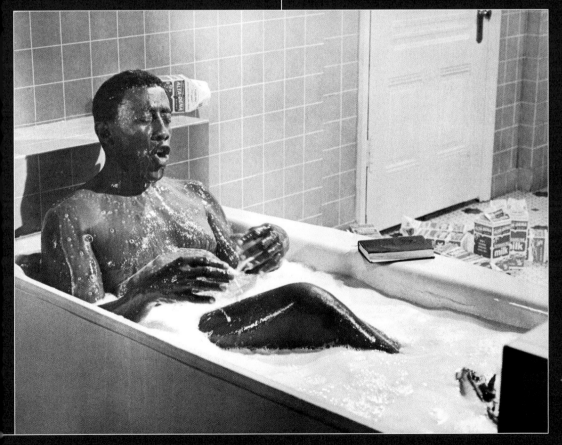

Godfrey Cambridge tries to wash the black out in *Watermelon Man*.

★ ★ ★ ★ ★ ★ **Linda Lovelace** ★ ★ ★ ★ ★ ★

GERARD DAMIANO'S DEEP THROAT

HOW FAR DOES A GIRL HAVE TO GO TO UNTANGLE HER TINGLE?

EASTMAN COLOR Ⓧ ADULTS ONLY

As far as I know there was one moment in history, and one moment only, when the upper crust of society, happily married couples, doctors, professors, movie stars, judges, accountants, professional athletes, and Ivy League club men all lined up in their finest evening clothes to see a down-and-dirty stag film shot in ratty motel rooms.

THE MOVIE WAS, OF COURSE, *DEEP THROAT*, and even after millions of words have been written about it, I still have no idea why this movie became the first mainstream smut flick. It was not the first hard-core pornographic movie to be shown in American theaters, and in the context of the tens of thousands of porn movies made both before and after it, it ranks pretty close to the bottom in terms of cinematography, acting, entertainment value, and just plain sexual thrills. But it changed America's sexual attitudes more than anything since the first Kinsey Report, in 1948; it altered the lives of everyone associated with it; it supercharged the feminist movement; it gave the Mafia its most lucrative business since Prohibition, and it changed the nation's views of obscenity forever. We'll never

know exactly how much money it made—and continues to make—but estimates have gone as high as $600 million, which would make it one of the most successful motion pictures of any kind in any country in the history of the world.

Nations, like people, have moments when they just need to get drunk and party, and apparently something of the sort was happening in June of 1972, when, at almost the same moment, the Watergate burglars broke into the offices of the Democratic National Committee, and *Deep Throat* opened at the New World Mature Theater in New York City. *Deep Throat* was not just a dirty movie. It was a cause, and it was so popular that most film critics were afraid to deprecate it for fear of seeming unhip. It's hard to imagine today a theater full of sophisticates keeping a straight face during the scene in which Linda Lovelace and an actor identified as "Mr. Fenster" pour Coca-Cola into her most private place and then share sips of it from a very long plastic tube while at the same time having sex (the logistics of this are hazy) while grooving away to a scratchy soundtrack featuring the song "I'd Like to Teach the World to Screw." Ed McMahon, the sidekick of Johnny Carson on *The Tonight Show*, was such a fan of the movie that he showed up with six friends and a case of beer, then stood outside the theater afterward enthusing with the public. Frank Sinatra was one of the early audience members, along with Vice President Spiro Agnew, Warren Beatty, Truman Capote, Shirley MacLaine, Nora Ephron, Bob Woodward, and Sammy Davis Jr., who grew so enamored of Lovelace that within the year he and his wife would be having group sex with Lovelace and her husband.

Deep Throat is finally one of those movies that really can't be explained. It was simply there at a certain crazy time, and it brought out every suppressed urge of a public starved for sensation. One of the most thoughtful reviews of the phenomenon was written, oddly enough, by straight-laced Vincent Canby, the chief film critic of the *New York Times*, who said that the only really fascinating thing about the movie could be summed up with a single question: "How does she do it?"

"It," of course, was the film's sole gimmick and, if truth be known, the main reason anyone wanted to see *Deep Throat* in the first place. Lovelace, one of the loosest women in New York and Miami at a time when people were competing to be promiscuous, had been trained by her husband to perform fellatio on some of the largest male members on the planet in such a way that the organ literally vanishes into her mouth. If you want to get clinical about it—and we might as well, since this is the "donkey show" trick that made her so famous—she appears to do something with her throat about halfway into the act, a sort of esophageal anterior repositioning that allows her to glide it on down. Thanks to the closeup lenswork of director Gerard Damiano—a veteran producer of Mafia-funded peep shows—we see the trick twice in all its lurid-color glory. The first time is about twenty-seven minutes into the film, when she achieves nirvana with Harry Reems, who went on record in interviews as saying he had a full ten inches worth of male equipment. Over and over again she does it to Reems, with occasional cutaways to his mock-terrified face, to the point that you sort of wonder what the sheer mechanics of it are. The second time is in the concluding—I hesitate to say "climactic"—scene, in which she does it to an actor identified as William Love, who appears to be even bigger than Reems. Reems would become famous as a result of the movie, while Love would disappear into the ultimate obscurity of porn pseudonyms—which just goes to show, I suppose, that even in a movie called *Deep Throat*, size is not everything.

Lovelace may be the only American celebrity to publish *four* best-selling autobiographies. The first two celebrate free, uninhibited sex as the most liberating form of human expression since man learned to speak. The last two describe pornography as legalized rape, a menace to the future of civilization, and the very essence of evil. In this one desperately unhappy woman, we have both the yin and the yang of the sexual revolution played out before our eyes. How did she do it? And, more importantly, why?

LINDA BOREMAN—HER REAL NAME—STARTED down the road that would turn her into the world's most famous sexual performer on a day in 1970 when she was recuperating from a car accident at her parents' condo in Fort Lauderdale, Florida. She and a girlfriend were relaxing poolside in their bikinis—despite scars all over Linda's body—when a bar owner and sometime pimp named Chuck Traynor spotted her and offered the two girls a joint and a ride in his Jaguar. She was twenty-one. He was twenty-seven. In a matter of weeks she had moved in with Traynor, and she soon found out that opposites truly attract. He was the rough and possessive type, part of the small-time criminal underworld; she was the protected daughter of a cop. He liked oral sex; the idea of it disgusted her. But she would learn to like it, he told her, and he introduced her to hypnosis in an effort to teach her sword-swallowing techniques and to change her sexual appetite.

Lovelace had grown up in Yonkers, New York, the daughter of a New York City police officer father and a domineering mother who believed in frequent corporal punishment. At Catholic school she got the nickname "Miss Holy Holy" because she wouldn't put out. When she was sixteen, her parents retired to Florida, and she finished high school there without making many new friends. She lost her virginity at age nineteen and gave birth to a baby at twenty. (She claimed her mother tricked her into giving the baby up for adoption by having her sign papers she didn't read.) She returned to New York to enroll in computer school and was planning to open a boutique when a nasty car accident left her with a broken jaw, broken ribs, and a lacerated liver. That's when Traynor walked into her life.

The hypnosis apparently worked, because within a few weeks Lovelace was turning tricks. Traynor owned a bar, the Vegas Inn in North Miami, but when business dropped off, he returned to pimping. For her initiation he took Lovelace to a Holiday Inn, where she serviced five men. He then beat her because one of the men complained that she didn't seem to enjoy it. He eventually had her working parties for up to twenty men at a time, and he got a special delight out of hooking her up with especially ugly customers. In later years, Lovelace would claim that she was a virtual prisoner during her prostitution years, from 1970 to 1972, and that she was frequently beaten and threatened with a gun. The truth is difficult to determine, because Traynor freely admits to beating her but says it was part of mutual sexual games—Lovelace was a masochist—and that he did carry guns but he never threatened to use one on her. He also claims she could have left at any time. As late as 1974, Lovelace was declaring in public interviews that she loved Traynor.

Traynor eventually married Lovelace—so she couldn't be forced to testify against him on drug charges, according to her. Both became habitual users of marijuana and methamphetamine, and Traynor increasingly came to think of her as his meal ticket. Eventually he moved her to New York, where he hoped to sell her services to the most famous madam of her day, Xaveria Hollander, the "Happy Hooker" herself. But Hollander turned down Lovelace as an employee, and it's not difficult to see why. Lovelace was not a particularly attractive woman, especially by the standards of the call-girl world. She had frizzy hair and a square mannish face; her breasts were fake, the result of illegal silicone injections she had gotten in 1971, before implants had been invented. Her sole appeal, according to those who worked with her, was that her personality came off as winsome and girl-next-doorish. There was also a little bit of the hippie "free love" spirit about her. And there was, of course, her special talent.

Undeterred by Hollander's rejection, Traynor turned to the next best thing—"loops." These were five to ten minute filmed sex acts that were also known as stag films, smokers, peeps, and beaver loops. They were all illegal, filmed secretly with 8-millimeter cameras in New York City apartments with anonymous actors, anonymous crews, and anonymous moneymen supplied by the Colombo crime family. Lovelace made several of these, many directed by a guy named Ted "Tom" Snyder, who wore cowboy hats, gold chains, and a gold pinky ring with "Ted" spelled out in diamonds. He liked to pretend to be an Italian mobster, driving a Rolls and flying a private airplane in later years, although he was actually Jewish and not entirely trusted by the mob. In 1989, he was gunned down on his front lawn in Los Angeles, a vial of cocaine in his hand. His wife Sharon was charged, but not convicted, of hiring the assassin.

When Traynor and Lovelace met Snyder in 1970, he was working out of a filthy apartment on 48th Street, in the Times Square area, and frequently used an actor named Rob Everett as Lovelace's partner. Everett said Lovelace was not only a willing participant in the filming, but "She loved sex." Her fellow actors, responding later to charges that she was forced into the business, even went further to say that she loved prostitution, multiple partners, and especially any kind of rough sex.

Under Traynor's guidance, the loops got more and more freaky. Lovelace appeared in loops featuring urination, "foot insertion," and eventually bestiality. In a loop called "Dogarama," she performs oral sex on a German shepherd, then the dog mounts her. In one of her autobiographies, she said that this was one of the moments when she was threatened at gunpoint, but the six people on the set that day were interviewed by film historian Jim Holliday, and all except Lovelace claim that she not only did it willingly, she seemed to enjoy it.

Traynor and Lovelace got their big break at a cocktail party. There they met Gerard Damiano, a director of soft-core porn who was casting hard-core scenes for a new movie called *Changes*. With jaded guests looking on—this was no ordinary party—Traynor had Lovelace demonstrate her oral sex skills for Damiano, and he was so impressed that he wrote a script especially for her. That script would become *Deep Throat*, but first Damiano would have to convince his Mafia bosses to use her.

Stag films had been around for decades, and the Mafia had had a direct interest in making them at least since 1965, but it was not much more than a penny-ante sideline until 1971. That's when Reuben Sturman, working under the protection of the Gambino family, imported the first peepshow machines from Copenhagen and installed them in murky theaters around Times Square. The peepshow machine was a Super-8 projector enclosed in a wooden booth that locked from the inside; the customer would pay a quarter for each minute of film, and what he did in the privacy of his own booth was nobody's business. The device had been invented by Lasse Braun, an Italian known as "King of the Euroloops" who had already staked out a successful porno business in Amsterdam and Stockholm as early as 1962. The peep show liberated porn from the "raincoat crowd"—guys who wore raincoats over their clothes so they could secretly masturbate in adult theaters—and made it four times as profitable as any previous dirty-film business.

The control of this exploding business segment naturally settled on the Colombo family. John "Sonny" Franzese, a "made" Colombo member, had been selling 8-millimeter stag films since the late sixties. The Colombo outfit even controlled its own plant for processing film, called All-State Film Labs, in Brooklyn. The official owner of the lab was Louis "Butchie" Peraino, a Colombo associate, and the actual operations were run by Michael Zaffarano, "Mickey Z," a capo in the Bonnano family. The films were sold out of automobile trunks, coffee catering trucks, unmarked warehouses, several restaurants, a chain of meat markets, and a Brooklyn candy store.

It was Peraino who had to approve the budget for Damiano's *Deep Throat* script, and the 300-pound "Butchie" was not impressed at first by Lovelace. He knew her as the star of the "M" series of loops, and he thought she should stay there. He wanted Carol Connors, a big-breasted blonde, to play the lead in what was, for him, a major investment of his father's money. But he changed his mind when Damiano had Lovelace demonstrate her technique—on Butchie himself. It was an audition he would ask to be repeated many times over during the coming months, and it kept her career, such as it was, going.

It's doubtful that Lovelace knew just exactly who the men were in this business, but anyone with any knowledge of New York organized crime would have instantly recognized the name Peraino. Giuseppe Peraino had been a member of the Profaci family when he was killed in 1931 in the famous Castellamarese War in Brooklyn, which established Lucky Luciano and Vito Genovese as the kings of the underworld. Giuseppe left a widow, Grazia, and two sons, Anthony and Joseph, who would both be taken into the Colombos, where they became made men. Butchie Peraino was the grandson of Giuseppe and son of Anthony (better known as "Big Tony").

Butchie was an associate, not a made man (indicating the low priority given to porn in the sixties), when he was set up at All-State Film Labs. But that would change after *Deep Throat* fell, literally and figuratively, into his lap.

At the time he met Lovelace and Traynor, Butchie Peraino had no criminal convictions and only one arrest—for chasing his wife down the street with a gun—but the people working for him weren't so clean. His primary sales rep, for example, was Cosmo Cangiano, whose rap sheet included larceny, forgery, mail theft, and interstate shipment of stolen securities. Cangiano sold porn in New York, Pittsburgh, South Carolina, and Baltimore, as well as counterfeit Chanel perfume, Omega watches, DMV documents, false IDs, registrations, birth certificates, and Social Security cards. But when Lovelace ventured into bestiality, she was also getting into the territory of a Gambino family member named Roy DeMeo, who controlled all child porn and animal porn. (This specialty was carved out for that family.) It's estimated that by the end of the seventies DeMeo's gang had killed about 100 people in various business disputes and turf wars.

ALL TRAYNOR KNEW IS THAT LOVELACE WOULD be paid $1,200 to appear in the new film, which was titled *The Doctor Makes a Housecall.* To give it a bigger look than the usual loop, Damiano filmed it in Miami with $23,000 of Big Tony's money. One of the crew members making the trip with Damiano was Herbert Streicher, a twenty-five-year-old Jewish kid from suburban New York who had done Wheaties commercials and off-Broadway theater but was still struggling to make it as a legitimate actor. He had turned to porn—both behind and in front of the camera—to pay the bills, and had even made a couple of loops with Lovelace. On this trip he was hired strictly as a grip and a gaffer. Streicher liked Lovelace, and would always defend her as a sweet, trusting person, even though he pooh-poohed her accounts of being forced into porn. "She's a beautiful person," he would say later. "As far as a personality, Linda has got that magnetic ability to draw an audience or anybody in a room directly to her, that twinkle in the eye, that real smile without phoniness or presumptuousness. Linda's a sweet, sweet girl, a very together person. She's not super bright, and she's not an actress, but she's totally open and free sexually. She's got this thing where sex is to be enjoyed and not slandered, and she follows it. She really believes it. Linda loves to deep throat, it's a turn-on for her, that's where she's at. But there's not a lot of contact and warmth and lubrication in that kind of technique. It's 'Look what I can do.' It's nothing special."

If anyone knew what he was talking about, it was Streicher: His screen name was Harry Reems. When Damiano couldn't find anyone to play the key role of the doctor, he took Streicher/Reems off gaffer duty, bought him a white coat at a barber-supply house, and film history was about to be made. The cast and crew settled into the Voyager Inn on Biscayne Boulevard and spent an uneventful six days shooting scenes that could just as easily have been shot in Brooklyn. Lovelace would later claim that she was savagely beaten by Traynor on the night before shooting began, but no one else noticed anything strange about his or her behavior. If anything, they thought Lovelace was a little too much in love. "She doted on [Traynor]," said Damiano. "She loved him, she was close to him, she was never out of his sight." In fact, Damiano discovered that she was so protective of Traynor's feelings that she would try to disguise the fact that she was enjoying the on-screen sex. After a while, they started sending Traynor out to get cigarettes when they needed a "money shot"—"and the sex got five times better because she relaxed," recalled Reems.

Of course, the other way to interpret that is that she was an abused, intimidated slave—the way she would be portrayed by feminists Andrea Dworkin and Gloria Steinem, among others, in later years. For example, Traynor ordered her to wear cutoff denim shorts that were so skimpy they exposed her labia—then, if anyone stared at her, he blamed her and punished her. But at the time, the cast and crew assumed it was some kind of S&M game that the two of them played together and both enjoyed. For the same reason, they also ignored the occasional marks on Lovelace's body.

THE FILM ITSELF IS ACTUALLY FOUR STANDARD loops, shot mostly without sound, and then hooked together with connecting material shot in New York. (Carol Connors, the best-looking actress in the film, didn't even go to Miami.) The story, such as it is, involves a woman who has never had a real orgasm, despite her worldly best friend's

trying to initiate her at an afternoon orgy. (The best friend was played by Dolly Sharp, who would be remembered for the movie's most famous line: "Mind if I smoke while you're eating?") So the sexually frustrated Linda—who feels "tingly" during sex but wants "bells, bombs, and dams bursting"—goes to a goofball doctor who examines her and discovers that her clitoris is actually located in the bottom of her throat. She gets orgasmic with the doctor—the first time we see Linda's talent—then signs on as a sexual therapist so she can get orgasmic with the rest of the cast. At last she meets a wimpy fetishist who has a thirteen-inch penis: She samples the goods, agrees to marry him, and the movie ends.

From the opening titles, when Lovelace is seen driving aimlessly around Miami with a deadpan expression, to the horrid wakka-chicka folk-rock soundtrack to the grainy jump cuts to the cheesy cutaways to fireworks and rocket launches, it was the longest sixty-two minutes that millions of people would ever sit through. The sex scenes aren't even particularly well edited or shot, so you have difficulty getting your bearings or even knowing, in a couple of cases, who's having sex with whom. Yet it's partly the sheer awfulness of it that has made it high camp in some circles. The soundtrack album is a collector's item worth about $300, even though no one knows who the musicians are. (Supposedly the FBI has their names in a file somewhere.) It features the excruciating title theme, "Love Is Strange," and, of course, the actual *Deep Throat* anthem, which I'll quote in its entirety so that you can vicariously experience the suffering of the masses: "Now I'm going to tell you the way it has to be, / And pay attention, I'm sure that you will see, / If you relax your muscle and once you hit that spot, / Keep right on pushing and give it all you got. / Now we found your tickler, the solution is quite clear, / For if we both can hit it now, the bells you'll surely hear, / Deep throat, / Deeper than deep your throat, / Deep throat. / Deep throat, / Deeper than deep your throat, / Deep throat. / Don't row your boat, / Don't get your goat, / That's all she wrote, / Deep throat." In retrospect, the most inspired decision Damiano made was to rename the movie *Deep Throat*. Nothing else could possibly explain its success.

The poster for the movie announced "Linda Lovelace Is Deep Throat!" And, in fact, both her stage name and her character in the movie are named Linda Lovelace, presumably in an effort to make her a star. The grand opening at the 48th Street New World Mature Theater benefited immediately when the film was slapped with an obscenity charge, then named public enemy number one by Mayor John Lindsay in his effort to clean up Times Square. But as the case made its way through the courts, *Deep Throat* was already a media sensation, called a "major happening" and "porno chic" by New York reporters. Lovelace was fodder for Johnny Carson on *The Tonight Show*, further stoking the interest of socialites, students, swingers, and the curious. You can get a sense of the New York dinner-party buzz in Ang Lee's movie *The Ice Storm* (1997), set in 1972, in which upper-middle-class table talk switches effortlessly from Watergate to Linda Lovelace. The book *Sinema*, by Kenneth

Turan and Stephen F. Zito, summed up the effusive prose of the day, praising Lovelace's "fresh carnality, the air of thoroughly debauched innocence, the sense of a woman exploring the limits of sexual expression and feeling. Linda Lovelace is the girl next door grown up into a shameless . . . woman."

The obscenity trial itself was a circus, of course. The heavyweight witness for the defense was Arthur Knight, the *Saturday Review* film critic who had been a judge at another "porno chic" happening, the first International Erotic Film Festival in 1970. Knight was enthusiastic about such things as "the clarity and lack of grain" in the photography (what was he smoking?) and the message of the movie—you can imagine everyone leaning forward in their seats to hear this—that "there's more than one way to have sex." Also weighing in on the side of "socially redeeming value" was Dr. John Money, a professor of medical psychology at Johns Hopkins University, who said the movie creates sane, healthy attitudes about sex by showing people there is nothing shameful about it and, on a feminist note, "indicates that women have a right to a sex life of their own." Sociologist Ernest van den Haag, on the other hand, testified for the prosecution that "I not only regard [*Deep Throat*] as being without redeeming social value; I regard it as highly antisocial."

Alas, Criminal Court Judge Joel E. Tyler came down squarely on the side of the police, setting some new standards in purple prose himself. The movie, he said, was "a feast of carrion and squalor . . . A Sodom and Gomorrah gone wild before the fire . . . One throat that deserves to be cut . . . A nadir of decadence . . . It does, in fact, demean and pervert the sexual experience, and insults it, shamelessly, without tenderness and without understanding of its roles as a concomitant of the human condition."

His verdict: a three *million* dollar fine. The film was withdrawn and the World Cinema was hung in black bunting under the marquee: "Judge Cuts Throat, World Mourns."

As it turned out, Judge Tyler's decision was overturned by the Court of Appeals, and that decision had the effect of legalizing hard-core porn in New York forever. The floodgates were open: If *Deep Throat* had been proven in court to have "redeeming social value," then virtually anything qualified. By February of 1973, *Deep Throat* was playing on the tony Upper East Side at the Trans-Lux 85th Street Theater, with ads trumpeting "The film that has become the symbol of freedom of the screen," "one of the most talked-about pictures of the decade," and "a 'must' by many experts, a 'no-no' by others, a personal decision for you."

Deep Throat was actually the culmination of a twenty-year trend toward sexual explicitness on the screen. Burlesque films started it, in the early fifties, when strippers were filmed with locked-down cameras, albeit with pasties over their breasts. *Garden of Eden*, a nudist-camp film, introduced nonpastie breast nudity in 1954. It was banned in New York but was later ruled acceptable by the New York Court of Appeals, in 1957. This resulted in a flood of nudist films from Europe, followed by Russ Meyer's *The Immoral Mr. Teas* in 1959 and more

than 150 homemade "nudie-cuties" between 1960 and 1963. That fad wore off and gave way to "kinkies" (mild S&M movies with names like *Satan in High Heels*), which in turn gave way to "roughies"—movies like *The Defilers* and *Love Camp 7*, which used violent, drug-fueled rape scenes that were much darker and certainly more disturbing than *Deep Throat*. Up to this point, all of these films were seen almost exclusively in "grind houses" that catered to a 100 percent male audience. Pubic hair was seen for the first time in 1968, along with group sex and lesbianism, and perhaps the most important test case came that year when *I Am Curious (Yellow)* was imported from Sweden and seized by New York customs officials. The movie had full-frontal nudity, both male and female, including an erection. A jury ruled it obscene, but once again the Court of Appeals overturned that verdict, calling it an "intellectual effort."

t HE MAFIA LOVED THESE WORDS— "intellectual effort." At first they used them to import documentaries from Copenhagen, where all pornography laws had been rescinded in 1967. Alex de Renzy's *Censorship in Denmark* was made for $15,000 in 1969 and grossed $2 million. Copycat pseudo-documentaries quickly followed: *Sexual Freedom in Denmark*, *SEX U.S.A.* (with Linda Lovelace and Harry Reems, working together for the first time), Gerard Damiano's *This Film Is All About . . .* , Donn Greer's *101 Acts of Love*, Alex de Renzy's *A History of the Blue Movie*, Bill Osco's

Hollywood Blue, and, in 1970, the first porn feature to be advertised in a New York newspaper, *Electro Sex '75*. The common denominator of all these films is that they made some pretense to education, normally with a voice-over narrator or a medical expert explaining something about sex.

Man and Wife was the first 35-millimeter porn film to get national distribution. Directed by Matt Cimber (Jayne Mansfield's husband at the time of her death and much later the founder of Gorgeous Ladies of Wrestling), it uses the "expert sexual researcher" premise—claiming phony Swedish credentials from a "Centre of Sexual Research"—that Damiano would lamely co-opt for *Deep Throat*. In fact, *Deep Throat* was a combination of *Man and Wife* and another 1970 film called *Mona the Virgin Nymph*. *Mona* was directed by Bill Osco, heir to the Osco drug chain, and is regarded by some as the first real "classic" of porn. Mona, played by Fifi Watson, refuses to have actual intercourse but, under the tutelage of her father, will fellate anyone. *Mona*, in fact, delivers a lot more raw action than *Deep Throat*, including incest, nymphomania, lesbianism, masturbation, orgies, oral sex, bondage, S&M, and sex toys. Damiano's script was a watered-down version of *Mona*, so he was basically recycling stuff that had been around for three years.

In the heady months after the *Deep Throat* premiere, there seemed to be a whole new porn future opening up for the underworld bosses accustomed to paying pimps to let them film scenes with their dope-addled hookers. The most amazing thing about the *Deep Throat* craze is that, for the first time in porn history, many of the customers were women. Russ Meyer had supposedly invented "couples porn" with his 1968 softcore flick *Vixen*, starring Erica Gavin, but no one really believed it would catch on. But now the Mafia looked at its business in a whole new way. Even women would pay money for this stuff? Their eyes lit up with dollar signs, and the Mafia did a major reorganization to turn porn into a priority business.

First they moved to protect their winnings. *Deep Throat* was owned by a company called Gerard Damiano Film Productions Inc. Damiano had a one-third interest in lieu of salary, and Butchie Peraino had two-thirds. But Damiano was told they wanted to buy out his interest in the film—for $25,000. He sold it. Quickly. Next they decided to make the business more legitimate by sending Butchie Peraino to Hollywood to turn their new company, Bryanston Pictures, into a mainstream motion-picture producer. Butchie's father, "Big Tony," and uncle, "Joe the Whale," would henceforth run All-State Film Labs and all the hard-core operations out of New York and Miami. Butchie would make "class" films on the West Coast. In Hollywood, Butchie was greeted by the trade papers as the new mogul in town, even after he installed Joseph "Junior" Torchio as his director of finance, which was a big step up from Torchio's former position as a skilled auto-break-in artist.

But so-called "couples porn" would turn out to be one of those filmmakers' phantoms—like "mainstream horror" and "crossover gay cinema"—that everyone would chase for years without any real success. Porn was a male medium, and *Deep Throat* turned out to be, for many women, their first, last, and only exposure to it. There were occasional theatrical hits that moved away from the sleazy grind houses and were seen by Middle America. Damiano scored again with the first porn horror film, *The Devil in Miss Jones*, starring Georgina Spelvin, always considered the best real actress ever to work in adult flicks. From the West Coast porno capital of San Francisco, the Mitchell brothers hired Marilyn Chambers, famous as the Ivory Snow soap girl, to star in *Behind the Green Door*, scoring near *Deep Throat*-level profits. But these were exceptions; most efforts to draw women and couples back to the theater were colossal failures. Casting about for female-friendly gimmicks, they made porn fairy tales (*Cinderella* and *Alice in Wonderland*), a porn disaster film (*Deluge*, the first in a series of one), and Damiano even did an X-rated tribute to the Muppets called *Let My Puppets Come*. One director, Radley Metzger, tried to do literary porn, using real stories that had a beginning, middle, and end, with efforts like *The Opening of Misty Beethoven* (featuring Spaulding Gray!) and *Naked Came the Stranger*. (Another phantasm of the porn business is its periodic attempt to do a "real movie" that happens to have raw sex in it, but after thirty years of trying, it's obvious that the genre won't accommodate a plot.) With every genre failing, porn producers turned to carnival marketing, using performers with enormous sexual organs—Candy Samples and her boobs, Long John Silver and his long john—and curiosities, such as a performer with a three-inch clitoris and an amputee nymphomaniac. John Holmes was perhaps the biggest star of this anything-goes era, with his thirteen inches of acting ability.

But not a single one ever recaptured the couples market. "Porno chic" lasted less than a year. The films returned to the tatterdemalion theaters on 42nd Street and retrofitted drive-ins in the deep South, where strapped owners were given new economic life when they discovered that a parked car served the same function as a peep-show booth. In 1974, *Emmanuelle* was imported from France and scored big numbers with women, but it was not technically pornography at all, since it didn't show penetration. After that, the only thing that fueled the porn business was the now virtually unlimited right to show any kind of pornography virtually anywhere in the United States. The raincoat joints were back, but this time they were just as legal in Omaha as they were in Times Square.

That right was tested only once, by an ambitious federal prosecutor in Memphis, who indicted Louis, Anthony, and Joseph Peraino in August 1974 for transporting obscene materials—namely *Deep Throat*—across state lines. Prosecutor Larry Parrish was counting on a June 1973 Supreme Court decision that apparently changed the standard for obscenity from "socially redeeming value" to "community standards." Called the Miller Decision, it had not only panicked the mob, but frightened Hollywood lobbyist Jack Valenti, who feared it would lead to a new wave of local censor boards across the country. If Parrish had limited his indictments to mob figures, he might have had a more lasting effect on the ability of the government to prosecute porn, but he also indicted Harry Reems, and intellectuals were outraged by that. Even though Reems was a very small part of the prosecution case, it became known as the Harry Reems trial, and in the court of public opinion, that was a bad call for the government. Warren Beatty and Jack Nicholson led a petition drive to raise money for Reems's legal defense funds, and as it turned out, Reems would need every penny. With evidence supplied by the FBI, the IRS, and the Department of Justice Organized Crime Strikes Force in Brooklyn and Miami, Parrish was able to get convictions on Butchie and Joe the Whale, each receiving a one-year sentence, but Big Tony went mysteriously missing. Reems was convicted as well, but his sentence was eventually overturned in an appeal that helped make his lawyer, Alan Dershowitz, famous.

In April 1976, a month after the Memphis trial, the mob closed down Bryanston Pictures and got out of legitimate film production altogether. Bryanston had released several hits, including *Andy Warhol's Frankenstein* and Bruce Lee's *Return of the Dragon*, but their biggest score came from *The Texas Chain Saw Massacre* in 1974. (With typical mob flair, they concealed most of the profits from the hapless Texas investors, who called the Perainos "the Piranha Brothers.") Most of Bryanston's other pictures—including *The Human Factor*, *The Devil's Rain*, and *Echoes of a Summer*—had been turkeys. In searching for legitimate businesses to launder porn cash, the mob apparently decided Hollywood wasn't

the place. Instead they used the *Deep Throat* profits to buy garment companies in New York and Miami, investment companies, and possibly a drug smuggling operation in the Caribbean—all businesses that made them more comfortable.

Butchie wasn't finished with showbiz, though. Fresh out of prison, he "bought" a Los Angeles music company in September 1977—the owner was given an offer he couldn't refuse—then established Arrow Film & Video to produce porn in both New York and Van Nuys. By the late seventies the business was getting a little messy, though. There were three mob hits in Los Angeles associated with porn debts. And when the young John Landis, fresh off the success of *The Groove Tube*, announced he might like to dabble in porn himself, two goons showed up at his house and suggested he reconsider. He reconsidered.

MEANWHILE, POOR LITTLE LINDA Lovelace, now an international celebrity, never quite figured out how to handle it. She got a little more than her allotted fifteen minutes of fame, though. She may be the only celebrity in history who was profiled by *Women's Wear Daily* and Al Goldstein's *Screw* magazine in the same month. To the former, she came off as "a simple girl who likes to go to swinging parties and nudist colonies." In her interview with Goldstein, she said, "Yeah, I have an orgasm every time I get screwed in the throat."

"Do you enjoy the taste of sperm?" asked the never-shy Goldstein.

"I love it," said Lovelace. "It's caviar to me. I can't understand why other chicks get turned off by it."

Everything peaked for Lovelace about a year after the movie's release. She appeared on the cover of *Esquire* and in a *Playboy* pictorial. She and Traynor reportedly demonstrated some bestiality at the Playboy Mansion, then left in a huff when Hugh Hefner turned down Traynor's suggestion of an ongoing business relationship. There were orgies and parties and eventually a Percodan habit. She published her first autobiography, *Inside Linda Lovelace*, and stated in the opening chapter, "I live for sex, will never get enough of it, and will continue to try every day to tune my physical mechanism to finer perfection. . . . Nothing about sex is bad. That should be repeated over and over . . . and perhaps the truth will eventually be seen." She also claimed that she had devised a sophisticated system of oriental and mystical self-discipline, bolstered by hypnosis, in order to achieve her secret techniques for satisfying men and herself. In August 1973, she told *Bachelor* magazine that her breasts had grown larger—not because of silicone but because of hypnotism. She crashed the Oscars and was invited to the American premiere of *Last Tango in Paris*, which she pronounced "disgusting." She turned up at the Cannes Film Festival, where she posed for the paparazzi, and she spent a lot of her time testifying at obscenity trials, where she was frequently asked for her autograph by attorneys on both sides.

What's odd, in retrospect, is that she failed to do the one thing that would have provided her with long-term income. Although she did occasional single-scene appearances in other porn movies, always displaying her oral skills, she only made one other full-length film—the sequel to *Deep Throat*—then swore off hardcore altogether. The Linda Lovelace films that did flood the market were actually her old loops that had been strung together to make choppy compilations like *The Confessions of Linda Lovelace* and *Linda Lovelace Meets Miss Jones*. The *Deep Throat* sequel, on the other hand, was released in a soft-core version only, and by the time it came out, in 1974, with an R rating, audiences were infuriated that it didn't deliver the goods. (Supposedly the hard-core scenes had been removed because of a tricky legal situation, but that footage was stolen from a vault in New York City and was never seen again.)

The beginning of the end came when Lovelace was arrested at the Dunes Hotel in Las Vegas in January 1974 for possession of cocaine and amphetamines. She was just starting out on what she had hoped would be a legitimate night-club and theater career. The Aladdin Casino booked her for a play called *My Daughter's Rated X*, but it closed after a week when, once again, audiences were disappointed to see that she didn't get naked. She tried dinner theater in Philadelphia, bombing in *Pajama Tops*. And sometime during this ill-advised night-club period, she and Traynor broke up, and she instantly moved in with her producer and choreographer, David Winters. Winters became her new Svengali, setting up a new book deal for her that led to her second autobiography, *The Intimate Diary of Linda Lovelace*, and a movie called *Linda Lovelace for President*, which ended her dreams of mainstream stardom for good. (*Linda Lovelace for President* came out in 1976 and was a *Groove Tube* ripoff featuring dozens of lame sight gags, cameos by Mickey Dolenz and Joe E. Ross and a full-frontal-nudity sendup of K-Tel records commercials by Vaughn Meader, the JFK satirist who did the best-selling *First Family* album. Bill Margold's review was typical of the withering notices: "Linda is best on her knees with her mouth full. Letting her talk is enough to turn a stud into a eunuch.")

Perhaps the most revealing passages in her first two books have nothing to do with all the pseudo-mystical free-love folderol she spouts. In the first book she says (falsely) that she lost her virginity to Traynor, and describes that moment with "the awesome Chuck Traynor" as follows: "The fat rocklike muscle tore into me like a battering ram, and I nearly fainted from the shock. I came in seconds." But in her second biography, Winters has become the greatest lover in the world: "With a tremendous thrust, he put that surging, gorgeous cock inside me. A pulsating jackhammer that kept driving, driving, plowing into me, over and over." When you look at everything she wrote, and claimed to write, in context, she was just an insecure girl who needed the attention of men.

Even more revealing, though, was an interview she gave to Eric Danville for Penhouse.com in which she sounds like a country girl lost in the big city. "After I got away from Traynor," she said, "it was a lot more fun, because I wasn't being sexually abused. I was walking around with transparent clothes on, but that wasn't too bad. I didn't think looking sexy was a terrible thing. I had many, many good times when I was with David. When I was with David I had an awesome time. I met a lot of people and had a lot of fun at that point. I went to see my first play. I saw Richard Chamberlain in *Cyrano De Bergerac*, I saw *Grease* in Manhattan. I saw the Alvin Ailey Dancers. I became cultured, I guess. I'd never been cultured."

By 1976, when *Linda Lovelace for President* ended her career, she had called it quits with Winters and run straight into the arms of another man, a construction worker named Larry Marchiano. By 1980 she had become a mother of two, a born-again Christian, and a feminist—and was living on welfare as her husband tried to make ends meet as a cable installer. She had already become the feminist poster child for the demeaning effects of pornography, turning up in Andrea Dworkin's 1979 book *Pornography: Men Possessing Women*. And now it was time to tell her story for a third time, in the book *Ordeal*, which was cowritten by Mike McGrady, the writer who had planned the *Naked Came the Stranger* hoax of 1969. (The publisher, perhaps leery of McGrady, was so concerned about libel suits that Lovelace was required to take an eleven-hour lie-detector test before they would go ahead with it.) This is the book in which she made her most serious charges, accusing Traynor of virtual white slavery and the porn business as a whole of legalized rape. The book is full of horror stories like the time she says Traynor put a garden hose up her

XXXXXXXXXXXXXXXXXXXXXXX

rectum and threatened to turn on the water if she didn't strip and perform publicly. "When you see the movie *Deep Throat*," she told the *Toronto Sun* in 1981, "you are watching me being raped. It is a crime that movie is still showing; there was a gun to my head the entire time." She hit the lecture circuit, talking about the evils of porn for $1,500 per speech, and eventually testified before the Meese Commission on Pornography in 1986.

Her old friends in the business never really took the allegations seriously. "After *Deep Throat*, the business simply passed Linda by," said Eric Everett, her original sex partner in her loop days. "She wasn't particularly attractive nor could she act. If she'd told the truth about her life, her book may not have sold as well as making up a story that claims she was forced to do these disgusting things."

Harry Reems became almost as famous as Lovelace, but he kept a much lower profile, continuing to work in porno films after *Deep Throat* but telling Al Goldstein, "Pornography is not my way of life. It's a thing I do for income." In fact, he was making $30,000 a week in the seventies, but the lifestyle eventually got to him as he became addicted to alcohol and cocaine. He retired from the business in 1976, then returned in 1982 when Reuben Sturman, the original importer of the peep-show machine, paid him $75,000 to have sex with twelve women in *Society Affairs*. The shoot didn't go well. The once potent Reems had trouble performing. In the eighties Reems was in and out of detox centers, dealing with tax problems and bad debts, and even spent time in mental institutions and, briefly, in jail.

He fell in love with porn star Brandy Alexander, but she refused to marry him, and he ended up sleeping behind a grocery store dumpster in Malibu with a two-quart-a-day vodka habit. A friend literally saved his life when he pulled him out of a gutter on Sunset Boulevard. He eventually got into a twelve-step program, managed to stay sober for eleven months, and in 1990 proposed marriage to a redheaded waitress he had met eight years before in Park City, Utah. He got religion, became a real estate salesman and a trustee in the Methodist Church, and now lives the quiet life of a family man.

Traynor, on the other hand, hooked up with Marilyn Chambers, the second superstar in porn, and stayed with her through the eighties, living in Vegas and running an indoor shooting range. After *Behind the Green Door*, Chambers scored another hardcore hit with *Insatiable* in 1980 and even starred in two kinky S&M movies, *Never a Tender Moment* and *Beyond De Sade*. As late as the mid-nineties she was still making softcore porn, although her body was puffy and her breasts looked more than a little artificial from having been enlarged more than once.

Carol Connors would continue her porn career, then become a regular on Chuck Barris's *The Gong Show*, then return to porn to star in the hit *Candy* series. The cinematographer on *Deep Throat*, a man named Joao Fernandez who used the all-purpose porn pseudonym Harry Flecks, would become perhaps the most successful of those associated with the film. He crossed over to do mainstream cinematography, worked on many Chuck Norris and

148

Fred Williamson action films, and is known as a competent journeyman with the camera. (Arthur Knight would be proud.)

Lovelace, in contrast, continued to be haunted by the film. In the early eighties she was still in demand as a professional witness for antiobscenity movements—she appeared on *Donahue* and testified before the Minneapolis City Council when it was considering a law defining pornography as discrimination against women—and in 1986 she wrote her final autobiography, *Out of Bondage*, with an introduction by Gloria Steinem. Mostly she used the book to describe her poverty-ridden circumstances and to counter attacks on her credibility that resulted from *Ordeal*. She portrayed herself as a typical rape victim who gets raped all over again in the court of public opinion when she decides to tell the truth.

Just as the book came out, though, her health fell apart. First she entered the hospital for a double radical mastectomy, which the doctors assured her was necessary due to the silicone injections she'd gotten in 1971. But during the procedure, doctors discovered that her liver was malfunctioning, the result of a blood transfusion she'd had after her 1969 car accident. Apparently the original blood donor had Hepatitis C, and barring a liver transplant, Lovelace would die. A liver did become available in March 1987, and she underwent a fifteen-hour procedure at Presbyterian-University Hospital in Pittsburgh, followed by two months of convalescence. She was told that for the rest of her life, she would need an anti-rejection drug that costs $2,500 a month.

In 1990, her husband's drywall business collapsed and they moved to Colorado. She worked for a while at Albertson's drug store but had to quit because of varicose veins that made it difficult for her to stay on her feet all day. (She said this was the result of Traynor's repeated beatings and rapes, which allegedly caused permanent damage to the blood vessels in her legs as well as internal damage.) In 1993, she went to work for a computer company, doing purchasing and record-keeping for $9.45 an hour, but she was fired a year later for falsifying a time card. Her third marriage broke up in 1996. Continuing her pattern of vilifying her exes, she described Marchiano as an emotionally abusive alcoholic that she had loved for only the first two years of their marriage. Using an interesting choice of words, she told a Denver reporter, "I prostituted myself [to Marchiano] so I could have my kids. They were the most important thing to me. They were all I ever wanted." At the turn of the millenium, she was living in Denver in a small condo and working in "user support" for an investment company and cleaning office buildings at night. She became a grandmother in 1998, when her daughter Lindsay gave birth at the age of seventeen.

THE VIDEO REVOLUTION OF THE LATE SEVENTIES had changed the pornography business forever, making it both more accepted and less visible, as consumers retreated into the privacy of their own homes and bought porn videos in numbers undreamed of by even the most optimistic assessments of the industry. (Today more than 10,000 porn videos a year are produced in Southern California alone.) The last real theatrical crossover attempt was Chuck Vincent's *Roommates* in 1981. After that, the business became all video, all the time, and those directors who still wanted to work with film switched to horror films or other low-budget offerings on the fringes of Hollywood. At one point in the seventies, there were more than a thousand adult theaters nationwide, but by 1991 there were fewer than twenty-four.

The Colombo family was not able to keep its monopoly on the porn business, though. By 1976, organized crime controlled 80 percent of all porn production and distribution, and there were families from Chicago, New Jersey, and Florida involved as well as the traditional New York families. Eventually it was Carlo Gambino who proved the most aggressive and persistent of the mob competitors. Gambino had had a hand in porn ever since 1971, when his operative Reuben Sturman imported the peep-show machine, and in the late seventies he moved into video production long before anyone else. Eventually he got into pornographic books, magazines, toys, movies, and massage parlors, operating through his lieutenants Ettore "Terry" Zappi and Zappi's son Anthony. The porn profits were recycled into various vertical monopolies, including garbage collection, vending machines, trucking, construction, garment manufacture, restaurants, and restaurant-supply companies. Gambino was simply becoming bigger than everyone else. And as the Colombos and the Gambinos began to fight over porn turf, there were about two dozen more killings.

During the eighties, porn suffered a temporary retreat as it found itself under attack by the federal government, feminists, and Christian fundamentalists all at the same time. The feds made their most devastating strike against the pornographers in a sting operation called MIPORN, with FBI agents posing as video pirates, and on February 14, 1980, 400 agents arrested 58 people, including Butchie Peraino and his uncle Joe the Whale. Their operations man, Michael "Mickey Z" Zaffarano, had a heart attack during his arrest and died on the spot. In the ensuing trials, Butchie got a six-year prison term, Joe the Whale got three, and Butchie's father, Big Tony, was finally nailed for his original *Deep Throat* conviction and sentenced to ten months for bail jumping.

This marked the end of the Perainos' dominance of the porn businesss. In November 1981 Joe the Whale was wounded outside his home in Brooklyn by men with 9-millimeter handguns, but when police interviewed him at the hospital, he claimed he didn't know who the men were. The following January he was attacked again by two gunmen while walking with his son Joseph Jr. in the Gravesend section of Brooklyn. Running into a duplex to escape, they were both cut down by gunfire and Joe Jr. was killed, along with an innocent bystander, a fifty-three-year-old former nun and social worker. Joe the Whale once again refused to identify his attackers. The hit men weren't identified until 1993, when Salvatore Miciotta turned state's evidence and entered the federal witness-protection program. He told the FBI that he and

Vincent "Jimmy" Agellino had been the triggermen, and that they were working under direct orders of Carmine "the Snake" Persico, the godfather of the Colombo family. The Perainos were on the outs with their own family. The reason: a dispute over movie profits.

Joe the Whale and his brother Big Tony must have patched things up with the family, though, because they managed to keep Arrow Film & Video, running it through dummy corporations. In 1987 they released *Deep Throat II*, followed by part three in 1990, and a fourth and final installment in 1991. In 1997, with Big Tony on his death bed, Butchie sold Arrow to a producer named Raymond Pistol just before the twenty-fifth anniversary of *Deep Throat*. Pistol then held a series of regional deep-throat contests, billed as a search for the new Linda Lovelace, in which aspiring actresses demonstrated their oral skills on inanimate objects. A stripper named Hayley Huntington was so enthusiastic that she almost choked to death on a ripe banana in the finals at a Las Vegas topless club, but she edged out porn star Jacklyn Lick for the title, and Pistol proceeded to produce a four-film series called *Deep Throat: The Search* that was, if possible, even harder to sit through than the original.

EVEN AS THE VERY LAST SMIDGEN OF controversy seemed to have been milked out of *Deep Throat*, Ron Howard, the Hollywood producer and director, optioned the rights to *Ordeal* for $3,000. So given the growing Hollywood fascination with all things sordid, we may see her story told one more time. Until then, she'll mostly be remembered as the "How did she do it?" girl among the people who saw the film, and the "Bad men made me do it" girl among feminists and Christian crusaders. The porn industry has coined its own term, "the Linda Syndrome," to describe porn stars, such as Angel Kelly and Samantha Fox, who become stars and then disavow their porn past and embrace feminism.

For the generation born after *Deep Throat*, the term has entered the vernacular as a synonym for oral sex and the name of several cocktails. (All of them are served in a shot glass with either whipped cream or Bailey's on top.) But even Generation X, for whom oral sex is more or less common, knows who Linda Lovelace is, as her daughter Lindsay found out in high school. "I'm not ashamed of my mother," she said. "I'm never going to say, 'Oh, no, that's not her.' . . . I just have to deal with it when it comes into my face."

Lovelace was the longest surviving member of her liver-transplant support group, so it's ironic that she died alone after losing control of her car on April 3, 2002, and hitting a concrete post. For almost three weeks, she remained on life support. When it was finally turned off, her parents were at her bedside, along with Marchiano and their two grown children. It was a car accident that led her into porn, and it was a car accident that finally released her. In both cases, she never knew what hit her.

FOR FURTHER DISTURBANCE

Deep Throat was the beginning of mainstream hardcore pornography in America, but there were earlier sex films that paved the way for it. Most important were GARDEN OF EDEN (1954), a nudist-camp film that established the legal precedent allowing nudity on screen; THE IMMORAL MR. TEAS (1959), Russ Meyer's groundbreaking attempt to take advantage of the new situation; Doris Wishman's NUDE ON THE MOON (1962), the most entertaining of the excruciatingly awful nudie-cuties of the early sixties; SATAN IN HIGH HEELS (1962), illustrative of the "roughies" period, which made rape fantasies explicit for the first time; I AM CURIOUS (YELLOW) (1968), a Swedish film that employed full-frontal nudity for the first time; VIXEN (1968), the Russ Meyer film regarded as the beginning of couples porn; Alex de Renzy's CENSORSHIP IN DENMARK (1969), the first feature to show hard-core intercourse; Matt Cimber's HE AND SHE (1970), representative of the fake "sex research institute" films and the first porn film to get national distribution; Mike Henderson's ELECTRO SEX '75 (1970), first porn feature to be advertised in newspapers; and NECROMANIA (1971), the only hard-core film by the notorious Ed Wood Jr. Bill Osco's MONA THE VIRGIN NYMPH (1970), is regarded as the first "classic" narrative porn feature. It stars Fifi Watson as an oral-sex expert in a story that's remarkably similar to *Deep Throat* and yet delivers more sex.

After *Deep Throat* was released, the porn industry kept trying to repeat history with films that crossed over to a mainstream audience. None of them ever acquired the same cachet, but a few got close—namely BEHIND THE GREEN DOOR (1972) with Marilyn Chambers, Gerard Damiano's THE DEVIL IN MISS JONES (1973) with Georgina Spelvin, ALICE IN WONDERLAND (1976), THE OPENING OF MISTY BEETHOVEN (1977), CANDY STRIPERS (1978), and DEBBIE DOES DALLAS (1978). The last attempt to make a couples crossover film was Chuck Vincent's ROOMMATES (1981).

Mainstream filmmakers in Europe and Hollywood, adapting to the new sexual freedom, became more daring as well. From Italy came Bernardo Bertolucci's LAST TANGO IN PARIS (1973). From France came EMMANUELLE (1974), based on a popular banned novel. It could be argued that 9 1/2 WEEKS (1986) and UNFAITHFUL (2002) would have been impossible had it not been for porn opening up the limits of the screen, and yet most American films, even when dealing with sex as a legitimate plot element, have shied away from hard-core coupling.

The loops Linda Lovelace filmed for director Ted "Tom" Snyder have become collector's items, but they can be seen in the compilation tapes SCREAMING DESIRE (date unknown), NAKED NIGHT (date unknown), THE CONFESSIONS OF LINDA LOVELACE (1974), and LINDA LOVELACE

MEETS MISS JONES (1975). Her fetish loops are legendary, especially DOGARAMA (date unknown), her bestiality loop, but they're not widely available. Easier to find is the first film starring Lovelace and Harry Reems, SEX U.S.A (1970), also directed by Damiano.

DEEP THROAT: THE SEQUEL (1974), which exists today only in an R-rated version, recycled Lovelace footage from the original film, but by then she had opted for a "legitimate" career orchestrated by her second husband, David Winters. He produced her soft-core follow-up film, LINDA

LOVELACE FOR PRESIDENT (1976), which was not a success, leading her back to hard-core porn for single-scene appearances, notably in EXOTIC FRENCH FANTASIES (1974) with John Holmes. Ignoring the first sequel, Arrow Entertainment released DEEP THROAT II in 1987, DEEP THROAT III in 1990, and DEEP THROAT IV in 1991, each time using a new actress.

Chuck Traynor continued to produce porn after he broke up with Lovelace, and he later married Marilyn Chambers, the star of *Behind the Green Door*. Among the more famous films they did together were the blockbuster INSATIABLE (1980) and two sadomasochism flicks, NEVER A TENDER MOMENT (1979) and BEYOND DE SADE (1979).

Bryanston Pictures, the mob-controlled Hollywood film studio run by Louis "Butchie" Peraino, released a number of nonporno pictures that manage to end up frequently on late-night TV, including THE HUMAN FACTOR (1975), THE DEVIL'S RAIN (1975), and ECHOES OF A SUMMER (1976). And the company had bona-fide independent hits with RETURN OF THE DRAGON (1973) starring Bruce Lee, ANDY WARHOL'S FRANKENSTEIN (1973), and THE TEXAS CHAIN SAW MASSACRE (1974).

Most members of the *Deep Throat* cast were never seen again. Carol Connors worked in porn for many years and is best known for CANDY (1983) and its sequels. Harry Reems starred in a slew of films in the years just after *Deep Throat*, retired for six years, then returned in 1982 in *Society Affairs*.

Bob Chinn's 1978 classic *Candy Stripers.*

WILLIAM PETER BLATTY'S "THE EXORCIST" STARRING ELLEN BURSTYN · MAX VON SYDOW · LEE J. COBB · KITTY WINN · J.
SPECIAL EFFECTS BY MARCEL VERCOUTERE   ORIGINAL MUSIC BY JACK NITZSCHE   DIRECTED BY WILLIAM FRIEDKIN   WRITTEN BY WILLIAM PETER BLA

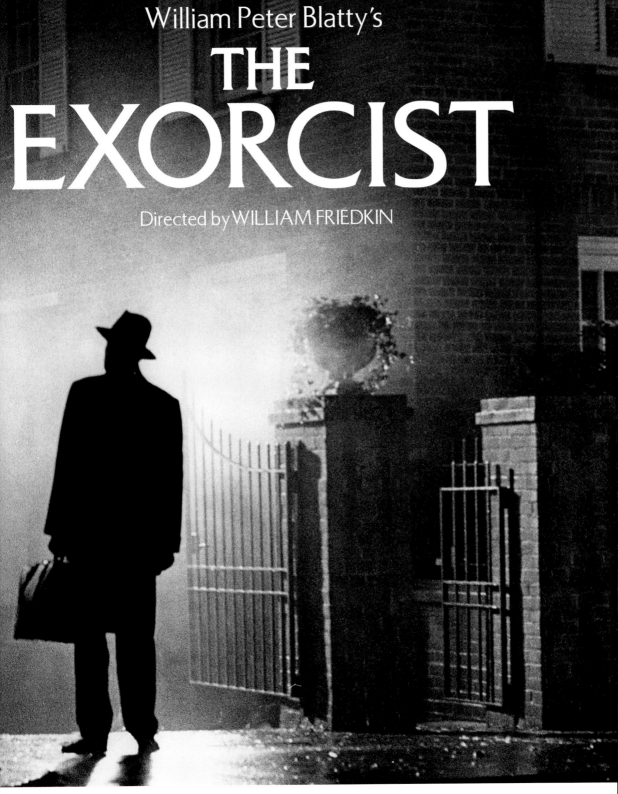

William Peter Blatty's

THE
EXORCIST

Directed by WILLIAM FRIEDKIN

CGOWRAN · JASON MILLER · LINDA BLAIR · REVEREND WILLIAM O'MALLEY · BARTON HEYMAN
DUCER **WILLIAM PETER BLATTY**   EXECUTIVE PRODUCER **NOEL MARSHALL**   ASSOCIATE PRODUCER **DAVID SALVEN**

R | **RESTRICTED**

Catholic demon slayers!
Possessed children!
Green pea soup!—
it was all anyone could talk about in the winter of 1973-74,
when the ultimate Upchuck Jubilee epic hit the screens.

THERE HAVE ONLY BEEN TWO HORROR FILMS, really, that caused the whole country to go nut-zoid. One was the original *Frankenstein*, in 1931, starring Boris Karloff, and the other was *The Exorcist* forty years later. People would throw up when they went to see this movie. People fainted. People claimed they had to have psychiatric help. Several people used it as a murder defense. "I don't know why I killed him, but it was right after I saw that movie." It started the whole "devil made me do it" thing. The video was banned in England for more than a decade. It inspired heated denunciations, including one from a Church of Scotland official who said he'd "rather take a bath in pig manure than see the film." Billy Graham preached sermons against it—which is very odd, because the Catholic Church cooperated all the way on it. It's sort of the ultimate evocation of medieval Catholic gloom fused with a contemporary pubescent girl singled out by a devil who's a little bit too successful to make the clergy comfortable. *The Exorcist* grossed $160 million in an era of $3 movie tickets and turned Satan himself into a Hollywood high concept.

And it has its basis in fact. *The Exorcist* came from a novel by William Peter Blatty that was a study of an authentic exorcism in 1949. Strangely enough, until he wrote *The Exorcist* Blatty was basically a comedy writer. He was considered, in fact, a master of light comedy. He wrote *A Shot in the Dark* for Blake Edwards—the first Pink Panther movie. He wrote humorous pieces for the *Saturday Evening Post*. He wrote movies like *What Did You Do in the War, Daddy?*, *John Goldfarb, Please Come Home*, *Promise Her Anything*, and *The Great Bank Robbery*. But then that sort of frothy sixties comedy played itself out, and Blatty found himself out of work because the studios didn't consider him serious enough to write drama. So in the summer of 1969, he got a cabin at Lake Tahoe and started writing *The Exorcist*, based on an article he'd read in the Washington Post back when he was a student at Georgetown University, in 1949. It became a best-seller, which in turn became the top-grossing horror film of all time. (Three or four years later, a studio head was having a meeting to discuss a comedy he wanted to make. When Blatty's name came up, he shouted, "William Peter Blatty! The guy who wrote *The Exorcist*? You want me to hire him for a comedy?!" So Hollywood still wouldn't hire him.)

Blatty's book stayed very close to the actual facts in the case, and director William Friedkin followed suit, even going so far as to have actual Jesuit priests on the set to ensure accuracy. (Blatty produced the film himself, and the dictatorial Friedkin, known for treating actors like cattle, was not his first choice. He went to Friedkin only after Mike Nichols, John Boorman, and Peter Bogdanovich all turned it down.) What we know about the historical version is that a psychotic fourteen-year-old boy lived in Mt. Rainier, Maryland, just across the line from Washington, D.C., and after the medical community all but gave up on curing him, his mother turned to the church. First he was taken to Georgetown University Hospital and worked on by the Reverend Albert Hughes, the assistant pastor at St. James Catholic Church. But the boy seriously wounded the priest with a bedspring wire, and they had to call in a priest who had handled exorcisms in tribal Africa—William Bowdean, a Jesuit from St. Louis. He did the exorcism rite for about three months before pronouncing the boy free of the devil. And all that time, the kid spoke in a weird language that they think was Aramaic, the language of Jesus, which is all but extinct in the modern world. The priest would never talk about the case, citing the family's need for privacy, and he maintained his silence right up until his death in 1980. But people who knew that priest did talk about it,

so Blatty was able to piece the story together. He protected the identity of the boy by changing him to a girl—fortunately for Linda Blair's career.

Although tourists still travel to the Georgetown section of Washington to see "the Exorcist House," that is merely a location used for the movie. The real residence of the demon-possessed boy was 3210 Bunkerhill Road in Mt. Rainier, a house where many inhabitants died violent deaths before it became vacant and then burned down during a fire-department training exercise. Even after that, the neighborhood has continued to have a high incidence of strange murders. That could be interpreted as spooky, but then again, it's practically Washington, D.C., you might be able to go two blocks over and get the same crime statistics.

At any rate, this movie made such a pile of money when it came out that the thirteen-year-old Blair became the superstar child actress of the seventies, and it affected everyone else who worked on it as well. Ellen Burstyn, who played Blair's stressed-out mom, became one of the hottest stars of the seventies, and actor-playwright Jason Miller's portrayal of the unhappy Father Damien Karras would haunt him for the rest of his alcohol-riddled life.

Miller was actually very happy at the time he made this movie, though, because he had just won the Pulitzer Prize for his Broadway hit *That Championship Season*. Blatty had wanted Marlon Brando to play the guilt-ridden priest, but Friedkin vetoed the choice. Jack Nicholson desperately wanted the part, but Friedkin chose Miller, who

---

Following pages: Linda Blair as inhabited by Satan.

And it wasn't until the movie came out
and every weirdo in the universe
started coming up to her
in the street that she realized,
"Oh, the devil was inside me!
And people like that."

had never acted in a film. Friedkin's explanation: "I just can't see Jack Nicholson as a Catholic priest." The studio also wanted Audrey Hepburn as the mother, but Friedkin wouldn't take her, either. Instead he hired Burstyn, who had been nominated for the Oscar for *The Last Picture Show* the year before. (She was nominated again for this role, and then won Best Actress for *Alice Doesn't Live Here Anymore*, in 1975.) But Burstyn was already forty years old when stardom struck. She'd been working for years under a variety of stage names. When she was eighteen years old she changed her name to Edna Rae to become a model. She worked in a Montreal night-club chorus line under the name Keri Flynn, then got a screen test in the fifties and changed her name again—to Erica Dean. Next she got a part in a Broadway play and changed her name to Ellen McRae. Finally, after marrying for the third time, she took the name of her husband, which was Burstyn, and she's been that ever since. In the late nineties, a Broadway producer, still trading on her *Exorcist* fame, cast her in a show as a nun trying to become a priest. It closed after a few weeks. *The Exorcist* remains her most famous role, although she was nominated for yet another Oscar in 2000 for her work in *Requiem for a Dream*.

Bᴜᴛ ɪᴛ ᴡᴀs ᴛʜᴇ sᴘᴇᴄɪᴀʟ ᴇꜰꜰᴇᴄᴛs ᴛʜᴀᴛ astounded and horrified early audiences, many of whom had never heard the word "exorcism" before. And, oddly enough, the number-one gross-out scene is not the actual exorcism. It's the closeup spinal tap near the beginning when doctors are trying to treat the girl for apparent brain dysfunction. Even Blatty couldn't handle that scene. He watched it one time when the film was being edited and never watched it again. This is the "walker" scene, the place during the film when people fainted, asked for their money back, and had subsequent nightmares. Blair's frequent use of the f-word when she gets injected with the drug made it all the more unpleasant and caused an uproar. She cusses like a psycho sailor throughout the film, using gross sexual terms, and there were numerous editorials outraged that a thirteen-year-old girl was allowed to use such language in a movie.

When she gets really nasty, though, it's not even her voice. It's the voice of Mercedes McCambridge, the veteran of classic movies—*Giant, Touch of Evil, Suddenly Last Summer, All the Kings Men*—who was even better known in the thirties as the woman Orson Welles called "the world's greatest radio actress." So she was more than a little skilled in making frightening noises. In addition, Friedkin put all kinds of subliminal noises into the soundtrack, just to make the audience even more nervous. The first possession scene is delayed for a full forty minutes, and it's not until the sixty-five-minute mark that someone finally says "What about exorcism?" Yet the audience is already scared to death.

In later years Linda Blair would claim that, while making the movie, she had no idea how freaky she was being. She was basically ordered around by Friedkin, who told her, "Here, go spend three hours in makeup. Here, let us strap you into the bed. Here, smile at Jason Miller. Here, open wide!" And it wasn't until the movie came out and every weirdo in the universe started coming up to Blair in the street that she realized, as she later said, "Oh, the devil was inside me! And people like that." Blair was nominated for the Oscar for this performance, and then she did TV movies throughout the seventies. (Remember *Sarah T.: Portrait of a Teenage Alcoholic*?) She also did some of the best B movies of the eighties—*Hell Night*, *Savage Streets*, *Chained Heat*, and the immortal *Roller Boogie*—but blames *The Exorcist* for ruining her career. She would always be "the pea soup girl." Today she works occasionally in TV movies, lives in Connecticut, and rides show horses professionally.

In her two climactic exorcism scenes, there were three grossout effects that had never been seen before. The spooky 360-degree headswivel was, of course, the biggest sensation, but the intensity is created by Blair repeatedly stabbing herself between the legs with a crucifix while saying some very nasty sexual things to Mom. (That effect may be the single most disturbing of the film.) And finally, there was the projectile vomit. In reality, the on-screen puking was done by a girl named Eileen Smith. When they were making the film they asked Smith not to tell anyone that they were using a stunt vomiter, but later she got upset that Linda Blair was getting all the attention for what was rightly her vomit, so she sued the film company, trying to get vomit credit.

But then Friedkin was the kind of director who would be proud of his vomit. This and *The*

When they were making the film they asked Smith not to tell anyone that they were using a stunt vomiter, but later she got upset that Linda Blair was getting all the attention for what was rightly her vomit, so she sued the film company trying to get vomit credit.

French Connection (1971) are his two best movies, partly because he was so obsessive about detail. He spent an entire year making *The Exorcist*, making mincemeat of a 105-day shooting schedule and ballooning the cost from $2 million to $12 million. He spent a whole month in Iraq shooting the spooky gargoyle scenes at the archeological site—for less than four minutes of screen time. The actual Max von Sydow exorcism takes about fifteen minutes of screen time, but it took three months to shoot. And Friedkin used a special refrigerated room so that you could see the actors' breath. He would cool the room down to ten degrees below zero, then when they turned on the lights and started shooting, it would warm up to zero. Makeup man Dick Smith did an extraordinary job on the pitted, pock-marked, contorted face of Blair, but he did just as much makeup on von Sydow. Von Sydow was only forty-three years old when he made this. He looks at least eighty-three. (Of course, he made all those Ingmar Bergman movies, in which where you spend two hours watching bored Swedish people yell at each other. That'll make you old.) And Friedkin treated his actors the same way he treated his sets. When Father William O'Malley, a real Catholic priest, gives absolution to the dying Father Karras, he's trembling—because Friedkin had just smacked him across the face to get a better performance out of him. When Linda Blair whacks her mother across the face and against the wall, Friedkin kept redoing it, having a stunt man jerk Burstyn off the bed with a rig attached to her midriff that ultimately injured her spine.

THE OVERLOOKED PERFORMANCE IN THE MOVIE is Lee J. Cobb as the creepy detective who's always hanging around. For some reason, he disappears before the end of the movie, creating a pretty sizeable loose end. Are we assuming he just doesn't care to know how the two priests died?

The answer could lie in the twenty minutes of film that Friedkin left on the cutting-room floor, forever angering Blatty. For years, Blatty begged the studio to put out a special cut with the original footage in, but Friedkin never liked the idea. Blatty thought the additional footage—including a shot of Blair walking up and down the stairs like a spider and a scene explaining why the devil chooses to possess an innocent girl—would help flesh out the story. He finally got his wish with *William Peter Blatty's The Exorcist*, which had a brief run in theaters twenty-seven years after the original release, only to be snickered at by a younger generation of horror fans who couldn't figure out what all the fuss was about. It's still one of the greatest horror movies ever made, and it spawned two sequels, which are among the worst horror movies ever made.

And to answer the question everyone asks: Yes, it was pea soup. Green pea soup. Not Campbell's. Anderson's pea soup. And Blair said she hated vegetables at the time, so it did make her throw up.

FOR FURTHER DISTURBANCE

The word "exorcism" was hardly even known to the general public before 1973, but over the next two years it would become a movie cliché, more often used in comedies than supernatural horror films. There were so many rip-off versions immediately after the film's appearance that Warner Bros., anxious to put out a sequel, reportedly paid director William Friedkin and writer William Peter Blatty $500,000 just to come to a pitch meeting. Even with all that money on the table, there were too many "creative differences" for them to work together again. Instead, Warner Bros. hired director John Boorman, hot off *Deliverance* (1972), and writer William Goodhart to make what they thought was a can't-miss follow-up, loading it up with big-name actors like Richard Burton and James Earl Jones, return performances by Linda Blair, Kitty Winn, and Max von Sydow, and a score by Ennio Morricone.

On opening night of EXORCIST 2: THE HERETIC (1977), audiences laughed out loud, causing the studio to pull all the prints so that Boorman could reedit. The new cut did no better, and the film ended up as one of the standard entries on everyone's ten-worst-movie lists. Singled out for special abuse was the wooden, ponderous performance of

Richard Burton. The confusing metaphysical mumbo-jumbo plot has Regan (Linda Blair) as a hot teen being taken care of by a shrink (Louise Fletcher). Burton plays a priest sent by the Vatican to investigate Father Merrin's (Max von Sydow) death, and he journeys through Regan's mind to find his answers. Fletcher's character hypnotizes the girl and attaches some kind of metal mind-melder called a synchronizer to her head, and somehow we end up in Africa searching for the locust-loving demon that controls her. James Earl Jones helps out as Kokumo, a previous victim of the demon, and the whole thing tends to fall apart after the midpoint.

No wonder, then, that the Spooky Supernatural Catholic Priest genre was appropriated by others. LISA AND THE DEVIL (1974) was rushed over from Italy—where they know their Catholic priests—and is one of Mario Bava's better horror films, although it has little to do with exorcism. It was actually made in 1972, but some new footage was shot with Elke Sommer and Robert Alda, as a priest, to get demon possession into the plot, making it possible for it be shamelessly renamed *The House of Exorcism* in 1975. It also stars Sylva Koscina, Eduardo Fajardo, Alessio Orano, Alida Valli, and Telly Savalas. The 1972 version, minus the disembowelment of Sommer and her frequent vomiting, is far superior, as fifteen minutes of Bava's original footage was deleted to make room for the exorcism.

Much more impressive was Richard Donner's THE OMEN (1976), with Gregory Peck as a diplomat whose young son, Damien, turns out to be the son of Satan, able to control the minds of Rottweilers and to cause his first governess to hang herself during his birthday party. As the boy's mayhem increases, the deaths get ever more gory (the impalement of a priest is an especially memorable image) until Peck decides he must kill his own son by trying to stab him to death with ritual knives on a church altar. Also starring Lee Remick, Billie Whitelaw, Patrick Troughton, and David Warner, *The Omen* was a huge hit, leading to the fairly decent DAMIEN: OMEN II (1978), with William Holden and Lee Grant playing the parents, and the awful THE FINAL CONFLICT (1981), with Sam Neill as a grown-up Damien now running the United Nations Youth Council. No wonder that ten years passed before OMEN IV: THE AWAKENING (1991), which was a mere TV movie.

William Peter Blatty had already discovered that the genre was played out after he fought for years to be allowed to write and direct his own sequel. It finally came out in 1990 as THE EXORCIST III and was based on his 1983 novel *Legion*. Despite excellent performances from George C. Scott as a police lieutenant and Brad Dourif as the creepy Gemini Killer, it lacks suspense, and even though it uses plot elements from the original—pretending that *Exorcist II* never happened—by the time of its release, the story had ceased to resonate. Nicol Williamson is trucked in at the climax as the priest who performs the obligatory exorcism scene.

Still, Blatty remained obsessed with the idea of restoring the original version of *The Exorcist*, without Friedkin's cuts, and finally achieved his

expanded rerelease in 2000, but young audiences seemed bored by a film that now looked clearly dated, and the box-office returns were disappointing.

Meanwhile, Blatty's 1980 film THE NINTH CONFIGURATION—originally called *Twinkle, Twinkle, Killer Kane* and edited so much that there are five different versions—had become a sleeper cult hit after being ignored on its first release. It's one of those love-hate flicks, a wholly original story starring Stacy Keach as a marine colonel brought in to head the psychiatry department in a converted remote castle in the Pacific Northwest where soldiers who are suspected of feigning mental illness to avoid military service are treated. As the audience starts to guess which loony is really crazy—Scott Wilson as a psychotic astronaut; Jason Miller as a lieutenant who spends his days rewriting the works of Shakespeare for canine actors; Moses Gunn as a major who believes he's Superman; Robert Loggia as a lieutenant who believes he's being held captive by shape-shifting Venusians; William Blatty himself as a patient who thinks he's the medical officer—they realize that perhaps the colonel in charge has his own inner demons. The film is difficult—some would say exasperating—but always good for a debate.

Curtis Harrington's RUBY (1977) is an uneven tale of supernatural possession, starring Piper Laurie as an aging gun moll who runs a sleazy Florida drive-in where her sixteen-year-old daughter (Janit Baldwin) turns out to be responsible for all the creepy killings going on. REPOSSESSED (1990) is the inevitable send-up of the genre, with Linda Blair good-naturedly reprising her swivel-head vomit-spouting scene, Leslie Nielsen spoofing Max Von Sydow, and Ned Beatty and Lana Schwab doing a thinly disguised version of Jim and Tammy Faye Bakker. Unfortunately, writer-director Bob Logan's script is meandering and full of leaden puns and sight gags, so it runs out of steam after a few minutes.

At some point, satanic possession plots became inextricably linked to apocalyptic plots, as in THE SEVENTH SIGN (1988), the stylish thriller starring Demi Moore that's a mix of ROSEMARY'S BABY, *The Exorcist*, and every mystical religious text ever created, and SEVEN (1995), the thriller starring Morgan Freeman and Brad Pitt that starts out as a police procedural about two cops tracking a serial killer, then suddenly spins toward the day-uh-vuh's work.

Proving it's the studio where hope springs eternal, Warner Bros. recently announced yet another installment, a "prequel" called EXORCIST: THE BEGINNING, starring Stellan Skarsgard as the young Father Merrin, with direction by Paul Schrader.

Harvey Stephens is Damien in *The Omen*.

NAZI OF THEM ALL!

ILSA

SHE-WOLF OF THE SS

EVEN THE SS FEARED HER!

en by **JONAH ROYSTON** • produced by **HERMAN TRAEGER** • directed by **DON EDMONDS**

A DIFFERENT KIND OF

No one under the age of 18 will be admitted

X

"Once a prisoner has slept with me,"
says Ilsa, She-Wolf of the SS,
"he will never sleep with a woman again.
If he lives he will remember only
the pain of the knife."

"The knife?" gulps her lover,
tied naked on a wooden operating table.

"Castrate him."

AND ACTUALLY, THAT'S NOT EVEN THE WORST thing we see happen to this guy.

In the world of the underground cult movie, *Ilsa, She-Wolf of the SS* occupies a rare place of honor. It's considered beyond the pale of even the most daring late-night cable networks and may never be seen on any form of satellite or broadcast television. There are only a few of these "too grisly for cable" classics, most of them made in the seventies, including *Bloodsucking Freaks* and *I Spit on Your Grave*. And what they all have in common is that they are so subversive, breaking down unwritten moral codes of what should and should not be seen, that they amount to a sort of pornography of violence.

With sexual pornography, the precise limits were set long ago: actual visual penetration is the dividing line between hard-core porn and movies that are simply racy. But the few filmmakers who have gone all the way with violence, especially sado-masochistic violence, have been condemned more often than not for what they *haven't* shown. We don't actually see the castration of the prisoner in this opening scene of *Ilsa*, nor do we see the disturbing follow-up to it, in which Ilsa herself relieves him of the rest of his sexual organs. But we see the blood and we hear the screams, and the camera lingers a little too long for the squeamish. In 1974, any censor board in America would have banned this movie after watching the first three minutes.

And yet these movies weren't banned. These movies were all released during the golden age of exploitation, from about 1972 to 1983, when flicks destined for downtown grind houses and drive-ins were routinely passed by the MPAA classification board and given "R" ratings, apparently under the assumption that no one except the already depraved would see them. The video revolution changed all that, not because public taste changed, but because movies that once required a visit to the seediest part of town could now be rented, collected, and, most important, monitored by the prying eyes of outraged mothers. These movies became a little too available for comfort.

Ilsa, She-Wolf of the SS had an uneventful theatrical release. It set minor box-office records at one theater, on New York's 42nd Street, but otherwise it was noticed only by a fanatical audience of males who liked their nudity served with bizarre, bloody fetishism. American popular culture being what it is, yesterday's Nazi porn becomes today's cult classic, and *Ilsa* started circulating in various pirated copies as soon as VCRs became commonplace in the eighties. What's surprising, in light of Holocaust sensitivities, is that this most raunchy of all films set in concentration camps wasn't hounded by the Simon Wiesenthal Center. Perhaps the reason is that it is so luridly realistic. Ilsa, one of the most barbaric and depraved Nazis in film history, is exactly the image of National Socialism that a Nazi hunter would love. It's also supposedly based on the real story of Ilse Koch, a Gestapo officer known as the "Bitch of Buchenwald," and as we'll see, there's more than a little truth to the characterization.

Prison and white-slavery movies were nothing new, of course, dating back to the vice-racket road shows of the twenties. But *Ilsa* belongs to a particularly graphic group of films called "kinkies,"

launched in 1964 when a movie called *White Slaves of Chinatown* established what would become the women-in-prison genre. *White Slaves* featured numerous scenes of physical abuse of inmates, including closeup rope burns, injuries with metal bridles, flagellation, lesbianism, clothes ripping, slapping, whipping, and burning with cigarettes. But the principal innovation of *White Slaves of Chinatown* was to make the sadistic warden a female—in this case a Commie named Olga, played by Audrey Campbell with such panache that she would star in several sequels, such as *Olga's Girls*, *Olga's House of Shame*, and *Olga's Massage Parlor*.

The kinkies that followed—*Confessions of a Psycho Cat*, *Spiked Heels and Black Nylons*, *The Brick Doll House*—did not always follow the prison formula, but it became apparent after a time that audiences loved nothing more than a sadistic female prison warden, especially if she had lesbian tendencies. Why? I don't think it's been studied in the literature of abnormal psychology yet, but just as the "final girl" in the slasher movie must be a spunky, virginal female with some male character traits, so the villain in a kinky must be a sadistic, jaded female with some male character traits. In extreme cases—movies like *Obscene House* and *Invitation to Ruin*—the filmmaker even used a gigantically fat dominatrix, but these appear to be aberrations. In the most successful titles, the warden had to be attractive as well as ruthless. The common denominator of all these movies is the fear of castration—never shown but always suggested, as in *The Daughters of Lesbos* (1967), in which angry women take revenge on a rapist, or *Slaves of Love* (1969), in which men are held captive by voracious Amazons who use them sexually and then emasculate them.

UP UNTIL *ILSA*, ALMOST ALL THESE MOVIES had come out of New York, where two fetish magazines—*Bizarre* and *Erotique*—spawned a ready supply of young bondage models. (The most famous, of course, was Bettie Page, the raven-haired pixie who posed for fetish and bondage photos sold through the mail by the brother-sister team Irving and Paula Klaw.) But *Ilsa, She-Wolf of the SS* actually originated in Canada, where two producers, Andre Link and John Dunning, had been inspired by the success of a movie called *Love Camp 7* in 1969. *Love Camp 7* would today be regarded as a more or less standard women-in-prison movie, with Jewish women turned into sex slaves at a Nazi concentration camp, followed by a successful revolt and their bloody revenge on the Gestapo. (*Love Camp 7* was produced by Bob Cresse. According to Eddie Muller and Daniel Farris, authors of *Grindhouse*, Cresse "apparently never cast an actress he didn't want to whip." He cast himself

as the Nazi commandant.) Link and Dunning, the owners of Cinepix, commissioned their own Nazi script, careful to avoid any direct references to Jews, and then hired David Friedman, the veteran B movie producer who was no stranger to graphic violence, having produced the very first gore film, *Blood Feast*, in 1963 (see pages 84–99).

It was not to be a happy partnership, though. "Cinepix constantly played a money game with me," Friedman reminisced later. "They had this script that was as thick as an encyclopedia with scenes with the Allies attacking 2,000 German soldiers, storming the camp, and so on. And the budget was only $150,000! I said for that money there would be no 2,000 soldiers—just one soldier running into the camp shouting 'The Allies are coming!'—and we'd shoot off some firecrackers, and that's it! At any rate, I dug up some equipment and rolling stock—German half-tracks and so on from a private collector I knew, assigned Don Edmonds to direct, and sent him . . . up to Canada to close the deal."

Don Edmonds had spent ten years trying to make it as an actor—his main credits were *Gidget Goes Hawaiian* (1961) and the hayseed sixties TV

The common denominator of all these movies is the fear of castration— never shown but always suggested.

series *Petticoat Junction*—then turned to directing soft porn with *Wild Honey* in 1971 and *Tender Loving Care*, a teenage nurse flick released the same year as *Ilsa*. He knew what he was doing, though. Despite being made for pennies, the film has a slick, big-budget look, with realistic sets, costumes, and special effects, and much better acting than normally found in a movie of this type. The credit for that belongs to both Friedman and Edmonds, who took advantage of several lucky breaks. In 1973, when the project was put together, the popular American sitcom *Hogan's Heroes* had long since finished its sixth and final season, and its Stalag 13 prison-camp set was abandoned and waiting to be demolished so the property could be sold for development. Friedman asked if he could use the set, and the owners agreed because they knew he was planning to burn it down in the film's final sequence, saving them the cost of dismantling the buildings where Bob Crane and Werner Klemperer once roamed.

THE SECOND KEY DECISION WAS BORN OF necessity. The lead role of *Ilsa* had been given to Phyllis Davis, the stunning star of *Beyond the Valley of the Dolls* and *Sweet Sugar*, but when she read the script she said she couldn't do one particular scene, in which a German general asks Ilsa to degrade him in a most disgusting way. Since the scene is pivotal to the climactic sequence of the movie, Friedman and Edmonds had to find a new Ilsa at the very last minute. Friedman called a showgirl he knew from Las Vegas, and a few days later Dyanne Thorne showed up, ready to ride herd over Medical Camp 9. Perhaps Thorne's chief asset was that she looked the part of a ruthless Gestapo femme and yet was still gorgeous. Enhancing her zaftig Teutonic looks were enormous breasts on a voluptuous Marilyn Monroe–style frame.

Thorne would come to be called, somewhat inaccurately, "the female Bela Lugosi," but in fact she didn't have a German gene or a sadistic bone in her body. She was also, by the standards of the softcore sex film, much too old for the part. At forty-two she was already nearing the point of retirement for most casino dancers, but she had that certain pizazz that, in the perfect time and place, makes for instant stardom. Hers was a limited stardom, of course, and in fact many of her friends shunned her after the movie came out. But a large part of the movie's success has to be credited to her performance as the oversexed Gestapo mama. It wasn't an accident that she pulled it off. She had been classically trained in New York and even performed Pinter on Broadway. She had tried her luck in Hollywood, but landed only bit parts in B movies and episodic television (including two episodes of *Star Trek*), almost always playing the busty sexpot. In Vegas she worked chorus lines and as a straight woman for Tim Conway, playing the Eastern European bombshell who delivers lines like "Vee go to motel now, ja, sveetie boss?"

For Thorne the film was a lark, but for Friedman it was a nine-day nightmare. Cinepix would only send $10,000 at a time to make the movie, and

Following pages: One of Ilsa's experiments.

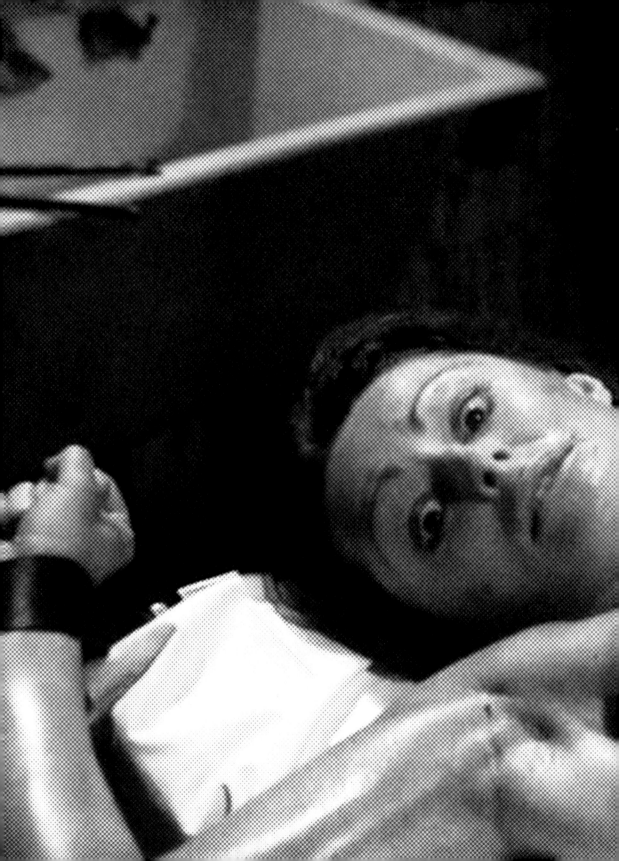

The super-soldiers of the future
will be women,
not men, because they can
endure any level of torture."

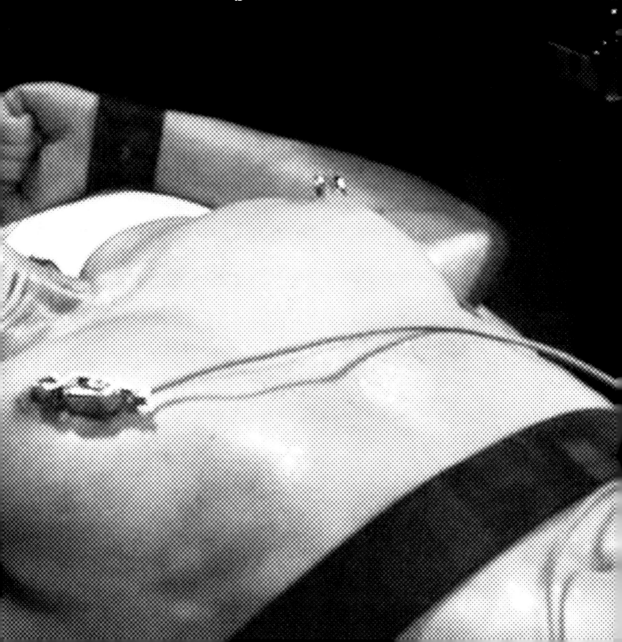

when Friedman asked for more, there would be long delays while he fretted and stalled. At one point the cash dried up entirely, and then, to his horror, Cinepix asked him for a personal loan. When he threatened to quit, they finally wired the full budget from the Bank of Nova Scotia, but he got frustrated with their frame-by-frame notes on the footage Edmonds was shooting, and eventually he just sent a rough assembly to Canada and told the producers to edit it themselves. He even took his name off the film, using the pseudonym Herman Traeger, and refused to have anything to do with the two official sequels. Even so, Cinepix's editing job was very good: What could easily have been a mind-numbing succession of atrocities is actually well-paced and never dull.

One more element that would make *Ilsa* a success was the hiring of a young aspiring makeup man who had been knocking around Hollywood for seven years trying to make a name for himself. Joe Blasco had worked as a sales rep for Max Factor, run a special-effects makeup school out of his apartment, and done more or less standard makeup jobs at CBS television, working on *The Red Skelton Show* and *The Jim Nabors Show*, before going on the road for two years with comedian John Byner's variety show. Friedman and Edmonds liked what he'd done on his only feature, *The Touch of Satan* (1970), primarily some old-age makeup, and they hired him for the gruesome effects that lie at the heart of *Ilsa*. Blasco would create not only the standard gunshot wounds, head injuries and whip burns, but build the illusions of skin cancer,

radiation burns, syphilis, and other horrors while using only liquid latex rubber and coloring. Although later viewers would complain that the blood is so red it seems unreal, Blasco's work was plenty horrifying.

THESE EFFECTS, AND EDMONDS'S STRAIGHT-ahead direction, made it clear that *Ilsa* was not meant to be camp. (The fact that it became camp is what ruined the sequels, in which Ilsa's character is softened and the horror is ruined by wildly implausible plots.) The only thing that makes you think the filmmakers might have their tongues in their cheeks is the opening type crawl, a classic "square-up," which rolls over the sound of a Nazi orator speaking in German:

"The film you are about to see is based upon documented fact. The atrocities shown were conducted as 'medical experiments' in special concentration camps throughout Hitler's Third Reich. Although these crimes against humanity are historically accurate, the characters depicted are composites of notorious Nazi personalities, and the events portrayed have been condensed into one locality for dramatic purposes. Because of its shocking subject matter, this film is restricted to adult audiences only. We dedicate this film with the hope that these heinous crimes will never occur again. Herman Traeger, Producer."

As the crawl closes, the soundtrack echoes with a crowd chanting a chorus of "Sieg Heils."

Cut to . . . Ilsa having sex—she's on top, of course—in an elegant bedroom where a radio plays chamber music. Our stunning white-blonde commandant is nude and screaming with pleasure, until she stops abruptly. "You should have waited," she says—leading to the terrifying castration scene.

What follows is the story of a concentration camp commandant who uses the male prisoners for her private sexual amusement and the females for her cruel medical experiments, which include infecting them with diphtheria, typhus, tetanus, plague, and syphilis to test experimental drugs on them. Only one man—a handsome American prisoner named Wolfe, played by Gregory Knoph—manages to sleep with Ilsa yet evade the castration chamber, thanks to his "freak of nature" sexual stamina, which she tests in every way possible. As the prisoners conspire to escape, Ilsa carries out a series of increasingly diabolical tortures, many of them centered on the doomed Anna—played by Maria Marx—who has such a high threshold for pain that Ilsa believes she's on the verge of a scientific breakthrough proving that the supersoldiers of the future will be women, not men, because they can endure any level of torture.

For cult enthusiasts, the film is full of classic scenes: Ilsa examining a new group of naked female prisoners, separating them into Third Reich prostitutes or medical guinea pigs while watching them get their privates shaved with a straight razor; Ilsa striding down the ranks of naked males saying "You call yourselves men? I see no manhood between your legs!"; Ilsa watching as an assistant systematically breaks the toes of a naked woman to prove the "feminist" principle that "a carefully trained woman

can withstand pain better than any man"; Ilsa ordering a girl to be gang-raped by laughing, grotesque men as punishment; Ilsa with her favorite toy, a giant electric cattle prod; Ilsa boiling a girl alive in a hyperbaric chamber (Uschi Digard, one of Russ Meyer's favorite actresses, in an uncredited role); Ilsa at her surgical table, attaching electrode nipple clamps and plunging a fiery implement into a woman's flesh, flaying open her leg; Ilsa administering electroshock to a prisoner's temples; Ilsa showing her superior how she has infected maggots with typhus by letting them breed in an open wound; and, perhaps most disturbing of all, a dinner celebration for a visiting Gestapo general, at which the entertainment is a naked girl with a noose around her neck, standing on a block of ice which slowly melts as the soldiers engage in an orgy.

OBVIOUSLY THERE WAS NO REAL MEDICAL Camp 9 where all of these atrocities took place—and yet there was a real Ilsa. Born in Dresden in 1906, Ilse Kohler was by all reports a beautiful woman with long red hair, although you wouldn't know it by her photos in various Holocaust books, taken after she had been imprisoned and her face had become puffy and severe. Everyone who knew her agrees that she flaunted her sexuality and could make herself alluring even in full SS regalia. Soon after Hitler's rise to power, she had been given a job in the Sachsenhausen concentration camp, where she worked her feminine wiles on the commandant, Karl Koch. At the time she met him,

Koch was already famous in Gestapo circles as the commandant of Columbia House in Berlin, where the Gestapo extracted confessions. Among Koch's favorite techniques were confining prisoners to dog-houses and forcing them to bark on command, bloody beatings, and stopping up prisoners' anuses with hot asphalt then forcing them to drink castor oil. In May 1937, he took Ilse as his bride, and when Koch was reassigned to a brand-new "special pun-ishment camp" for political prisoners, she went with him. The new camp was to be constructed by prison labor on a beautiful slope of Ettersberg Mountain, five miles north of Weimar. Once there, she was named the SS-Aufseherin, or overseer, of the prison that was named by Heinrich Himmler himself. It was to be called Buchenwald.

The Kochs ruled Buchenwald for four years, and from what we know, they used prison labor to build a life of luxury for themselves. Anything that was sent to the prison—wood, copper, bronze, gold, silver, wrought iron—was diverted for the benefit of Koch and his officers. Ten villas for the Gestapo were built by prisoners, with house servants chosen from imprisoned Jehovah's Witnesses. The prison workshops were devoted to the production of lux-ury articles like decorative objects, inlaid wood furniture, paintings, busts, and sculptures. If Koch found a competent craftsman or talented artist, he would loan him out to Berlin or to other cities—for money, of course—so that SS officers could have the luxury goods they craved. The sculpture studio at Buchenwald made a desk set of green marble that was presented to Heinrich Himmler as his Christmas present in 1939. Koch also constructed a personal falconry for Hermann Goring in 1940 (although Goring never used it). It included an

The video revolution changed all that, not because public taste changed, but because movies that once required a visit to the seediest part of town could now be rented, collected, and, most important, monitored by the prying eyes of outraged mothers.

aviary, hunting hall, fireplaces, trophies, gazebo, a house for the falconer, deer pens, and wildcat cages, with the whole complex maintained by landscape gardeners. Koch also ordered the construction of an elaborate entrance gate with the inscription "My Country Right or Wrong."

The orgy scene in *Ilsa* is not far removed from reality at Buchenwald. From the very beginning, Commandant Koch instituted monthly "comradeship evenings" for headquarters staff, and these were all-night riots of eating and drinking, usually ending in wild orgies. One of Koch's fellow black marketeers, an SS sergeant named Hans Schmidt, was fond of urinating in champagne glasses at these gatherings, and he was not above ordering prison servants to wash his penis, even as his wife and daughter looked on. The officers lived like kings. After Allied forces raided the camp in 1945, they found, in Koch's house alone, thirty hams, sixty smoked sausages, several hundred jars of fruits and vegetables, and 500 to 600 bottles of wine and champagne.

In 1938, Ilse's husband ordered construction of a park area for SS guards, with a birdhouse, a water basin, a zoo for four bears and five monkeys, and a falconry for the pet birds of prey kept by the officers. There was also a movie theater for the inmates, a prison library with 14,000 books, and a camp brothel employing fifteen prostitutes. At first, Buchenwald was a labor camp for political prisoners, with mostly German Communist inmates who were employed making weapons and other war material. These prisoners were later joined by Slavs,

resistance fighters, homosexuals, handicapped people, gypsies, and Jews. Although designed for only 8,000 prisoners, Buchenwald would eventually house more than 60,000 and, in the latter years of the war, become a death camp with a quota of eighty gas-chamber executions per day. All these prisoners knew who Ilse was, and they came to despise her as "Die Hexe von Buchenwald," or the Witch from Buchenwald. (This was transformed into the Bitch of Buchenwald by American reporters who accompanied the Allied liberators in 1945.)

There's no question that Ilse was a nymphomaniac. While living with her husband, she managed to carry on affairs with two other Gestapo officers, Dr. Waldemar Hoven by day and Deputy Commandant Hermann Florstedt at night. She would spend entire days in her bedroom while also finding time for trysts with the occasional SS guard. She was fond of horses and rode through the camp each day exposing her cleavage or her legs—but if a prisoner looked at her, she would order him whipped by guards. She liked to bathe in expensive Madeira wine, poured into the tub by her personal valet, a prisoner who was also expected to take care of her children (including wiping their bottoms), feed and walk her dogs, make coffee, and take it to Frau Koch in the morning as she luxuriated in the nude. (When one of her servants was caught stealing a bottle of wine, he was whipped in the face, forced to crawl over two high mounds of road gravel, strapped to a whipping block and given twenty-five lashes on the butt with a horsewhip, forced to do 100 deep-knee bends, ordered to stand motionless

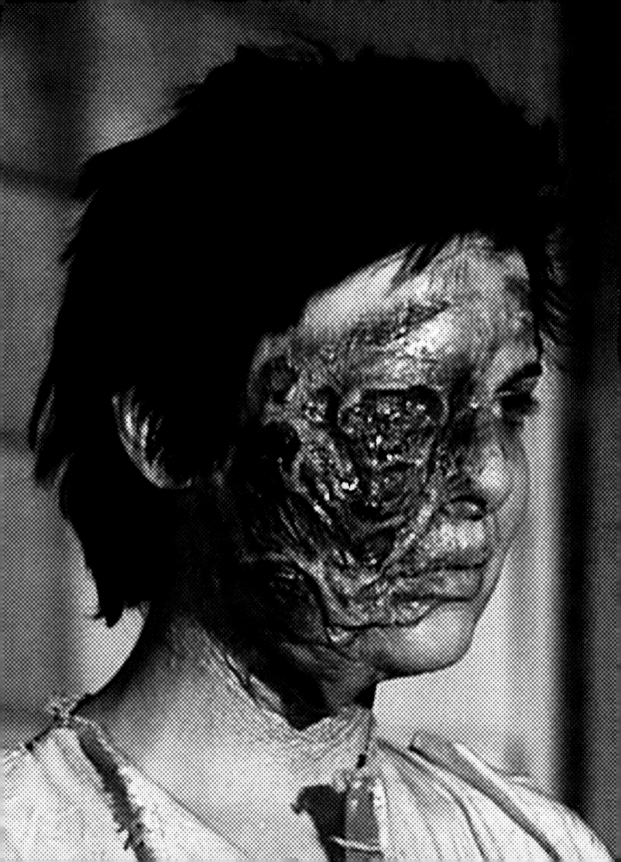

for hours on a mound of gravel in the glaring heat, and finally hung from the steel door of his cell block, arms tied behind his back, for three hours.)

In 1940, Commandant Koch had the inmates build an indoor equestrian arena especially for Ilse, and prisoners later claimed that the work was so hard and dangerous that it resulted in perhaps thirty deaths. She was the only person who ever used the football-field-sized arena, taking her morning ride there while the SS band stood on a special platform, playing music for her. Its walls were lined with mirrors so she could admire herself.

Her life as the Queen of Buchenwald was interrupted only slightly in August 1941, when her husband was charged with black-market activities and inciting the murder of two prisoners. The charges were made by SS General Prince von Waldeck-Pyrmont, Koch's superior, who never liked Koch but was blocked from disciplining him because the Buchenwald commandant was a favorite of SS General Theodor Eicke, inspector of all concentration camps. Waldeck-Pyrmont was finally able to make the charges stick after Eicke was transferred to the front. The specific charges were that Koch had ordered the execution of two German Communists, Walter Kramer and Karl Peix, who were working as hospital attendants. (Koch had ordered them shot because they had treated Koch for syphilis and he wanted to eliminate them as witnesses.) While awaiting trial, Koch was demoted to the Majdanek concentration camp for Soviet prisoners in Lublin, Poland, but Ilse decided to stay in Buchenwald with her number-one lover,

the powerful and feared Dr. Waldemar Hoven, who was not above poisoning or lethally injecting inmates if they proved troublesome or dangerous. If you treat *Ilsa, She-Wolf of the SS* as a combination of the crimes of Ilse Koch, the crimes of Karl Koch, and the crimes of Dr. Hoven, you come closer to docudrama than you might first imagine.

But Ilse's days were numbered. The same man who prosecuted her husband, a law-and-order SS officer named Dr. Konrad Morgen, continued to monitor her activities and those of Dr. Hoven, and in August 1943, Ilse, her husband, and both her lovers were arrested for cruelty to prisoners, embezzlement, and forgery. Karl Koch was also charged a second time with murder and making threats to officials. Ilse moved to Majdanek, where her husband continued to work while awaiting his final judgment.

Karl Koch was tried and condemned to death on both murder counts, but Ilse was acquitted—and moved back to Buchenwald in her capacity as overseer. Hermann Florstedt, Ilse's other lover, was recalled from his commandant position at the Majdanek camp and also received a death sentence. Dr. Hoven was convicted of murdering anti-Communists by lethal injection, raising the suspicion that he was a Communist spy, but his death sentence was commuted due to a doctor shortage. (He was tried again by a United States military tribunal in 1948 and executed, partly because of Dr. Morgen's testimony. Hermann Pister, Koch's replacement as commandant at Buchenwald, was also convicted by an American court in 1947 and executed in 1948.)

A survivor in Ilsa's camp serves to caution new arrivals.

✱ ✱

AT THE TIME BUCHENWALD WAS LIBERATED by the Americans in 1945, Ilse was still living in her spacious villa near the camp. She was not important enough to be tried at Nuremberg, but she was judged by a 1947 tribunal, where the principal charge against her was that she had used the flesh of dead inmates to make lampshades for her personal use. One prisoner testified that she had ordered all the inmates to be assembled on the Appelplatz and stripped naked so that she could examine each one and choose tattoos that she liked. Presumably the prisoner would then be killed so she could use his skin to make decorative leather objects. Another testified that in her villa she had light switches made from human thumbs.

None of these charges were ever proven, however, and it was difficult later to determine what had really happened and what had been embellished by American newspaper reporters who became fascinated with the only woman Gestapo officer tried for these sorts of atrocities. It now appears that the allegations about tattooed human skin were the result of the obsessions of a Nazi doctor named Wagner, who wrote a doctoral dissertation on tattooing and had the camp searched for interesting tattoos, which he photographed. Nevertheless, in 1947, at a trial that got massive press coverage in the states, Ilse was sentenced to life in prison.

Two years after the trial, American General Lucius B. Clay ordered an investigation into her case and determined that the famous human-skin lampshades were actually made of goat skin. Even if they had been made of human skin, he said, those types of objects were found in other officers' quarters and didn't prove that she had ordered them, asked for them, or caused anyone to be killed. (Her husband, for example, had a watch fob made out of gold from teeth.) Clay reduced her sentence to four years. It was not a popular decision. The outrage in the popular press resulted in U.S. Senator Homer Ferguson of Michigan conducting a Congressional investigation, and soon thereafter, Ilse Koch was rearrested by German authorities and given a new trial on atrocity charges. In 1951 she was again sentenced to life, and this time it stuck. She was held in the Bavarian prison at Aichach, where she committed suicide in 1967.

It appears, in retrospect, that Ilse Koch was punished more severely than male officers convicted of similar crimes, mostly because of the human-skin

"You call yourselves men? I see no manhood between your legs!"

lampshade stories that gained wide circulation. It's well documented that many of the Nazi doctors at Buchenwald engaged in bizarre practices like shrinking the heads of dead inmates. (A letter exists from Gestapo headquarters ordering a stop to the practice.) It's also clear that many SS officers owned objects made from human skin. What's less clear is whether Ilse Koch had anything to do with the creation of those objects. It seems that her primary crimes were simply emotional cruelty. In one instance in February 1938, for example, the prisoners were forced to stand naked for three hours while SS men searched their clothes, and for much of that time Ilse and four other officers' wives stood at a barbed-wire fence staring at the men. There are documented instances of Ilse ordering men to be beaten, but that was such a common camp punishment that it's hardly remarkable. She may have gotten her life sentence as a signal that anyone that close to the leadership of a camp where 43,045 people had died simply deserves no mercy.

She also may have received punishment as a substitute for her husband. With the U.S. Third Army closing in on Buchenwald in April 1945, the Gestapo set about getting rid of anyone who had a motive to testify against them. Karl Koch, who had become a millionaire through his exploitation of concentration-camp workers, was shot one week before the liberation of Buchenwald, the execution being carried out by his original accuser, von Waldeck-Pyrmont, Higher SS and Police Leader of Thuringia. Dr. Konrad Morgen, the original prosecutor of Koch's crimes, more or less vindicated Ilse

Koch in the subsequent trials. And the American general in charge of tribunals, Lucius Clay, was sufficiently disturbed by the lack of evidence against her that he made it a special point to revisit the case twenty years later, even after she was dead.

"As I examined the record," wrote Clay, "I could not find her a major participant in the crimes of Buchenwald. A sordid, disreputable character, she had delighted in flaunting her sex, emphasized by tight sweaters and short skirts, before the long-confined male prisoners, and had developed their bitter hatred. Nevertheless these were not the offenses for which she was being tried and so I reduced her sentence, expecting the reaction which came. Perhaps I erred in judgment, but no one can share the responsibility of a reviewing officer. Later the Senate committee which unanimously criticized this action heard witnesses who gave testimony not contained in the record before me. I could take action only on that record."

Clay pointed out that she had not even lived at Buchenwald during the years of its worst atrocities, 1943 to 1945, and that most of the allegations made in the press—that she had a "family journal" bound in human skin featuring a chest tattoo of a four-masted ship—were not proven. He thought that she may have owned "medical specimens" cut from dead inmates, but that there was no evidence that she had ordered any murders. The Secretary of the Army, Kenneth C. Royall, agreed with Clay's decision. "I hold no sympathy for Ilse Koch," he said as late as 1976. "She was a woman of depraved character and ill repute. She had done many things reprehensible and punishable, undoubtedly, under German law. We were not trying her for those things. We were trying her as a war criminal on specific charges."

The German court that tried her the second time had more substantive charges: one count of incitement to murder, one of incitement to attempted murder, five counts of incitement to severe physical mistreatment of prisoners, and two counts of physical mistreatment. Even these charges, though, appear to involve crimes largely committed by her lovers and husband. It could be that she was a femme fatale who could get men to do nasty things for her, and if so, that was probably the view the court took. "She had been destroyed," said General Clay, "by the fact that an enterprising reporter who first went into her house had given her the beautiful name the 'Bitch of Buchenwald,' and he had found some white lampshades in there which he wrote up as being made out of human flesh. Well, it turned out actually that it was goat flesh. But at the trial it was still human flesh. It was almost impossible for her to have gotten a fair trial."

Indeed, to this day, if you visit almost any Holocaust museum, you'll find a picture of Ilse Koch and brief biographies like this one at the Museum of Tolerance in Los Angeles: "Married to the commandant of Buchenwald, Karl Otto Koch, Ilse Koch was known for her extreme sadism. She selected living prisoners whose skin she wanted, and after they were killed she used their tattooed skin for lampshades." So despite all her real crimes

and cruelties, the legend of the lampshades still gets most of the attention.

OF COURSE, NO ONE WHO SAW *ILSA, She-Wolf of the SS* thought for a moment that it was a docudrama, but Dyanne Thorne might possibly have gotten more respect as an actress if the movie were promoted more accurately. *Ilsa* led to a series of movie roles for her, but they were all more or less variations on *Ilsa*. Two of them were sequels: *Ilsa, Harem Keeper of the Oil Sheiks* and *Ilsa, The Tigress of Siberia*, neither of which made any pretense of being historical, both of which glossed over the fact that Ilsa had been killed at the end of the first movie. (A long-standing cult-movie rumor is that the Arab oil baron in *Harem Keeper* is played by Spaulding Gray in heavy makeup. Although Gray admits to making porno movies in the seventies, he's never specifically confirmed this.) There's even a fourth movie, *Ilsa, the Wicked Warden*, that was actually filmed by Jess Franco, the Spanish B-movie king, as *Greta, the Mad Butcher*, with the title changed later to take advantage of Thorne's notoriety. Franco's wife, Lina Romay, plays the heroine, who gets used as a human pin cushion. There were occasional attempts to revive the franchise, but by 1980 the world had had all the *Ilsa* it was going to swallow. Unfortunately, we never got to see *Ilsa Meets Bruce Lee in the Bermuda Triangle* or *Ilsa vs. Idi Amin* or *Ilsa: Nanny to Royalty*, all of which were in development at various times.

Dyanne Thorne eventually returned to Vegas and the burlesque world, starring in the *Sex After*

40 afternoon show at the Aladdin (sample line: "I'll show you my Schweppes, you can show me your Canadian Club"). She married Howard Maurer, one of the supporting actors in *Ilsa, the Wicked Warden*, and became an activist in the Screen Actors Guild. For the last two decades, she and her husband, both ordained ministers, have owned a Vegas wedding service called "A Scenic Wedding: The Musical Ceremony," specializing in ceremonies conducted on mountaintops, at lakefronts, in helicopters, in hot-air balloons, and on horseback. Thorne will even appear in costume, if requested. She's never been asked to do an *Ilsa* wedding, although she has conducted ceremonies as Mae West. At the age of seventy she was still getting 200 letters a week from *Ilsa* fans.

Most of the other actors on the original *Ilsa* faded into obscurity. Gregory Knoph, the male lead who has all the *Ilsa* sex scenes, would never make another film. Tony Mumolo, as the superserious Mario, would also vanish, although he did turn up on *The Incredible Hulk* and *Kojak* TV series. Maria Marx and Jo Jo Deville, the two most prominent female inmates, would never be seen again. Nicolle Riddell, the "good girl" who escapes with Knoph, would make three more exploitation films, including the infamous *Blazing Stewardesses*, and then retire. One of the best actors in the cast—Wolfgang Roehm, who plays the Gestapo general—came back in the *Harem Keeper* sequel but is not credited with anything after that.

Although Friedman had produced hundreds of movies and would still be working three decades later, most of his famous titles were behind him. (He only contributed to eight projects between 1975 and 2002.) Edmonds would direct the *Harem Keeper* sequel, then an action film called *Bare Knuckles* and an oddity about a KISS lookalike band that mutilates its groupies called *Terror on Tour*. By the nineties, he was primarily a producer (*The Night Stalker, Skeeter*) and a TV director, having worked on the pilot for *Silk Stalkings*.

Perhaps the most successful *Ilsa* survivor is special-effects man Joe Blasco, who would go on to do makeup for David Cronenberg's pioneering gore films (*They Came from Within, Rabid*) and then return to TV as a personal makeup artist for Carol Burnett, Rona Barrett, and on many series (*Barney Miller, The Darkroom*).

Although *Ilsa* was made into a musical play in the nineties, it lives on mostly as an under-the-radar cult item, its reputation boosted temporarily by Quentin Tarantino citing it as one of his favorites of the seventies. But it was saved from any real entry into the mainstream by its bizarre ending, in which leading man Wolfe and his waifish girlfriend, the only two characters not scarred or deformed by Ilsa's cruelty, head for the hills, leaving Ilsa's maimed victims to die as they take revenge on the Gestapo but are finally mown down by the Nazi tanks. Besides being historically inaccurate—the Allies did liberate injured prisoners from Buchenwald—it's a fairly cynical message, as though the "freaks" of Nazism are better off dead. The pornography of violence takes no prisoners.

FOR FURTHER DISTURBANCE

WHITE SLAVES OF CHINATOWN (1964) is considered the first dominatrix-warden movie, with Audrey Campbell in the lead role as Olga Petroff, a Communist sympathizer smuggling drugs from China for the mob. It led to three sequels: OLGA'S GIRLS (1964), OLGA'S HOUSE OF SHAME (1964), and OLGA'S MASSAGE PARLOR (1965). Those led in turn to Olga ripoffs such as INVITATION TO RUIN (1968)—which features an off-camera hot-poker-to-the-vagina scene—and OBSCENE HOUSE (1969).

"Kinkies," also called "roughies," flourished from about 1964 to 1970, and most centered on the slavery and brutalization of women by various sadistic criminal organizations. Notable examples are VIOLATED LOVE (1963), TAKE ME NAKED (1966), LOVE: MY WAY (1966), SPIKED HEELS AND BLACK NYLONS (1967), THE BRICK DOLL HOUSE (1967), and CONFESSIONS OF A PSYCHO CAT (1968).

Less common were movies in which men were victimized by women, but THE DAUGHTERS OF LESBOS (1967) and SLAVES OF LOVE (1969) are both Amazonian fantasies with men paying the ultimate price—castration.

The immediate inspiration for *Ilsa* was Bob Cresse's LOVE CAMP 7 (1969), which is also set in a Nazi concentration camp, but with a male commandant (Cresse himself) and only female prisoners.

The first *Ilsa* sequel was ILSA, HAREM KEEPER OF THE OIL SHEIKS (1976), which managed to use the Glendale (California) Public Library as the sheik's palace. Don Edmonds directed, with Dyanne Thorne reprising Ilsa, this time as the guard of a harem that features Amazon twins played by Marilyn Joi of NURSE SHERRI (1977) fame and Tanya Boyd, who starred in BLACK SHAMPOO (1976). Also in the cast are George "Buck" Flower as a beggar with syphilis and Haji as the spy who gets her eyeball fed to the Roehm character and her leg covered in fire ants. Highlight scene: an exploding diaphragm timed to go off at the moment of male climax.

ILSA, THE WICKED WARDEN (1977) was released on video in the early eighties and initially mistaken for an *Ilsa* sequel. It was actually Spanish director Jess Franco's *Greta, the Mad Butcher*, which did star Dyanne Thorne—with a redhead perm!—as the warden of a jungle prison for nude sex deviants, but had nothing to do with the series.

The second official sequel was Jean LaFleur's ILSA, TIGRESS OF SIBERIA (1977), the movie in which Thorne costarred with her future husband, Howard Maurer. Ilsa runs a Russian gulag for Stalin in 1953. For forty-five minutes, she tortures the inmates and has threesomes with guards. When she finds out Stalin is dead, she tries to destroy the camp, causing a riot of carnage. Then the movie flashes forward to Montreal in 1977, where a former inmate spots Ilsa as the madam of a brothel. She's building up a mob empire, but it all collapses when Russian soldiers shoot it out with her gang. Highlights include a man chopped up by a snow blower, and an arm-wrestling match with running chainsaws on each side of the table.

As a struggling actress in the sixties, Dyanne Thorne had bit roles in WHO WAS THAT LADY? (1960) and SIN IN THE SUBURBS (1962), uncredited walk-ons in LOVE WITH THE PROPER STRANGER (1963) and THE PRESIDENT'S ANALYST (1967), and a small part in LOVE ME LIKE I DO (1970). But by the early seventies, she was a bona fide B movie queen, featured in POINT OF TERROR (1971), THE EROTIC ADVENTURES OF PINOCCHIO (1971), BLOOD SABBATH (1972), WHAM BAM THANK YOU SPACEMAN (1975), and THE SWINGING BARMAIDS (1975), which ran for years at drive-ins under the title *Eager Beavers*. She also starred in CHESTY ANDERSON, USN (1976) and appeared in UP YOURS (1979), HELLHOLE (1985), and REAL MEN (1987).

Joe Blasco, the specialist responsible for the gory effects in *Ilsa*, was noticed by Friedman for his work on Tom Laughlin's *The Touch of Melissa* (1970), also known as THE TOUCH OF SATAN, but his best work came later, when he hooked up with David Cronenberg in 1975 on *The Parasite Murders* (known in the States as THEY CAME FROM WITHIN) and RABID (1977). He also did the makeup effects work on GARDEN OF THE DEAD (1972), TRACK OF THE MOON BEAST (1976), and WHISPERS (1991).

Don Edmonds had directed WILD HONEY (1971) before making *Ilsa*, and would direct the first sequel as well as an Avery Schreiber comedy called SOUTHERN DOUBLE CROSS (1973), the Marilyn Joi sex comedy TENDER LOVING CARE

(1974), an action film called BARE KNUCKLES (1978), TERROR ON TOUR (1980), the 1991 pilot for the *Silk Stalkings* TV series, and TOMCAT ANGELS (1991). He was also the writer on *Tender Loving Care*, *Bare Knuckles*, and *Tomcat Angels*. He was the coproducer on Tony Scott's TRUE ROMANCE (1993) and the goofy killer-mosquito flick SKEETER (1993). Most recently he produced LARCENY (2001) with Andy Dick, Tyra Banks, and Kate Jackson.

David Friedman, the producer of *Ilsa*, was one of the most prolific B-movie filmmakers in Hollywood at the time, and his principal credits are detailed on pages 98–99.

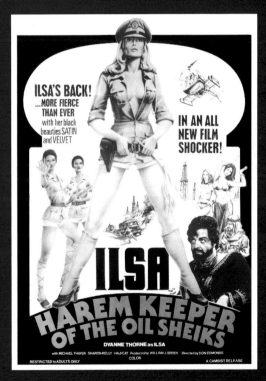

Who will survive and what will be left of them?

"THE TEXAS CHAIN SAW MASSACRE"

What happened is true. Now the motion picture that's just as real.

"THE TEXAS CHAIN SAW MASSACRE" A FILM BY TOBE HOOPER STARRING MARILYN BURNS · ALLEN DANZIGER · PAUL A. PARTAIN · EDWIN NEAL
JIM SIEDOW · WILLIAM VAIL · TERI MCMINN · ROBERT COURTIN AND INTRODUCING GUNNAR HANSEN as Leatherface
PRODUCTION MANAGER RONALD BOZMAN STORY & SCREENPLAY BY TOBE HOOPER · KIM HENKEL PRODUCED & DIRECTED BY TOBE HOOPER

| R | RESTRICTED |

America's most
bizarre and
brutal crimes!...

Five young people, travelling in a van, winding down strange country roads, encountering increasing levels of hostile Gothic weirdness as they move further into the wilderness...

T WOULD BE A CLICHÉ WERE IT NOT FOR THE fact that it was the first real youth-horror film. *Chain Saw* was the first baby-boomer shocker, in which pampered but idealistic suburban children, distrustful of anyone older than thirty, are terrorized by the deformed adult world that dwells on the grungy side of the railroad tracks.

The most enduring flick of the hippie era was made by twenty-eight-year-old Tobe Hooper, perhaps the most underappreciated horror director in history, who used $60,000 raised by an Austin politician to create a film that is still shown in almost every country of the world, and whose innovations have continued to influence the horror genre for the last thirty years. Its very title has become America's cultural shorthand for perversity, moral decline, and especially the corruption of children. (It remains the favorite example of congressmen calling for the censorship of television.) Yet the movie's pure intensity, startling technique, and reputation as an outlaw film have brought praise from a group as diverse as Steven Spielberg, the Cannes Film Festival, the inmates of the Pennsylvania State Penitentiary, Martin Scorsese (Travis Bickle watches it in *Taxi Driver*), William Friedkin, the Museum of Modern Art, Paul McCartney, almost every metal band of the past twenty years, and the Colombo crime family of Brooklyn, which gleefully ranked it right up there with *Deep Throat* as one of their major sources of income in the seventies. The film itself is a strange shifting experience, part Grand Guignol and part gritty realism. Early audiences were horrified, later audiences laughed, and newcomers to the movie were inevitably stricken with a vaguely uneasy feeling, as though the film might have actually been made by a maniac.

Chain Saw was conceived, shaped, filmed, edited, and released in a kind of mild doper's haze. Hooper would go on to direct *Poltergeist*, *Salem's Lot*, and many other films and television shows, but through it all he retained, like his friend Spielberg, a latent counterculture shabbiness, with his unruly beard, mop haircut, professorial wire-rim glasses, and gravelly, halting voice. (He rivals Dennis Hopper for the number of times he uses the word "man.") Hooper's scenarist, Kim Henkel, was a lanky, drawling textbook illustrator with a droopy handlebar mustache who had starred in Hooper's first feature, *Eggshells*, as a dope-smoking sexaholic poet who likes to write in the nude and discuss politics in the bathtub. Henkel was also living the Austin hippie lifestyle, and most of the *Chain Saw* cast had some connection to the counterculture. Allen Danziger, who played van driver Jerry, was a childhood friend of Stokely Carmichael's who had traveled from the Bronx to Austin to work with the mentally retarded in one of LBJ's Great Society programs. Dottie Pearl, the makeup artist, was a cultural anthropologist who had received government grants to make films about the Navajos. Gunnar Hansen, the 300-pound Icelandic-American who played the actual chain-saw killer, was the editor of the Austin poetry journal *Lucille* at the time he got the part.

Everyone involved felt permanently changed—or, in some cases, scarred—by the film. Ed Neal, who played the Hitchhiker, could never again speak about it without becoming enraged. Robert Kuhn, a criminal attorney who invested in the film, would waste years fighting for the profits that should have poured into Austin but were instead siphoned off by a Mafia distribution company that absconded with the funds. The late Warren Skaaren, who would become one of the highest paid rewrite men in Hollywood, could trace his whole career to his association with *Chain Saw*. Ron Bozman, the film's production manager, would ascend to the very pinnacle of the profession. He accepted the

1992 Academy Award for Best Picture as the producer of *The Silence of the Lambs*. Still, even he says that *Chain Saw* was the greater thrill: "It was by far the more intense experience—nothing compares to it for density of experience—it was just such a wild ride."

ALTHOUGH IT WAS THE FIRST REAL SLASHER film, it had no progeny. Its sequels were lackluster and its ideas used to more lucrative effect by other people—John Carpenter, with his *Halloween* movies; Sean Cunningham, with his *Friday the 13th* series; and Wes Craven, of *Nightmare on Elm Street* and *Scream* fame. *The Texas Chain Saw Massacre* changed many things—the MPAA ratings code, the national debate on violence, the Texas Film Commission, the horror film itself—but it remained a curiously isolated phenomenon. Hooper continues to fight today against the stereotype of being "just a horror director," and screenwriter Henkel became so frustrated with his "multipicture" Hollywood deal that he moved back to Port Aransas in the early eighties, where he's remained ever since as a part-time university film teacher. Marilyn Burns, the strikingly beautiful actress who became the prototype for the "final girl" in horror films, today sells cellular telephone service in Houston and never realized her great promise, partly because the film was a résumé killer. Gunnar Hansen continued with his writing career but has spent the rest of his life trying to stake out another identity. ("I'm happy I did it, but they'll probably put 'Gunnar Hansen—He Was Leatherface' on my gravestone.")

Yet for two decades now, the status of the film has been constantly on the rise. In 2000, the British Board of Film Classification finally lifted its twenty-five-year ban on the film's distribution in England. (The wording of the official announcement read almost like an apology.) Very few horror films survive the teen generation that first sees them, yet the myths and legends surrounding *Chain Saw* have continuously expanded. Many people believed, and still believe, that the movie is entirely true, in part because of its effective cinéma verité documentary style. In this respect, Tobe Hooper anticipated *The Blair Witch Project* by a quarter century, and he did it without the advantage of cheap video. Far from being an artless, shaky-cam documentary, *Chain Saw* is Hitchcockian in its complex editing: In a film less than ninety minutes long, there are a total of 868 edits, some of them as short as four frames, or one-sixth of a second. Forry Ackerman, the writer and film historian who has watched every horror film since 1922, said even his jaded eyes believed the actors were real people. "It's a watershed work," he told Brad Shellady in the video documentary *Texas Chain Saw Massacre: A Family Portrait*. "It brought a new dimension of reality to horror films."

THE FIRST VOICE YOU HEAR IS THAT OF THE narrator, John Larroquette, who would go on to TV fame in *Night Court* and *The John Larroquette Show*, but in 1974 was an unemployed actor Hooper heard about from a friend of a friend while furiously trying to finish the film in Los Angeles.

Hooper was an obsessive film geek who made his first film at age three and made ends meet in the sixties by shooting public TV shows, industrial films (including Farrah Fawcett's first commercial), and a documentary on Peter, Paul, and Mary. He got the inspiration for *Chain Saw* at Montgomery Ward, during the frenzied Christmas shopping rush, in December 1972. "There were these big Christmas crowds, I was frustrated, and I found myself near a display rack of chain saws. I just kind of zoned in on it. I did a rack-focus to the saws, and I thought, 'I know a way I could get through this crowd really quickly.' I went home, sat down, all the channels just tuned in, the zeitgeist blew through, and the whole damn story came to me in what seemed like about thirty seconds."

Before that epiphany, Hooper and Henkel had been working on an updated version of *Hansel and Gretel*. They augmented that original idea by studying the then-scant literature on real-life cannibals and serial killers, two in particular: Ed Gein, the Plainfield, Wisconsin, handyman who liked to dig up fresh graves, cut the skin off corpses, wear it on various parts of his own body, and dance in the moonlight; and Elmer Wayne Henley, a Houston teenager who had been arrested for recruiting victims for an older homosexual man.

The improbable financier of *Chain Saw* was a man named Bill Parsley, who was technically the vice president of financial affairs for Texas Tech University, but in fact was an Austin-based lobbyist for that school. Parsley had dabbled in the film business before, seeking tax shelters, and he was well known to Warren Skaaren, the nerdy, well-scrubbed Minnesotan who had become the first head of the Texas Film Commission. in 1971. Skaaren, who introduced Parsley to the filmmakers, would make his most lasting contribution to the film just one week before principal photography commenced that summer. He suggested that Hooper and Henkel throw out both of their working titles—*Head Cheese* and *Leatherface*—and call it *The Texas Chain Saw Massacre.*

U NDER A BLAZING WHITE-HOT TEXAS sun, principal photography began on July 15, 1973 with a cast assembled from area drama schools, community theater groups, friends, relatives, and local curiosity seekers. One of the latter was John Henry Faulk, the humorist and national radio talk-show host who had been blacklisted in the fifties by a Communist-baiting advertiser and was forced to return to Austin when his career dead-ended. A favorite "professional Texan" at liberal fund-raisers and a regular on *Hee Haw*, Faulk volunteered to appear in the graveyard scene near the beginning of the film. Teri McMinn, the leading actress that season at St. Edward's University, was starring in *The Rainmaker* each night and working days as Pam, the fearful, astrology-obsessed cutie in short-shorts who would be immortalized when she was impaled on a meat hook. ("That was always the number one 'walker' scene," says Henkel. "If the audience was gonna walk, that's when they walked.") University of Texas drama student William Vail played her strong,

jock-type boyfriend Kirk. Marilyn Burns, resplendent in figure-hugging white jeans and a long blonde mane, played Sally, who was destined to be the only survivor. Ed Neal, in his dirty and torn green T-shirt, clutching an animal pouch, his slick, greasy hair caked with God knows what, was the very essence of the hitchhiker you don't want in your car. (More than one critic called him a Charles Manson figure, "the subversive embodiment of the hippie youth culture.") Jim Siedow, the leering, cockeyed cook, was a Houston theater veteran who had worked with the WPA Theater before World War II, touring with Eve La Gallienne, and portrayed the most complex character in the film, a man on the edge of insanity trying to exercise control over his two clearly insane younger brothers. John Dugan, the eighteen-year-old nephew of Kim Henkel, had come down from Chicago, where he was working at the Goodman Theater, to play Grandpa, the preternaturally ancient patriarch of the cannibal clan. His makeup required eight hours to apply, and Hooper couldn't spare eight hours waiting on an actor to be ready. The result: one twenty-six-hour work day that frayed tempers to the breaking point and almost caused mass resignations. But the scene-stealing role belonged to Paul Partain. As Franklin, the whiny, corpulent, wheelchair-bound brother of Sally, Partain was obnoxiously brilliant. Partain, who had served in the Navy in Vietnam then done a stint at the UT drama school, threw himself into the role with such Method enthusiasm that the rest of the cast ended up despising him. His constant demand for attention,

The *Los Angeles Times* said it was

"despicable ...
ugly and obscene ...
a degrading, senseless
misuse of film and time."

his high-pitched cries of "Sally!," and his anger at everyone else for being ambulatory make him one of the most despicable handicapped people in film history. He's the only one who almost seems to deserve his death.

Hooper shot seven days a week, working anywhere from twelve to sixteen hours a day. It was an especially wicked Texas summer, better than 100 degrees most days, and inside the "cannibal house" it would get up to 115, baking the offal and animal carcasses and rotting meat that had been painstakingly assembled by art director Bob Burns. "We would do a scene," said Neal, "and then all run to the window so that we could throw up." To create a realistic slaughterhouse atmosphere, Burns indulged his lifelong fascination with animal bones by rounding up eight dead cows, two dogs, a cat, two deer, three goats, one chicken, an armadillo, and two real human skeletons. Everyone lived constantly with this grotesque menagerie, and since the whole story takes place in a twenty-four-hour period, everyone wore the same clothing for the entire five weeks. An Austin plastic surgeon, Dr. Walter Barnes, had been brought in to design the human-skin masks and special-effects makeup, and his messy concoctions stuck to the skin and increased the general level of misery. Virtually every cast member suffered some sort of injury, but no one was beaten, cut, and bruised more than Marilyn Burns. By the end of production her screams were real, as she'd been poked, prodded, bound, dragged through rooms, jerked around, chased through cocklebur underbrush, jabbed with a stick, forced to skid on her knees in take after take, pounded on the head with a rubber hammer, coated with sticky stage blood, and endlessly pursued by Hansen with his chain saw and Neal with his constantly flicking switchblade. Neal had his face burned by hot asphalt. Partain suffered a bruised and cut arm after rolling down a hill in one of the early scenes. For Partain's dying scene, Hooper and makeup artist Dottie Pearl stood on either side of the camera lens, spitting red Karo syrup into the air, attracting flesh-devouring mosquitoes. Hansen had no peripheral vision while wearing his mask and had a heart-stopping near-miss when his boots slipped while he was running and the chain saw flew up in the air and crashed to the ground, inches from his body. The heat, the miserable conditions, and the sheer pain of it all undoubtedly added to the atmosphere Hooper was trying to create.

LEGEND HAS IT THAT, ON A CERTAIN EVENING in October 1974, *The Texas Chain Saw Massacre* was sneak-previewed at a theater in San Francisco, where half the audience got sick and others pelted the screen, yelled obscenities, and demanded their money back. Fistfights broke out in the lobby, and the film became famous. The reality is probably less dramatic. The most credible version is that several members of the San Francisco City Council had gone to a special screening of the movie *The Taking of Pelham One Two Three* (1974), and it was a coincidence that *Chain Saw* was being sneaked as a second feature. The politicians were outraged, and therefore the press heard about it.

In the Leatherface mask, Gunnar Hansen had no peripheral vision while running.

Knowing what we now know about the film's distributor, Bryanston Pictures, very few things involving *Chain Saw* were coincidental. At any rate, a myth was born that night—that there was not only a horrific new movie, but a new kind of movie, a film with the unsettling name *The Texas Chain Saw Massacre* that was the most violent film ever made, a docudrama so nauseatingly and relentlessly gory that it tested the very limits of what the First Amendment allows. "The story is true," announced the poster with classic exploitation showmanship. "Now the movie that's just as real."

The movie was an overnight hit. No one will ever know precisely how many people saw it, but it made anywhere from $5 million to $10 million in its opening week—plenty high enough to make it the number-one release of that month, and easily a top-five movie, even in 2003 numbers. The critical reception ranged from disapproval (Johnny Carson's jokes) to backhanded compliments (Rex Reed called it "the *Jaws* of the midnight movie") to insane rage. The *Los Angeles Times* said it was "despicable . . . ugly, and obscene . . . a degrading, senseless misuse of film and time." Noting how angry people became when the film was praised by intellectuals, Bryanston stoked the publicity fires by getting the film accepted in the "Un Certain Regard" section of the Cannes Film Festival, then made a gift of a print to the film collection of the Museum of Modern Art in New York. The gift was hardly noticed at the time, but when MOMA started turning up in Bryanston's advertisements ("Part of the permanent collection of the Museum of Modern Art!"), reporters called the museum, where a spokesman confirmed that, yes, the film had recently been cataloged. Especially offended by this was Stephen Koch, a friend of Andy Warhol's. He called *Chain Saw* "a vile little piece of sick crap" and part of a growing "hard-core pornography of murder" that should best be compared to snuff films.

"We would do a scene . . . and then all run to the window so that we could throw up."

AFTER ALL THIS COMMOTION, IT WAS NATURAL that the actors and crew members—who had waived their salaries in exchange for a percentage of the movie—would say, "When do the first checks come in?" Calls were placed—first to Hooper, then to Henkel, then to anyone who would listen. "Three months, no check," said Neal. "Six months, no check. Nine months, a check for $28.45. We were angry." Soon thereafter they learned that the mob had absconded with most of the money—estimated by *Variety* as $12 million in less than a year—and that they would probably never be paid. For the next eight years, the film would be tied up in a tangled skein of litigation involving the bankrupt Bryanston, the several owners of the picture, and the subdistributors around the country who refused to release the prints because they hadn't been paid either. Yet in those same eight years, the $60,000 hippie horror movie grossed upward of $50 million. After a five-year censorship fight in France, the film opened on the Champs Elysées in 1982 and had grosses higher than *Superman*. For a 1983 rerelease by New Line Cinema, the gross was $6 million, an unheard-of figure for a nine-year-old film that had already been released on video. *Chain Saw* would end up being seen in more than ninety countries, sometimes dubbed, sometimes subtitled, sometimes marketed in an almost unrecognizable way. (In Italy, it was called *Non Aprite Quella Porta*, or "Don't Open That Door.") Its appeal, for better or worse, was universal.

But that was no consolation to the unpaid actors and the investors who lost millions to the mob. By the time they had finished their legal wrangling, it was too late. The sequel had been delayed for twelve years. And by that time, America had moved on. *Chain Saw* was famous, but it was famous in the way that bell-bottom pants were famous. The youth horror audience, which turns over every five years anyway, had already seen *Halloween* and *Friday the 13th* and *A Nightmare on Elm Street* and *Evil Dead*, all of which had higher production values than *Chain Saw* and all of which appealed more cynically to high-schoolers. America had entered the Stephen King era, and even the major studios were turning out horror films.

The famous cannibal family's house on Quick Hill Road in Round Rock, Texas, is gone. Quick Hill Road itself has been bulldozed, along with the mesquite break where Leatherface chased Sally. A sign on the nearest highway reads "La Frontera: 328 Acre Master-Planned Commercial Development." But if you drive a few miles to the southwest, to the little Hill Country lake town of Kingsland, and you go to the historic Antlers Hotel, you might want to eat at the restaurant across the street, which is located in a quaint "Victorian 1890s house" with a beautiful bay window where Bob Burns once built his "bone room" and a beautiful dining room where a cannibal family once dined for twenty-six hours.

FOR FURTHER DISTURBANCE

There are several movies based on the same real-life event—PSYCHO (1960), DERANGED (1974), MANIAC (1980), SILENCE OF THE LAMBS (1991), ED GEIN (2001), and *The Texas Chain Saw Massacre*—but *Psycho* gets most of the publicity. All of these screenplays derive from the case of Edward Gein, a handyman in Plainfield, Wisconsin, who was arrested in 1957 for graverobbing and murder. He confessed to two killings in his quest for "fresh" body parts, and on his property police found skulls on the bedposts, a human heart in a saucepan, and a lady in his barn dressed like a deer. All the members of his family had died, he had an unhealthy obsession with his dead mother, and he was suspected of killing his brother. He showed clear signs of being a transsexual—he always dressed in female body parts, especially breasts, vaginas, nipples, and the faces of women—and would spend the rest of his life in the Central State Hospital for the Criminally Insane, where he was known for the rock jewelry he made. He died in 1984. The closest version to the real story is Chuck Parello's *Ed Gein*, a true crime biopic. Jeff Gillen's and Alan Ormsby's *Deranged*, starring Roberts Blossom as the Ed Gein character, also follows actuality fairly closely. The least faithful, but one of the most entertaining, is

William Lustig's *Maniac*, starring Joe Spinell as the fat, balding New York psycho who scalps women then uses them to dress the family of mannequins he lives with in his claustrophobic apartment.

Chain Saw ushered in the era of the slasher film, and influenced everything from John Carpenter's HALLOWEEN (1978) to Sean Cunningham's FRIDAY THE 13TH (1980) to Wes Craven's A NIGHTMARE ON ELM STREET (1984) and SCREAM (1996) to Eduardo Sanchez and Daniel Myrick's THE BLAIR WITCH PROJECT (1999).

Among the films that influenced Hooper and his scenarist, Kim Henkel, were THE CURSE OF FRANKENSTEIN (1957), which Hooper had imitated in a student film while still in elementary school; George Romero's zombie classic NIGHT OF THE LIVING DEAD (1968); and the ultralow-budget THE LEGEND OF BOGGY CREEK (1972), made by Texarkana, Arkansas, real-estate man Charles Pierce.

Chain Saw created a vogue for cannibalism in horror plots, with notable efforts being the Italian THE GRIM REAPER (1981); Paul Bartel's EATING RAOUL (1982); and Rory Calhoun in the cult classic MOTEL HELL (1980). Interestingly, Laurence Harvey's last movie, WELCOME TO ARROW BEACH (1974), actually came out before *Chain Saw* but closed quickly. After the success of *Chain Saw*, it was rereleased, in 1976, as *Tender Flesh* in an attempt to ride the coattails of the movie it had already beaten to the punch.

Hooper's first feature, EGGSHELLS (1969), was a psychedelic hippie epic, shot in a communal house, starring his friend Henkel as a dope-smoking sexaholic poet who likes to write in the nude and discuss politics in the bathtub. Hooper, Henkel, production manager Ron Bozman, and Jim Siedow, who plays the Cook, had also all worked together on a hippie biker movie called THE WINDSPLITTER (1971), billed as "the Texas *Easy Rider*."

At the time *Chain Saw* was filmed, several of its crew members and actors, including Marilyn Burns and Paul Partain, had just finished working on a big-budget Columbia Pictures film called LOVIN' MOLLY (1974) that was directed in Austin by Sidney Lumet from a Larry McMurtry novel called *Leaving Cheyenne*, with Blythe Danner in the starring role. (Tobe Hooper was kicked off the set for stealing food.) Ironically, *Lovin' Molly* flopped so badly it's hard to find even on video, whereas *Chain Saw* put Austin on the filmmaking map.

The *Chain Saw* sequels didn't measure up to the original, partly because the franchise became tied up in litigation and the Hooper-Henkel team had split up by the time they came out. L. M. "Kit" Carson, best known for Wim Wenders's PARIS, TEXAS (1984), wrote THE TEXAS CHAINSAW MASSACRE 2 (1986) as a dark comedy, prefiguring the self-aware horror of the *Scream* films. His "horror version of *The Breakfast Club*" didn't fly with serious fans of the original. In it, Dennis Hopper plays a psychotic cop pursuing the cannibal family and Tom Savini provides some silly gore, although Caroline Williams is strong in the Marilyn Burns role and Bill Moseley is especially memorable as the brother who digs at the metal plate in his scalp with the end of a hanger. The serene Jim Siedow was the only

actor to appear in both the original and a sequel, reprising his role as the Cook.

LEATHERFACE: THE TEXAS CHAINSAW MASSACRE III (1990) was even worse, as New Line Cinema tried to milk the last life out of the franchise. Jeff Burr directed from a David J. Schow screenplay about a couple pursued by a new cannibal family, but it was shot in California, and the goriest scenes were cut as New Line struggled to get an R rating.

Kim Henkel wrote and directed the best of the three sequels, called RETURN OF THE TEXAS CHAINSAW MASSACRE (1994), starring then-unknowns Matthew McConaughey and Renée Zellweger (although top billing went to Tyler Cone and Robert Jacks). Before it could be released, both McConaughey and Zellweger became stars, and investors in the film are convinced to this day that their powerful agents squelched its distribution to protect their images. It was retitled twice, as *Texas Chainsaw Massacre IV* and *Texas Chainsaw Massacre: The Next Generation*.

After the original *Chain Saw* was released, Hooper directed the competent but utterly forgotten EATEN ALIVE (1976), in which Neville Brand runs a little swamp motel where he feeds the overnight guests to the alligators. Marilyn Burns once again starred, with Mel Ferrer, Stuart Whitman, and Robert Englund (who would later become Freddy Krueger) rounding out the cast. Alternate titles are *Horror Hotel Massacre*, *Legend of the Bayou*, *Death Trap*, *Horror Hotel*, *Murder on the Bayou*, and *Starlight Slaughter*.

Next Hooper filmed Stephen King's SALEM'S LOT (1979) as a TV miniseries. Steven Spielberg then hired him to direct the classic POLTERGEIST (1982), but there were constant rumors that Spielberg was "ghost directing," rumors that to some extent plague Hooper to this day and have kept him from bigger projects. Hooper remade the classic INVADERS FROM MARS (1986), which received a good critical reception but underperformed, and did an excellent sci-fi flick called LIFEFORCE (1985), which got mixed reviews but had poor box office. Hooper struggled after that, taking television work (*The Equalizer*, *Freddy's Nightmares*, *Tales from the Crypt*, movies-of-the-week) and making the occasional low-budget feature, such as THE FUNHOUSE (1981), SPONTANEOUS COMBUSTION (1989), and THE MANGLER (1995). By the nineties he was sufficiently well known to have his name above the title in the anthology film Tobe Hooper's NIGHT TERRORS (1993).

Warren Skaaren, head of the Texas Film Commission when *Chain Saw* was made, would become one of the highest paid rewrite men in Hollywood. After writing and directing a feature documentary called BREAKAWAY (1978), about a modern-day Thoreau living in the Brook Mountains in Alaska, he was given his big break when cocaine-addled producer Don Simpson fired all the writers on TOP GUN (1986) and paid Skaaren to finish it. It made Skaaren's reputation, and he went on to work on BEETLEJUICE (1988), BATMAN (1989), and DAYS OF THUNDER (1990) before dying of cancer in 1990, at age forty-five.

Ron Bozman, the film's production manager, would go on to accept the 1992 Academy Award for Best Picture as the producer of Jonathan Demme's *The Silence of the Lambs*. He has also produced PHILADELPHIA (1993), THE REF (1994), BELOVED (1998), FOR LOVE OF THE GAME (1999), AUTUMN IN NEW YORK (2000), and SISTER MARY EXPLAINS IT ALL (2001).

After flirting with Hollywood, Kim Henkel would return to Texas and write Eagle Pennell's LAST NIGHT AT THE ALAMO (1983), regarded as one of the finest independent films of the eighties. It's a

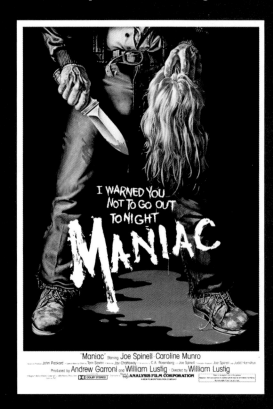

"Maniac" Starring Joe Spinell · Caroline Munro
Associate Producer John Packard · Screenplay by Tom Savini · Story by Joe Chatbawdy · Make up C.A. Rosenberg · Joe Spinell · Executive Producer Joe Spinell and Judd Hamilton
Produced by Andrew Garroni and William Lustig · Directed by William Lustig
DOLBY STEREO · Distributed by ANALYSIS FILM CORPORATION

dark and funny exploration of a little Houston bar called the Alamo, which is destined for demolition the following day to make way for a skyscraper, causing the regulars to sort through their illusions and dreams.

After *Eaten Alive*, Marilyn Burns landed the role of Linda Kasabian in the CBS production of HELTER SKELTER (1976), from Vincent Bugliosi's book on the Manson family, but that turned out to be her last performance of any stature.

Paul Partain, who played the whiny Franklin, appeared in three more films—RACE WITH THE DEVIL (1975), ROLLING THUNDER (1977) and OUT-LAW BLUES (1977)—before leaving the business to become a salesman.

Gunnar Hansen, the Icelandic-American actor who played Leatherface, did one more small part in THE DEMON LOVER (1976), then quit acting, returning to film in 1988 when he starred in the notorious Fred Olen Ray parody HOLLYWOOD CHAINSAW HOOKERS. Since then he's appeared in more than a dozen direct-to-video movies.

Bob Burns, the art director, became well known within the film community for his work on *Chain Saw*, and was hired for another cannibal movie, Wes Craven's THE HILLS HAVE EYES (1977). He also did the production design for THE HOWLING (1981), worked on the underrated chiller TOURIST TRAP (1979) starring Chuck Connors, and even starred in a movie called CONFESSIONS OF A SERIAL KILLER (1985), based on the life of Henry Lee Lucas.

One thing *Chain Saw* definitely introduced to horror iconography was the chain saw itself. Even though it's a clunky and impractical implement of death, it has since been used in Juan Piquer Simon's PIECES (1983), Sam Raimi's EVIL DEAD (1983), EVIL DEAD II (1987), Ronny Yu's BRIDE OF CHUCKY (1998), Brian De Palma's SCARFACE (1983), and, of course, MOTEL HELL (1980), in which Rory Calhoun brandishes a chain saw while wearing a pig's head. Variations on the saw motif include Dennis Donnelly's THE TOOLBOX MURDERS (1978), in which Cameron Mitchell uses every tool in the Black & Decker catalog, and Abel Ferrara's THE DRILLER KILLER (1979), in which Ferrara himself plays the frustrated New York artist who loses it and starts butchering homeless people with a portable power drill. The less said about THE NAIL GUN MASSACRE (1985), the better—but their heart was in the right place.

As this book went to press, New Line Cinema had just commenced production in Austin of a remake, produced by Michael Bay, starring Erica Leerhsen of BOOK OF SHADOWS: BLAIR WITCH 2 fame, Jessica Biel, Eric Balfour, and R. Lee Ermey. Hooper and Henkel were reportedly working together on the script, with cinematography by Daniel Pearl, who lensed the original.

JACKIE

DRU

"DRUNKEN MASTER" STARRING JACKIE CHAN • YUEN SUI-TEN • WANG JANG-LEE • DEAN SHEK • YUEN SHUN-YEE •

IN 1978, THE YEAR JACKIE CHAN BECAME AN INTERNATIONAL STAR, THE ONLY PLACES YOU COULD SEE HIS MOVIES IN THE UNITED STATES WERE CHINATOWNS (IN NEW YORK, CHICAGO, AND THE WEST COAST), TIMES SQUARE (AT A THEATER WHOSE MARQUEE HAD BEEN COVERED WITH THE PERMANENT SIGN "ALWAYS THREE KUNG FU HITS!"), AND AT DRIVE-INS IN THE DEEP SOUTH.

THE MOVIES WERE NEVER REVIEWED, MUCH less advertised in the mainstream media. But I saw the movies in all three places, and what amazed me was that, depending on the audience, the same movie could be a drama, a comedy, or a soldier-of-fortune how-to manual. In Chinatown, for example, audiences rocked with laughter when *Drunken Master* first played. It was obviously a sendup of the martial-arts superhero movies they had grown up with, and Freddy Wong, the Jackie Chan character, was an irreverent spoof of Wong Fei-hung, the Chinese Robin Hood. In Times Square, on the other hand, the audience was three-quarters black, and this was the era of violent black exploitation films. They occasionally laughed—especially when Gold Thunderfoot sets Jackie's pants on fire and sends him running down the road in his underwear—but mostly they took it as a straight action flick, frequently yelling at the screen when a fighter would score an especially devastating blow to the head. At the Gemini Drive-In in Dallas, the most likely remark around the concession stand was, "That little Chinaman is messed up, but he can fight like a sonofabitch." Jackie Chan was probably single-handedly responsible for more young karate students than any other person in the seventies and eighties, especially in areas where there was no sizeable Asian population.

After *Drunken Master* broke all kinds of box-office records around the world, Jackie Chan naturally assumed that he would move to America and become the next international action star. I can remember a publicity tour he made in 1982 when he was being billed as "Wacky Jacky" (he changed the spelling later), the first slapstick comedy kung-fu star, but I was the only person in Dallas who even wanted to interview him. His efforts at both American comedy (*Cannonball Run*) and American drama (*The Big Brawl*) were pretty much greeted with "Huh? What? Who is he?" I don't know of another case in which a bona fide star had so much trouble getting accepted in America, even after his films became the most popular long-running features in Times Square—which is, after all, where the New York Times is located. It would take him eighteen more years of making movies back home in Hong Kong before *Rumble in the Bronx* was picked up by New Line Cinema in 1996 and released with great fanfare in the states. He was the slowest developing overnight star in film history.

Drunken Master, originally released as *Drunken Monkey in the Tiger's Eye*, may not be the first or the best martial-arts comedy, but it's certainly the most influential. The idea of a kung-fu fighting style that only works when you're staggeringly drunk was so amusing to young boys in Hong Kong that they drove their mothers mad careening around the house, weaving, falling down, and executing loopy leg kicks—trying to be like Jackie. It was one of those films that was so politically incorrect it became a guilty pleasure for the young and old alike, making it even stranger that what was essentially a family comedy would be taken seriously at some venues in the states. The only explanation I can come up with is that the movie's villain, Korean kickboxer Wang Jang-lee, is so terrifyingly agile, with kicks and leaps that are higher even than Bruce Lee's, that it's impossible not to feel that Wacky Jacky is in real danger. It's like watching Jerry Lewis fight Mike Tyson; you know that Jerry will probably win because it's his movie, but you know that a single real blow would not only end the film, but probably end his life.

MOVIES LIKE *DRUNKEN MASTER* WOULD be impossible to make in the United States, because a) the talent pool doesn't exist for guys who can fight *and* do acrobatics *and* act *and* do comedy (Jackie even sings and dances), b) safety rules on American sets would make some of the dangerous stunts illegal, and c) even big-budget American films can't afford to spend an entire month on a single fight scene, as Chan often does. Most of the great kung-fu fighters came out of Hong Kong's Peking Opera School, where training in gymnastics, acrobatics, martial arts, weaponry, singing, dancing, mime, comedy, and performance art were drilled into young children nineteen hours a day in an atmosphere that included corporal punishment, the withholding of meals, and other practices that would constitute criminal child abuse in the West. Chan spent ten years at the school, from age seven to seventeen, and was featured at the Peking Opera spectacles as part of a boy group called the Seven Little Fortunes. Although the Peking Opera is what made it possible for him to accomplish all of his amazing physical feats, he describes it now as a dark and Dickensian experience. "I would never put my kids through it," he says, "and would never tell anyone to do the same thing."

It's possible to make anyone look superhuman with Hollywood magic—stunt men, cutaways, computer imaging, multiple cameras, speeded-up film—but the impressive thing about *Drunken Master* and the other kung-fu features made around the same time is that the fight scenes are frequently photographed in medium shots with minimal closeups, meaning that what you see is exactly what the actors were doing. The choreographer on a Hong Kong film holds a position of honor and respect, just one step below director, and a good one is said to have *ling-gan*, a word which means the ability to conceptualize, establish a mood, understand the tempo of a scene, and be willing to improvise. An American choreographer works out moves in a rehearsal studio, but a Hong Kong choreographer works on the set, like a speed-chess master, visualizing as he goes. He works with the prop master, especially in a Jackie Chan film, where any object can suddenly become a weapon, a shield, or a missile. (In *Drunken Master*, Chan fights with, among other things, a cucumber, a rice bowl, and a pair of chopsticks.) Once the fight is set, it will be repeated dozens of times, with slight variations, in classic Peking Opera style, and then it will be shot with the usual amount of camera coverage, meaning every stunt has to be repeated a dozen or so times to get the angles and shots the editor will use to put it together. Next to a chase scene, two men fighting is probably the most cinematic thing a filmmaker can shoot. Two men fighting within a chase scene—a frequent occurrence in Jackie Chan films—is the Super Bowl of directing, choreography and editing. Chan then adds a wild-card element—comedy—to make those magical moments that flicker onto late-night cable channels and are instantly identifiable as scenes that only he would do.

When Ang Lee's *Crouching Tiger, Hidden Dragon* won a number of Oscar nominations in 2001, it was praised for its mysticism and original plot, with many critics saying it wasn't "typical" of kung fu features. I'm not sure what this means, because I've never seen a typical kung-fu feature. One reason people continued to haunt the moviehouses in Times Square and Chinatown is that the plots were always wildly imaginative—so imaginative that the story line in *Mad Monkey Kung Fu*, to recall one example, would take this entire page to summarize. Even when you saw something similar to what you'd seen before—like a training sequence, or a brawl in an open-air bazaar—it was never choreographed in quite the same way. *Crouching Tiger, Hidden Dragon* actually has several themes recognizable from those martial-arts hits of the seventies—namely, the disgraced family, the quest for a totem, the master of the black arts, and the aging fighter who has to make one last effort. It also has a number of computerized special effects, which are breathtakingly beautiful but would have violated the code of the seventies. The directors of that era wanted the audience to know that the fighting was real. But a case can be made that *Drunken Master* actually started a cycle that has its culmination in *Crouching Tiger, Hidden Dragon*, because what Chan did, more than any other single star, was to open up the martial-arts film to pure fantasy. If you watch the much more serious Bruce Lee films of the early seventies, with their armies of warriors and their fierce battles to the death, what you miss is any kind of real personal relationships among the fighters and any supernatural elements. Lee was a more charismatic figure and a more graceful fighter, but Chan has more heart.

Bruce Lee, in fact, almost ended Chan's career before it started. Chan had worked as a stunt man with Lee twice in the early seventies—playing a villainous vanquished fighter in both *Fists of Fury* and *Enter the Dragon*—although the two men never really socialized. ("One day he gave me a great kick," said Chan. "He asked me if I was fine and I say, 'OK.'") But just as Lee's movies were breaking out all over the world, the great fighter died, in 1974, of a mysterious brain hemorrhage, and every panicked Hong Kong film company was suddenly scrambling to find "the next Bruce Lee." Chan was the great hope of a producer named Lo Wei, who signed him to do one of the many Bruce Lee

sequels, *New Fist of Fury*. It was a flop, as was everything else Lo Wei tried to do with Chan. *Shaolin Wooden Men* (1976), *Dragon Fist* (1978), *Killer Meteors* (1978, with Chan in one of his rare villain roles), and even a 3-D film called *Magnificent Bodyguards* (1978) were all pale imitations of Bruce Lee's glory, even after Lo Wei paid to have Chan's eyes surgically widened (a common operation among Hong Kong film stars) and his cracked teeth fixed. Chan also shaved his dorky pencil mustache and bulked up to look more heroic, but he was simply no Bruce Lee. "Nobody can imitate Bruce Lee," Chan recalled. "[Lo Wei] wants me to do the same kick, the same punch. I think even now nobody can do better than Bruce Lee. After he died, nobody as handsome, right? Lo Wei won't listen, wants every girl to fall in love with Jackie. I'm not a handsome boy, not James Dean. I'm just not this kind of person. It's totally wrong, and none of them are a success."

The best film he made in this period was *Snake and Crane Arts of Shaolin* (1978), with an excellent sequence in which he takes on three spear-wielding assailants, but it still underperformed at the box office and Lo Wei finally gave in to Chan's demands to try one film his way. The result, *Half a Loaf of Kung Fu* (1978), was an uneven comedy that Lo Wei promptly pronounced "rubbish" and refused to release. Discouraged, Chan was ready to drop out of the business entirely and move back to Australia, where his parents lived.

Everything changed when fight choreographer Yuen Woo-ping cast Chan in what was to be Yuen's directorial debut, *Snake in the Eagle's Shadow*. It was pretty much Chan's last shot, and both actor and director decided to go against the conventional wisdom and let the audience see the wise-cracking goofball that Chan was in real life. Yuen Woo-ping talked producer Yuen Ng-see into "borrowing" Chan from Lo Wei. (Say that five times fast.) "N.G.," as Yuen Ng-see preferred to be called, had a new company called Seasonal Films that had made a splash with its two *Secret Rivals* films, pitting Chinese kickboxer John Liu against Korean kickboxer Wang Jang-lee. The distributors liked Seasonal's product, but they begged him not to use Chan. "No film he has starred in has ever been a hit," they told him. But N.G. trusted his director, and they started casting what would turn out to be a new genre of kung-fu movie.

In *Snake*, Chan plays a country-bumpkin orphan who's the janitor at a cruel kung-fu school. Most of the comedy involves his relationship with an old hobo who teaches him how to fight using various "animal" styles. (By this time virtually every animal in the jungle had a martial arts style named after it, but this was the first parody of the trend). They searched all over Hong Kong for an old man who could both act and fight, and then one day N.G. said to his director, "What about your father?" Simon Yuen Sui-ten was a sixty-seven-year-old retired Peking Opera star who had brought up twelve children, most of them involved in the kung-fu business, and, as it turned out, he was delighted to be offered a job in his son's directorial debut. He still had amazing agility for an elderly

man, and his occasional flashes of fighting brilliance would delight audiences and lead to dozens more film roles for him. The only conventional character in the film is Wang Jang-lee as the Fu Manchu villain who terrorizes the old hobo with his "eagle claw" henchmen. Chan's snake fist can't defeat Wang's eagle claw, so he has to come up with a new way of fighting with the help of the old man. Chan sees a cat fighting off a cobra, then starts jumping around like a cat, hissing. The old man then teaches him how to mingle his new cat style with his snake fist to defeat Wang Jang-lee in the final battle.

But it wasn't so much the story that made *Snake in the Eagle's Shadow* different. It was Chan's manic screen presence. "I kid around," he said. "Totally opposite to Bruce Lee. When Bruce Lee acts like hero, I act like underdog. Nobody can beat Bruce Lee, everybody can beat me. He's not smiling, I'm always smiling." Many of Chan's best fighting moments are evasive instead of aggressive, as he uses his speed and agility to simply avoid being hit at all. When he does get hit, he lets the pain register on his face. And instead of classic kung-fu weapons, the only things he uses are ordinary objects.

THE FILM WAS A BIG MONEY MAKER for Seasonal Films, and they instantly planned a follow-up with the same cast and crew, this time going all-out with the comedy. It was Chan who suggested that they do a parody of the most revered fighter in Chinese history, Wong

Fei-hung, who had been the subject of ninety-nine classic and beloved films between 1947 and 1968. (The character has been revived several times since then, notably in a series of Jet Li films for the Shaw Brothers studio.) Wong Fei-hung was a real person, a sort of folk superhero who was loved by the people and feared by the emperors. He lived from 1847 to 1924, but his legend dominated Cantonese entertainment for all of the twentieth century. His father was one of the Ten Tigers of Canton but refused to train him. So Wong was raised by his mother, who taught him kung fu so well that at age fourteen he killed a martial-arts master in a challenge match. Eventually he sought out his father's master, an old man by that time, and learned the Hung Kuen (Hung's Fist) method of fighting. He was also known for Chinese medicine (he devoted his life to healing), Confucian philosophy, and Lion Dancing. The ninety-nine Wong movies, beginning with *The True Story of Wong Fei-hung*, were the first Chinese martial-arts films to use real kung fu, as opposed to swordplay and magic, and they take place at different stages of Wong's life, from childhood to old age, and always conclude with him defeating the forces of evil on behalf of the weak and downtrodden. (The village elder in the series was played by a fighter named Lee Hoi-chuen. His son, Lee Siu-loong, would become Bruce Lee.)

Chan's idea was simple: What if the great Wong went through a rebellious period as a teenager? What if he were lazy, naughty, headstrong, and kind of a pain in the ass before he became this Chinese hero? And what if the only man who could teach him anything was an old drunk?

"I like it," said N.G. "I shouldn't like it, but I like it."

Drunken Master was born. Although it follows the traditional kung-fu arc, telling the story of a novice's education and eventual victory, the interesting thing about Freddy Wong, Chan's character, is that he never truly reforms himself. It's Wang Jang-lee, as the hired killer Thunderfoot, who has a professional code of honor. Freddy cheats on his training, runs away, steals food from a restaurant, tricks girls into kissing him, and is so arrogant about his fighting skills that he gets roundly thrashed. At the beginning of *Drunken Master*, Chan is punished by his father by being forced to take the "horse stance" position for hours on end. The horse stance is the very foundation of the martial-arts system practiced by the real Wong Fei-hung, but Chan, of course, cheats by hiding a small chair under his butt. The only salvation for Freddy's aimless life is "Drunken Kung Fu," forced on him by his father's master (once again played by Simon Yuen Sui-ten), in which he gulps massive quantities of wine while

THERE'S SOMETHING ABOUT A MARTIAL ARTIST IN DRAG THAT ALWAYS SLAYS THE AUDIENCE.

learning the "Eight Drunken Fairies" fighting styles. He refuses to learn the eighth one—pretending to be a drunk, slutty girl—because he thinks it's "only for women." Of course, in the eighteen-minute climactic fight against Thunderfoot, he runs through all seven without winning and then has to improvise to become "the Drunken Goddess" for a wildly comic and athletic ending that would be used with variations in other Chan movies, because there's something about a martial artist in drag that always slays the audience.

There actually is a drunken kung-fu fighting style, by the way, but it's based on appearing to be drunk in order to get an advantage over your opponent. It seems to be a convention of kung-fu movies that the winning style will always be based on something involving subterfuge and cleverness, as opposed to brute strength. But in this case, the movie makes it clear that the Drunken Master really can't fight unless he's sloshed. At one point he gets watered-down wine because of Freddy's prank, and he has the shakes so bad that he almost gets killed by the King of Sticks. Many of the fight sequences include classic Three Stooges–type pratfalls, and Chan had already begun studying the films of Harold Lloyd, Buster Keaton, and Charlie Chaplin as he sought out new forms of physical comedy.

THE RESULT WAS AN INTERNATIONAL HIT THAT earned $8 million, out-grossing all of Bruce Lee's films, and was the second highest grosser for the year in Hong Kong. Later it was released in Japan, Singapore, and Malaysia, where it continued to break records. That final fight with Wang Janglee is still considered, after all these years, Chan's best sequence ever. "So successful was he," crowed the South China Post, "that Chan can be said to have revitalized the entire Asian film business. Many producers and their stars tried to imitate Jackie's new genre of comedy kung fu, but all came to realize that Jackie Chan—like Bruce Lee before him—was one of a kind, inimitable."

Suddenly all those Jackie Chan films that had flopped at the box office were rereleased, with new posters, and even Chan's weak films from the early seventies were shown all over Asia. His very first starring role, *Cub Tiger of Canton* (1973), had been deemed unreleasable, but now a Chinese distributor bought the existing Chan footage, shot extra scenes with a Chan look-alike, edited it together, and released it as *Snake Fist Fighter*. (It appears in video stores as *Master with Cracked Fingers*.) More important, with two hits under his belt, Chan was able to return to a now more supportive Lo Wei, who let him direct his first film, *The Fearless Hyena*, and raised his fee from $3,000 to $50,000 per picture. Chan instantly took on the lifestyle of a movie star, buying gold neck chains, expensive clothes, fancy cars, and seven Rolex watches, one for each day of the week. He traveled around Hong Kong with a huge retinue of stunt men, acquaintances, and hangers-on, and once walked into the elegant Peninsula Hotel clad only in shorts, just to prove he could. He also launched a lucrative singing career with a series of music videos aired on Asian TV.

He was a master of publicity, as he would prove to America in 1996 when he triumphed on Leno, Letterman, Conan (singing an Elvis Presley song karaoke-style), and Rosie (where he let Rosie crack a chair over his head). He quickly got the reputation of being the most daring stunt man in the world, and made sure the press had a precise chronicle of all his injuries. He had many head injuries, including a brain hemorrhage while making *Armour of God* that left him in a Yugoslavian hospital for three weeks. On *Drunken Master*, his brow ridge had been injured and he nearly lost an eye. (Wang Jang-lee's feet *were* lethal.) He's had his nose broken three times, his cheekbone dislocated, teeth kicked out, throat injuries, suffocation injuries, neck injuries, a dislocated shoulder, broken hand and finger bones, a sword slash on his arm, a dislocated sternum, near paralysis in *Police Story* (after which many stunt men refused to work for him anymore, deeming his methods too dangerous), a dislocated pelvis, crushed legs (between two cars), knee injuries, a burned arm while being dragged over hot coals, fractured ribs, fractured cheekbones, fractured shoulder blades, and a broken ankle.

GOLDEN HARVEST, THE LEADING HONG Kong distribution company, signed Chan for a big American production, to be directed by a Bruce Lee director, Robert Clouse. But when *The Big Brawl* appeared, in 1980, audiences stayed away in droves. The title and advertising campaign gave no hint of the comedy stunts, which apparently confused audiences. Actually, it was neither fish nor fowl. Golden Harvest had returned to the "next Bruce Lee" style of the earlier kung fu, with none of the elaborate set pieces that show off Chan's physical comedy. A second effort, called *The Protector*, directed by action veteran James Glickenhaus, was equally mundane, and Chan went back to Hong Kong, where his celebrity allowed him to write his own ticket. He directed, choreographed, and starred—not always at the same time—in a series of movies that featured increasingly daring stunts and exotic locations. *Project A* was a sword-fighting pirate film in the South Seas. In *Project A, Part Two*, he did an homage to Buster Keaton, recreating the famous gag from *Steamboat Bill Jr.* in which the wall falls over but leaves Keaton unharmed. Chan actually went Keaton one better, standing atop a fifty-foot billboard wall that is leaning to the right. As it falls, he runs down the other side, in the opposite direction to the fall, arriving safely on the ground as it collapses into the dust. Chan made a serious film, *Crime Story*, that was nominated for the Golden Horse, the Chinese Oscar. He reteamed with Ng See Yuen for *Drunken Master II* in 1994, but in yet another effort to crack the mainstream American market, it had disappointing box office.

Through all these years, he was more famous among filmmakers than the public. Certain Chan sequences, like his fight with Benny the Jet Urquidez in *Wheels on Meals*, the hospital fight in *First Mission*, and his battle against an army of monks in *Armour of God*, were "borrowed" for movies starring Sylvester Stallone and Jean-Claude

Van Damme. Quentin Tarantino was a fan. Michael Douglas tried to get him to play the villain in *Black Rain*, but even though he was flattered, he said his fans wouldn't accept him as a bad guy. His career was kept alive in America mostly by video fanatics influenced by Ric Meyers's 1985 book, *From Bruce Lee to Ninjas: Martial Arts Movies*, and Meyers's Chan-adoring fanzine. In 1988, *The Incredibly Strange Film Show* on England's Channel 4 did an episode on Chan, visiting him on the set of *Mr. Canton and Lady Rose* and showing the footage of his near-fatal injury on *Armour of God*. After that, the bootleg video business went crazy for Chan, accounting for the baffling array of titles, retitles and old supporting roles repackaged with Chan's name above the title. There were Jackie Chan film festivals at art houses in major cities, and a slew of new magazines with titles like *Oriental Cinema*, *Asian Trash Cinema*, and *Hong Kong Film Connection*. It all culminated with *Rumble in the Bronx*, which was panned in China for being plotless but got New Line's attention. *Rumble* earned $9.9 million on its opening weekend in America and $30 million in its first run. At the age of forty-two, Chan was finally accepted in the west.

In a repeat of *Drunken Master* mania, American distributors scoured Hong Kong for all the Jackie Chan films made in the eighties (even though all of them had already played in America, either in Chinatowns or at Jackie Chan festivals). Miramax rereleased *Supercop*, for example, but for some reason dubbed the lame disco hit "Kung Fu Fighting" on to the soundtrack. It earned only half of the *Rumble* take. New Line picked up another Asian hit, *First Strike*, and cut twenty minutes out to get a PG-13. At its premiere in January 1997, Chan put his hand and footprints in cement at Mann's Chinese Theatre. Distributors snapped up *Thunderbolt*, *Crime Story*, *Drunken Master II*, and *Mr. Nice Guy*, all of which had limited releases. But it would be an all-American production, *Rush Hour*, that would put Chan on the A list.

As the millennium dawned, Jackie Chan was still a hot commodity, known mostly for *Rumble* and his *Rush Hour* films, but, pushing fifty, he had reluctantly agreed to use two hand-picked stunt men for some of the more dangerous work. (Otherwise the studios couldn't get completion-bond insurance.) He wears a back brace now but still appears spry and energetic. He has five choreography assistants and still does painstakingly precise fight sequences. But he's never topped the finale of *Drunken Master*, and perhaps he never will. According to Bey Logan, author of the definitive *Hong Kong Action Cinema*, "*Drunken Master* remains the finest example of the kung-fu comedy genre." Chan himself knows that fame comes and goes and that nothing is permanent. "But if the books of film history have all these names," he says. "Charlie Chaplin, John Wayne, Steven Spielberg, and just a small footnote, Jackie Chan, then that's enough. I'm happy."

FOR FURTHER DISTURBANCE

Chen Gang-shen, better known as Jackie Chan, made his film debut in a family drama called BIG AND LITTLE WONG TIN BAR (1962) at the age of eight. As a stunt fighter, he's all but invisible in two Bruce Lee films—FISTS OF FURY (1972) and ENTER THE DRAGON (1973). But he had his first starring role in a formulaic kung-fu movie called CUB TIGER OF CANTON (1973), later rereleased as *Master with Cracked Fingers*, notable as the first time Chan worked with the legendary Simon Yuen. His first successful major role was in John Woo's HAND OF DEATH (1976), and his breakthrough-to-stardom role was SNAKE IN THE EAGLE'S SHADOW (1978), a less developed version of *Drunken Master*. Almost all of his early films were disappointments, with the arguable exceptions of SPIRITUAL KUNG FU (1978) and SNAKE & CRANE ARTS OF SHAOLIN (1978), which failed at the box office but garnered some critical acclaim. Less successful were EAGLE SHADOW FIST (1973), SHAOLIN WOODEN MEN (1976), NEW FIST OF FURY (1976), the 3-D flop MAGNIFICENT BODYGUARDS (1978), HALF A LOAF OF KUNG FU (1978), and DRAGON FIST (1978). One of his few villain roles also dates from this period, opposite Jimmy Wang Yu in KILLER METEORS (1978).

After *Drunken Master*, Jackie Chan expanded his popularity with the box-office hit THE FEARLESS HYENA (1979), which was also his directorial debut, followed by FEARLESS HYENA II (1980), THE YOUNG MASTER (1980), which features a climactic twenty-minute fight sequence, then a snoozer called FANTASY MISSION FORCE (1981), and DRAGON LORD (1982), in which he started doing the death-defying stunts he would become famous for.

In 1980, Chan tried to make it in the United States for the first time, but failed to break through in Robert Clouse's THE BIG BRAWL (1980) or James Glickenhaus's THE PROTECTOR (1985). His comic cameos in the star-studded THE CANNONBALL RUN (1981) and THE CANNONBALL RUN II (1984) seem out of place, as he was still unknown to Americans at the time.

Chastened, he returned to Hong Kong to make PROJECT A (1983), a South Seas pirate film with a lot of swordplay, followed by a Chinese-language remake of *The Protector* called POLICE STORY (1985). In PROJECT A, PART TWO (1987), he did his most memorable homage to Buster Keaton, improving on the famous gag from STEAMBOAT BILL JR. (1928) in which a wall falls over but Keaton (and Chan) is untouched. Throughout this period, he was injury-prone. ARMOUR OF GOD (1986) is one of Chan's most notorious films, mainly for the atrocious injuries he suffered doing the stunts for it.

Chan's American breakthrough, which he'd craved for fifteen years, finally happened in 1996, with RUMBLE IN THE BRONX, which broke records in Asia and got the attention of New Line Cinema. SUPERCOP (1992) was the biggest Chan film in Asia until that point, but had had only a limited release in America. It did establish the market, however, for *Rumble in the Bronx*, and in the wake of that film's success, distributors snapped up American rights to other Chan films, such as the race-car adventure THUNDERBOLT (1995), the James Bond–style adventure epic FIRST STRIKE (1996), CRIME STORY (1993), MR. NICE GUY (1997), and DRUNKEN MASTER II, which was made in 1994 but didn't make it to the states until 1997, where it was a disappointment.

Now an international star, Chan alternates between American and Chinese movies. In Hong Kong, he still makes pure action films, like ACCIDENTAL SPY and GORGEOUS, which consistently outperform his American roles in Asian markets.

Yuen Woo-ping, the director of *Drunken Master*, went on to make DANCE OF THE DRUNK MANTIS (1979) starring his brother Sunny Yuen, a Wong Fei-hung story called MAGNIFICENT BUTCHER (1979), and DREADNAUGHT (1981). Most of his career was spent as a producer and international stunt choreographer, directing fight sequences on BUDDHIST FIST (1980), ONCE UPON A TIME IN CHINA (1991) and THE MATRIX (1999), among others. But one of his finest directorial efforts was IRON MONKEY (1993), starring Donnie Yen as Wong's father.

Yuen Ng-see, the producer of *Drunken Master*, had several hits before hooking up with Chan, including BLOODY FISTS (1972), SECRET RIVALS (1976), BRUCE LEE: THE MAN, THE MYTH (1978), and THE INVINCIBLE ARMOUR (1977). Ng also produced Tsui Hark's first major feature, BUTTERFLY

Bruce Lee (*left*) in *Enter the Dragon*.

MURDERS (1979), and the second fake Bruce Lee film, GAME OF DEATH 2 (1981). He was the first Hong Kong producer to cross over to the English language, introducing Jean-Claude Van Damme in NO RETREAT, NO SURRENDER (1985) and Cynthia Rothrock in a sequel, RAGING THUNDER (1989). He made the two official sequels to *Drunken Master*, *Drunken Master II* and *Dance of the Drunk Mantis*. And he helped launch the early nineties kung-fu boom with *Once Upon a Time in China* and DRAGON INN (1992).

The first modern kung-fu film is generally considered to be CHINESE BOXER (1969), but the Wong Fei Hung series had begun in 1928 and comprised ninety-nine films ending in 1970. The one to watch is THE TRUE STORY OF WONG FEI HUNG (1949), which started the modern era of the legend and ultimately led to kung-fu films. Jackie Chan's only connection to the original series is that he sings its familiar theme song on the soundtrack of *Once Upon a Time in China*, which is also a serious treatment of the Wong Fei-hung story. In *Drunken Master II*, the biggest hit of 1994 in Southeast Asia, a major role is played by one of the original actors from the prewar series, Lau Kar Leung.

The lifestyle of the Peking Opera trainees can be seen in PAINTED FACES (1989), to get an idea of Chan's childhood.

No Chan collection is complete without a few lesser films that nevertheless had amazing fight sequences, including WHEELS ON MEALS (1984), FIRST MISSION (1985), and CITY HUNTER (1992).

The biggest international hits of Chan's life came very late in his career, with the *Rush Hour* series, costarring Chris Tucker. RUSH HOUR (1998 earned $141 million in the United States alone with RUSH HOUR 2 (2001) making $225 million and counting, and RUSH HOUR 3 scheduled for 2004. At the same time he started a second series, a comedy kung-fu western called SHANGHAI NOON (2000), costarring Owen Wilson, which also spawned a sequel, SHANGHAI KNIGHTS (2002). He also starred with Jennifer Love Hewitt in THE TUXEDO (2002) and had just completed HIGH BINDERS in Ireland as this book went to press.

"LET'S GO TO WORK!"

RESERV

STEVE BUSCEMI
AS

MICHAEL MADSEN
AS

TIM ROTH
AS

MR. PINK

MR. BLONDE

MR. ORANGE

"RESERVOIR DOGS" STARRING HARVEY KEITEL · TIM ROTH · MICHAEL MADSEN · CHRIS PENN · ST
CINEMATOGRAPHY BY ANDRZEJ SEKULA FILM EDITING BY SALLY MENKE CASTING BY RONNIE YESKEL PRODUCTION DESIGN BY DAVID WA
PRODUCER LAWRENCE BENDER EXECUTIVE PRODUCERS RICHARD N. GLADSTEIN · MONTE HELLMAN · RONNA B. WALI

IR DOGS

A FILM BY QUENTIN TARANTINO

HARVEY KEITEL
AS

EDWARD BUNKER
AS

QUENTIN TARANTINO
AS

MR. WHITE

MR. BLUE

MR. BROWN

SCEMI · LAWRENCE TIERNEY · RANDY BROOKS · KIRK BALTZ · EDWARD BUNKER · QUENTIN TARANTINO
ECORATION BY SANDY REYNOLDS-WASCO   COSTUME DESIGN BY BETSY HEIMANN   PRODUCTION MANAGER PAUL HELLERMAN
ODUCER HARVEY KEITEL   WRITTEN BY ROGER AVARY · QUENTIN TARANTINO   DIRECTED BY QUENTIN TARANTINO

THERE WAS A TIME IN THE NOT SO DISTANT PAST WHEN THE SUNDANCE FILM FESTIVAL IN UTAH WAS PRIMARILY . . . A FILM FESTIVAL. IT HAD A VAGUELY ACADEMIC TONE, AND AN ANTICOMMERCIAL ONE.

I T WAS WHERE PEOPLE WENT TO BE "ALTERNATIVE" in the way that "alternative rock" means the college radio station patronized by a small coterie of counterculture nerds. The only films that were cool at Sundance were the ones that Hollywood didn't want, and they tended to be liberal, pacifist, and neohippie in the same way that Robert Redford, the founder of the Sundance Institute, represented himself—as the anti-Hollywood Hollywood guy. The ideal Sundance film would be a socialist fable about oppressed miners who triumphed over evil, greedy strike-breakers, preferably with the help of lesbian feminist lawyers. If PBS owned a film studio, it would not be unlike what Sundance was set up to be. It was a place for wearing peasant dresses and sitting cross-legged on the floor while earnestly discussing Truffaut and the rainforest canopy. It was the kind of place where violence was treated tastefully and with restraint, where women and minorities were empowered, and where, above all, there was some common social good to be derived from filmmaking.

And then Quentin Tarantino happened. Tarantino at Sundance was like the local Ku Klux Klan chieftain showing up at a Save the Whales flower show. *Reservoir Dogs* didn't win the top prize at Sundance in January 1992, but it was the elephant at the dinner table that no one could ignore. In fact, the film was premiered at the Holiday Village Cinema, one of the worst venues in town, with the wrong aperture plate on the projector, so that the widescreen frame bled onto the curtain and made it impossible to see the actors at times. Tarantino was so upset that he raged up and down the aisles, screaming that this should not be happening. "Q," as his friends call him, had been part of the Sundance Directors Workshop the year before, so there was no question of not showing his film, but the film was decidedly un-Sundancelike, such a riot of nihilist black comedy, unrelenting violence and profanity, and overwhelming *maleness* that many in the audience couldn't get through it. It was so politically incorrect that it didn't have a single line of female dialogue and used the word nigger fifteen times, always in an offhandedly derogatory way. The dramatic midpoint occurs when a deranged armed robber and killer dances to "Stuck in the Middle with You" while cutting off a tortured policeman's ear—for the sheer fun of it. Nobody recalls who did win the Sundance grand prize that year—for the record, it was Alexandre Rockwell's *In the Soup*—but Tarantino was the sensation of Park City. The five screenings of the film generated such a buzz that scalpers were getting $100 a seat, and the Sundance jury was understandably perplexed about what to do with it. Tarantino got all dressed up for the Sundance award ceremonies, fully expecting to be acclaimed the new king of the indies, and was so crestfallen when he didn't win that he said he would never go to another awards ceremony: "I won't let myself be hurt like that again."

And there in a nutshell you have the dichotomy of Quentin Tarantino: the fierce slash-and-burn rage of an outsider and the hurt feelings of a little boy when the insiders don't accept him. Despite his jury snub, the wheels were already in motion for Tarantino to be acclaimed as a twenty-nine-year-old boy genius—the only parallel in film history is perhaps Orson Welles—but unlike the *enfant terribles* of previous generations, Tarantino was hard to figure out at first. With his crooked grin, thinning hair and lantern jaw, he didn't quite look the part. He was a geeky guy who grew up on comic books and exploitation films, and yet his movies were grown-up fables about manhood, guns, blood, the criminal life, and ultimately the utter lack of trust in

a world turned selfish and crazy. His debut film was so viscerally unsettling that even its silences were full of pregnant menace, and yet he also wrote and directed comic set-pieces that didn't seem to have any function except to make us appreciate how hip and witty he could be. He was a complete and utter show-off—and yet his films were ensemble pieces that seemed, at some deep, subterranean level, to value truth for its own sake. At times his movies seemed like they were patched together from all the movies of the past, like a self-referential film-school project, and yet their atmosphere was overwhelmingly *now*—and besides, Tarantino hated film schools. In many ways he was a creation of the media, and yet he was also a genuine auteur. Would he eventually crumble under the pressure like Orson Welles did, or would he become, like Hitchcock, one of the few "bankable" marquee directors who could control his own destiny?

Ten years later, we still don't know. People love him and people hate him. People think he's a pompous one-note wonder, and people think he's building a universe of overlapping stories that will be unlike any director's oeuvre in film history. What we do know at this point is that *Reservoir Dogs* altered so-called independent filmmaking for all time. The Idiot Savant Film Geek—Tarantino dropped out of school in the ninth grade and learned his craft during his five years of work as a video store clerk—would become the model for the next generation of wannabe directors. *Tarantino-esque* became an adjective meaning edgy, politically incorrect, violent, and male. When he scored again two years later with his follow-up film, *Pulp Fiction*, he was acclaimed at both the Cannes Film Festival and the Academy Awards (he was already too big for Sundance), and he was crowned the first American mass-appeal art-film director. He was simultaneously the darling of *Fangoria* magazine and *The Charlie Rose Show*. With the cost of film production declining, thanks to inventions like the digital video camera, thousands of film buffs fancied themselves the next Tarantino, and the market was glutted with instant boy geniuses, and even a few instant girl geniuses, many of them eagerly sought after by Hollywood studios that started trolling Sundance like a stock pond full of exotic fish that could be speared, marketed, and turned into blockbuster franchises. Tarantino, the ultimate indie filmmaker, is the same guy who probably killed the indie film—and Sundance would never be the same.

But Tarantino was hardly an overnight success. A frustrated actor, he had been trying to break into the film business for thirteen years. *Reservoir Dogs* was, in fact, his fifth script, most of the previous ones never making it past low-level studio "readers," who pronounced him too vile, too vulgar and too violent. (After the success of *Reservoir Dogs*, two of those scripts would be resuscitated as big-budget blockbusters in 1994—*True Romance*, directed by Tony Scott, and *Natural Born Killers*, rewritten by Oliver Stone so as to be almost unrecognizable, yet released to general critical acclaim.) But when Tarantino finally did get his chance, he made the most of it.

WHAT IS IT ABOUT *RESERVOIR DOGS* that inspires such adulation and such condemnation? *Reservoir Dogs* is, on the surface, a caper film, but it's also what I call an assemble-the-squad flick. In the classic assemble-the-squad formula—something like *Missing in Action* or *Ocean's Eleven*—a bunch of old criminal friends (or military friends, or ex-cops) are tracked down one by one and asked "Are you in?" on the biggest and final job of their careers. Then follows the planning, the rehearsal, the inevitable falling out and disagreements, the launching of the caper, the unexpected false moves and tragedies, and the eventual success, or ironic failure, of the scheme. What Tarantino has done in *Reservoir Dogs* is turn the assemble-the-squad formula upside down. First of all, the six men in the gang are the opposite of old buddies. They don't know one another at all and are only identified by color codes: Mr. White, Mr. Blonde, Mr. Pink, Mr. Blue, Mr. Brown, and Mr. Orange. The caper—in this case a jewelry heist—is not only not the climax of the film, but is never even seen on camera. (The actual crime occurs between the first and second scenes, and all we know is that something went horribly wrong and people were killed.) The caper is orchestrated by a hardened gangster named Joe Cabot, who works through his son, Nice Guy Eddie, so the six robbers are never masters of their own fate. And the whole movie takes place in a warehouse where the gunmen have agreed to meet after the holdup, whereas the traditional assemble-the-squad film unfolds before the crime. Once they get there the drama is not about the heist itself but who can be trusted, who will live and who will die, and, most important, who ratted out the gang. In a world where no one can trust anyone else, we gradually learn their real identities through flashbacks (although Tarantino hates the word flashbacks and prefers to call them "novelistic chapters"). Only in the final scene do they—and we—know the full truth, and by then all but one of them are dead. Tarantino has not only deconstructed the caper film, he's made the first disassemble-the-squad flick.

Reservoir Dogs is, then, an antimovie, a structural tour-de-force that upsets every single expectation we might have about any movie like this we've seen in the past. It's so cinematic that, as criminals, the characters' actions don't even make sense. They all wear identical black suits and tiny straight ties. There are too many of them. (Eddie Bunker, a San Quentin ex-con who plays the small role of Mr. Blue, says that among real armed robbers, such a heist would never use such a large gang—"because somebody is gonna talk to his wife"—and wearing uniforms would be considered insane.) Once the gangsters find out that the cops were tipped off, it's unlikely that they would assemble afterward at their usual meeting place. And the fact that one of the men turns out to be an undercover cop takes dramatic license to new levels of absurdity. Would a police force really allow its undercover guy to go through with an actual armed robbery? (There's some indication in the script that the inept backup cops simply arrive late, but it's still hard to believe they wouldn't have shut down the operation

outside the jewelry store, not inside, where innocent people can be killed.) And once the cops know two of their men have been captured, why wouldn't they move in with the SWAT team and rescue them from the warehouse?

The answer, of course, is that we're not in the real world. We're in Tarantinoland, a fantasy universe fashioned not from real life but from movie life. The reason we accept it at all is that it outwardly resembles things we've seen before, but it works like a horror film: Its first goal is to surprise and shock. Screenwriters speak of "turning a scene"—the principle that no scene should ever develop the way the audience expects it to develop—but with Tarantino he turns each scene, then twists it, spins it, turns it inside out, temporarily restores it, interrupts it with pop-culture dialogue (these are gangsters who have watched a lot of sitcoms and have listened to a lot of bubblegum music), and then shoots it off into space so that we end up watching a new movie entirely. Part of the fascination of *Reservoir Dogs* is that you never know exactly what genre you're watching, or where it could possibly be going, and yet you know that a train wreck is in progress, so you excuse every betrayal of traditional storytelling. It's also a very actorly movie: Everything is about behavior, so that the slightest physical movement carries with it the promise of a new complication and a new terror. The critics who have dissed it—for violence, for cynicism, for self-conscious artiness—are looking for moral and philosophical content in a film that has none. It's a horror film, but instead of one Jason Voorhees, we have eight of them. And the most sociopathic of them all—Mr. Pink, the character Tarantino modeled after himself—is the only one who gets to survive. It's a perverse masterpiece.

RESERVOIR DOGS HAPPENED BECAUSE TARANTINO was desperate. He wrote the script in three weeks in October 1990 as a last-ditch effort to make a movie—any movie—and get rid of the feelings of frustration and helplessness that had built up over the previous decade as he tried to become first an actor, then, when no one would hire him, a filmmaker so he could cast himself in his own movies. In the mid-eighties, he'd written an excellent script called *True Romance* and spent three years trying to get it financed through limited partnerships. (He'd gotten the idea from Sam Raimi, who financed *Evil Dead* that way, and the Coen brothers, who did the same with their first film, *Blood Simple.*) At the end of that time he'd raised nothing, and all he had to show for his acting career was a walk-on part as an Elvis impersonator on the sitcom *The Golden Girls.* He'd been to a hundred auditions and had never gotten any other jobs. He'd sent his script to everyone in town and couldn't get past the secretary. He wrote a second script, *Natural Born Killers*, which had a lower budget—only $500,000—and spent eighteen fruitless months trying to set it up, again with no results. Finally he decided he was going to write a film so cheap that it could be filmed in black and white on 16-millimeter film on a single location. He'd cast friends in all the lead roles, and he'd find five or ten thousand dollars to shoot it himself.

In 1989, one year earlier, Tarantino had quit the job he'd held for five years—as a clerk at Video Archives, a video-rental shop in Manhattan Beach, California—to get closer to Hollywood, where presumably he could scrounge up enough writing jobs to keep his head above water. First, he went to work at Imperial Entertainment, a Hollywood distributor that paid him to peddle its product to video stores. After a few months there, he moved to CineTel, a production company, where one of his first assignments was working on a Dolph Lundgren workout video. (Tarantino was assigned to clean the dog poop off the parking lot so Lundgren wouldn't get his trainers dirty.) Meanwhile, he continued to circulate *True Romance* and *Natural Born Killers* through the system, where they created just enough interest for him to get an occasional "script doctor" job, since he had a flair for pungent dialogue. Still, he'd never had any real money in his life, had frequently been in debt, and at one point had served ten days in the Los Angeles County Jail for nonpayment of $7,000 in parking fines. He was tired of being the goofy film geek no one takes seriously. He was going to make *Reservoir Dogs* himself and show everybody how it's done.

Then fate intervened, in the form of Lawrence Bender. Bender was a dancer turned actor turned producer, and when Tarantino ran into him at CineTel, he ended up being one of the first people who read *Reservoir Dogs.* Bender loved it—and told Tarantino not to shoot it on the cheap, but to let him produce it. "No, no, no, no, no," his new friend told him. He wasn't about to start down that frustrating begging-for-money road again. Bender asked for twelve months to show him he could raise the money and get it made, but Tarantino was skeptical. He told him to raise the money in two months or else he was going to shoot it himself—and then he dismissed Bender from his mind. In fact, he felt guilty about giving Bender the right to produce *Reservoir Dogs* at all, since his good friend Rand Vossler had been working for three years trying to set up *True Romance* and *Natural Born Killers*. But when he was honest with himself, he also knew that he was no longer interested in making those stories. They were like old girlfriends, he said; he thought of them fondly and wished them well, but he would never go back to them. To make the slate totally clean, he gave *Natural Born Killers* to Vossler, so he wouldn't be left out in the cold, and he sold the *True Romance* script outright, something he had vowed he would never do. He received the Writers Guild minimum for the sale—$30,000—and intended to use every cent of it filming *Reservoir Dogs*.

But he would never need to do that, because, in less than two months, Bender had created a full-bore Hollywood buzz around *Reservoir Dogs* and had the money in place. Like Tarantino, Bender was a lifelong acting student, and at the time he was taking classes from a teacher named Peter Flood. Flood's ex-wife was an acting teacher named Lily Parker, a member of the Actor's Studio. And through the Actor's Studio, she just happened to know the one man that Tarantino regarded as "my favorite actor in the world"—Harvey Keitel.

Bender told Flood he wanted to get the *Reservoir Dogs* script to Keitel. Flood called Parker. Parker called Keitel. The script was sent to the man himself. And a few days later, Keitel called from New York, leaving a message on Bender's answering machine. He had read it. He loved it. He was interested in helping set it up.

FROM THAT MOMENT, EVENTS MOVED QUICKLY. With Keitel attached, the script got into the hands of a director named Monte Hellman, who had made the horror sequel *Silent Night, Deadly Night 3: Better Watch Out!* and was looking for something to do. Hellman told Bender he wanted to direct *Reservoir Dogs*. Bender said that was probably impossible—Tarantino would never give up control—but encouraged the men to meet anyway. They got together at a diner, and Tarantino liked him so much that he brought him in as a producing partner. And that turned out to be the final key decision. Hellman took the picture to his friend Richard Gladstein, who had produced *Silent Night, Deadly Night 3* but was now vice president of production at LIVE Entertainment. LIVE specialized in small "niche" movies that were presold to video, cable, and foreign markets. Gladstein flipped over the script and told Hellman, "I want to meet this guy. And unless he's a total jerk, I want to make this movie." Fortunately for the talkative, outgoing Tarantino, he didn't come off as a jerk at the meeting, and Gladstein offered a budget of $1.3 million. It would eventually grow to $1.6 million. In a little more than three months, Tarantino had gone from being broke and feeling helpless to being a real director with a green-light project.

As the film moved into preproduction, Keitel was intimately involved at every stage. First they held auditions on the 20th Century Fox lot, but Keitel felt it was important to consider New York actors as well, so he came up with the money to fly Tarantino to New York and set him up at the Mayflower Hotel. It was there that Tarantino found Steve Buscemi, the actor who would play Mr. Pink. (Tarantino wanted to play the role himself, but reluctantly agreed it would be impossible to direct his first film at the same time he was playing one of the principals. Instead he cast himself in the small role of Mr. Brown. Ironically, Buscemi would also star in the film that defeated *Reservoir Dogs* at Sundance, *In the Soup*.) The cast came together fairly quickly, partly because Tarantino, who calls himself "the ultimate film fanatic," was already familiar with every tough guy on both coasts. One actor he definitely wanted was James Woods, and he was willing to hire him sight unseen. He was so anxious to have Woods, in fact, that he made five cash offers to Woods' agent, each one higher than the one before, but the agent never told Woods about them, thinking it was too small a film for such a big star. Two years later, Tarantino met Woods socially, asked him about the offers, and Woods ended up firing his agent.

Tim Roth was also high on Tarantino's list. Roth wanted one of the parts but didn't want to audition; he said he was a terrible actor in auditions and just couldn't do it. Keitel, an old-school New York actor, insisted that everyone audition, but Roth was adamant. Finally, Tarantino took Roth out one night, got him drunk, then convinced him to go back to Tarantino's apartment and read through the whole script. At the end of the night, Tarantino said, "So which do you want to play, Blonde or Pink?" But Roth surprised him by choosing Orange, the shot and bleeding undercover cop who spends most of the movie writhing around on the floor of the warehouse. (Tarantino later watched Roth's performance in *Vincent & Theo*, which he hated, and panicked, thinking he'd hired the wrong man.) Michael Madsen read for the part of Mr. Pink, but Tarantino convinced him to do the sadistic Blonde instead—giving him the most memorable scene in the movie, and the scene he'll probably be remembered for for the rest of his life. Kirk Baltz won the role of the tortured cop and asked Madsen to help him out with his motivation by locking him up in the trunk of a car and driving around Los Angeles for a few minutes. Madsen stretched the experiment to forty-five minutes, stopping at a Taco Bell and ordering a drink, driving over bumps, and gleefully enjoying the punishment of Baltz—which helped with his motivation. This set was obviously going to be Method-acting nirvana.

As it turned out, most of the cast did come from the Actor's Studio, including Lawrence Tierney, another longtime idol of Tarantino's from Tierney's heyday half a century earlier. Tarantino was so eager to have Tierney play Joe Cabot, the gang's behind-the-scenes godfather, that he hired him even after being told that he was troublesome to work with. (He even wrote an inside-joke line of dialogue for him. "Dead as Dillinger," says Joe Cabot near the end of *Reservoir Dogs*—a reference to Tierney's greatest role, in the 1945 docudrama *Dillinger*.) But by the end of production, Tarantino was not too fond of Tierney. "Lawrence Tierney is the big dirt," he said in the only interview he gave during the film's production. "Lawrence Tierney is insane. He should not be walking the streets. He should be in Bellevue with constant medication. If I ever meet Norman Mailer again, I'm going to kick his fuckin' ass. I met Norman Mailer before I cast Lawrence Tierney at a party for the Actor's Studio in New York. I said, 'Hey, you worked with Lawrence Tierney, I'm thinking about hiring him.' He said he was a problem. He said, 'Look, Lawrence will slow you down about 20 percent. If you allow for it, you'll be fine.' Fuck you, Norman Mailer! He slows you down 80 percent! What's this 20 percent bullshit? My friend said, 'Is he personally challenging you?' No, Lawrence likes me. He's a

nice guy. It's not that he's personally challenging me, he personally challenges the entire concept of filmmaking. . . . He's insane. The man is insane. You can't talk to him. He's that far from having a nervous breakdown. One night after shooting, Larry went home and got big-time drunk and unloaded a .357 Magnum in his apartment that went into the next apartment where a family was sleeping, so he was thrown in jail. He was taken from his bail arraignment to the set. He's got, like, five years hanging over his head right now. He's got a record that goes back forty years. He's a felon, he shouldn't be having a gun in the first place."

Tarantino gave this interview to *Film Threat*, an alternative film magazine in Los Angeles, and I'm quoting it because it reveals more about Tarantino than it does about Tierney, showing the intense, manic, bullying side of the boy wonder before he started sanitizing his media exposure. He said all these things—dropping Mailer's name and deriding him at the same time, slamming his own actor, telling stories that are borderline libelous—while he was still a total unknown. He was obviously

"FOR ALL HIS BRILLIANCE, SWEETNESS, AND SUDDEN BOUTS OF KINDNESS, HE IS ALSO SELFISH, GRANDIOSE, UNRELIABLE. AN ONLY CHILD, HE DOESN'T SHARE HIS TOYS."

loving the role of director, glorying in his power, and had the monomaniacal self-confidence of a filmmaker even before his later acclaim.

Rounding out the cast were Chris Penn as Nice Guy Eddie, Randy Brooks as Holdaway (the undercover cop's acting coach), and Penn's friend Eddie Bunker as Mr. Blue. (Bunker, at one time the youngest prisoner in San Quentin, had written the book *No Beast So Fierce* while still behind bars. It was later filmed, in 1978, as *Straight Time*.)

ONCE TARANTINO HAD HIS DREAM TEAM, HE spent two weeks just rehearsing, as though it were a play. (It actually reads like a play.) Several of the actors grumbled about that, including Madsen, who doesn't like to rehearse, but they all later agreed that the extensive rehearsal enriched the final performances. Very few low-budget films are willing to spend money on rehearsal time, so this fact alone indicates that Tarantino knew exactly what he was doing long before he shot his first frame of film. This was, after all, a film that begins with an eight-minute sequence in a diner where eight identically-dressed guys sit around a table talking about Madonna, seventies music, and the morality of tipping. In all that screen time, nothing happens and there's no indication of who each guy is or what they're doing there. Its only purpose, aside from fooling you into thinking they're old buddies (to deconstruct the assemble-the-squad formula), is to establish atmosphere. So why is there tension even during the diner scene? Because the dialogue is flawless. From their interplay, you discover eight guys who never back down. There's no false modesty or facade of politeness. Everything is rapid-fire assault, even during something as harmless as a joke or Mr. Brown's famous deconstruction of "Like a Virgin." ("It's all about a girl who digs a guy with a big dick. It's a metaphor for big dicks.") By the end of that scene, if you've been listening, you already know they're all sociopaths, but each is sociopathic in his own idiosyncratic way.

RESERVOIR DOGS STARTED SHOOTING ON July 29, 1991, in the Highland Park section of East Los Angeles, chosen because it's full of one- and two-story buildings that don't suggest any particular historical period but seem to be in the recent past. The opening scene—Uncle Bob's Pancake House in the script—is actually a place called Pat and Lorraine's on Eagle Rock Boulevard. The warehouse, where 80 percent of the action takes place, was an abandoned mortuary at Figueroa and 59th Streets. Tarantino shot for thirty days, slowed down only by Tierney's eccentricities and "the ear scene," which he ended up shooting three different ways because it was such a pivotal turning point. (Yes, there's an even more horrible and explicit version, which can be seen on the recently released DVD.) After he wrapped, Tarantino spent four and a half months in the editing room, using Steven Wright to dub in the voice of DJ K-Billy, the dopehead announcer for "K-Billy's Super Sounds of the Seventies"—and the final answer print of the film came out of the lab just three days before it was screened at Sundance.

FOUR MONTHS LATER, TARANTINO WAS THE toast of two continents, basking in the Mediterranean sun at the Cannes Film Festival, granting interviews to international film journals, talking about his next project, and saying the kinds of things—about his technique, for example—that first-time directors are normally too shy to talk about. "It's the characters who write the dialogue," he told *Cahiers du Cinema*, the Bible of French auteurists. "I just get them talking and I jot down what they say." He waxed poetic about Jean-Luc Godard, placing his own film in the context of the French New Wave. He talked about Brian De Palma, Sergio Leone, and Howard Hawks, as though he were the inheritor of their legacies. He was charmingly cagey when asked to explain the meaning of his title. "I don't like to say what *Reservoir Dogs* means," he would say, "because everyone has a different idea, and they're all right." (The more mundane truth is that, while working as a video clerk, he could never pronounce *Au Revoir les Enfants*, the frequently rented Louis Malle movie, so he started calling it *Reservoir Dogs*.) He hired a personal publicist with the colorful name of Bumble Ward. He was, in other words, a little hard to take at times. And yet I don't think it was false bravado. That's just how a film geek talks.

And Tarantino was the ultimate film geek. All he had known his whole life was movies. He was, in many ways, an arrested adolescent who continued to collect posters and action figures and comic books well into his thirties while consuming mass quantities of Cap'n Crunch, carbonated Yoohoo, and greasy diner food. He had been a pop-culture fanatic, by his account, since the age of five, when he watched *Abbott and Costello Meet Frankenstein* on TV one afternoon and thought it was the greatest movie ever made—because it was really scary and really funny at the same time. It's not stretching the truth too far to say that that's what Tarantino has been aspiring to ever since. Richard Gladstein, the LIVE executive who green-lighted *Reservoir Dogs*, described the film as "a very, very, very, very violent comedy." At the age of five, Tarantino had discovered his genre—and since the scary comedy wasn't ever a very popular genre, he was able to claim the territory as his own.

It was sheer chance that Tarantino had grown up so close to Hollywood, and you have to wonder what would have happened if he had remained in his birth city of Knoxville, Tennessee, instead. His mother Connie, a half-Cherokee, gave birth to him when she was sixteen, while a student at the University of Tennessee, but his biological father vanished immediately. Connie was reading Faulkner's *The Sound and the Fury* at the time, and named her son after Quentin Compson, Faulkner's deaf-and-dumb innocent whose sense of beauty can only be expressed to himself. When Quentin was two, she moved to Southern California, where she had gone to high school, and a short time later, she met and married a musician named Curt Zastoupil. Zastoupil adopted Quentin, and the three of them settled in Harbor City, in the shadow of Los Angeles International Airport, a middle-class neighborhood near the badass ghettos of Carson.

Tarantino hated every subject in school except history, which he liked because of its stories, and was a terrible student. He was hyperactive and disruptive, a schoolyard brawler, and he once got grounded for the summer for stealing a paperback from K-mart (Elmore Leonard's *The Switch*). His education came entirely from old movies—on TV, at the Carson Twin Cinema, and at the theater at Del Amo Mall. He watched everything, and the movies he liked he watched over and over again. His mother had a laissez-faire attitude about what he was allowed to see, taking him to *Carnal Knowledge* at age five and a double feature of *The Wild Bunch* and *Deliverance* at age nine. She indulged his movie mania and taste for monsters, comic books, and pulp fiction, although for a time she sent him to the strict Hawthorne Christian School, where exploitation films could hardly have been popular. When Quentin was eight, his mother and stepfather divorced, and after the ninth grade, he told his mom that he didn't really want to go to school anymore. All he had ever wanted to do was act. He would get a job, he said, and take acting lessons.

Surprisingly, she agreed, and was happy to learn that he had quickly landed a job as a movie usher. What he didn't tell her was that, at the age of sixteen, he had lied about his age and gone to work at a porno theater called the Pussycat in Torrance. Ironically, pornography was the only kind of film he didn't like. But he used the money from the job to take acting lessons with a Toluca Lake teacher named James Best. Best was known to the public as Sheriff Roscoe P. Coltrane in the goofy early-eighties series

The Dukes of Hazzard, but Tarantino knew him as the star of Sam Fuller's *Verboten!* and *Shock Corridor*. Best didn't teach classical acting so much as he taught audition techniques, but it was a beginning, and Tarantino formed a friendship there with a fellow student named Craig Hamann, who would become his first screenwriting partner.

Tarantino was always easily distracted, never learned to type, and wrote scripts by painstakingly printing barely legible notes on napkins and scraps of paper. Hamann would take the chicken scratches and turn them into actual screenplays. Their first one was a comedy called *Captain Peachfuzz and the Anchovy Bandit*, which they abandoned after twenty pages. When they both got kicked out of James Best's class—Hamann was a soul mate in more ways than one—they started a new script, a Martin-and-Lewis-type comedy called *My Best Friend's Birthday*. With a borrowed 16-millimeter camera, they would shoot scenes on weekends, working on it continuously for three and a half years. But when they finally got the footage back from the lab, Tarantino was devastated. The footage, he said, was "useless," the film unwatchable. "That was my film school," he would say later. "I found out how not to make a film."

Meanwhile, he was doing everything he could to get noticed as an actor. He changed his name from Zastoupil to Tarantino—the name of his biological father. He doctored a résumé, claiming Jean-Luc Godard's *King Lear* as one of his credits, figuring that no one in Hollywood would ever have seen it. He started acting classes again, this time with Allen

Garfield's theater group in Beverly Hills. Hamann introduced him to a manager named Cathryn James, who agreed to represent him, and indeed sent him out on numerous casting calls. (His now-legendary *Golden Girls* episode, aired on November 19, 1988, had him singing Don Ho's "Hawaiian Love Chant" in an Elvis costume.)

WHEN HE WAS TWENTY-TWO, TARANTINO walked into a store called Video Archives in Manhattan Beach and struck up a classic "film geek" conversation with Lance Lawson, the owner. Tarantino loved to argue about films and engage in the kind of one-upsmanship that was common in the video shops of the early eighties. Since he had seen virtually every movie available, knew who directed each one, who wrote them, and infinite detail about the casts, he was a natural to work there. When he returned the next day, to argue some more, Lawson hired him. He got $4 an hour and all the free rentals he wanted. Frequently he would close the store and then watch movies for the rest of the night. The customers loved him because he was such a character, always dressed in black, sporting dangly earrings, expounding on crime novels and comic books, expressing his love for Elvis and the Three Stooges, eager to recommend obscure titles that no one else had ever heard of. According to Lawson, Tarantino was the Steve Buscemi character in *Reservoir Dogs*, complete with his aversion to tipping. At one point Tarantino set up a whole "Heist Film" section of the store that included *Rififi*, *Topkapi*, *The Asphalt Jungle*, *The*

Thomas Crown Affair, and *Treasure of the Four Crowns*—all films he liked. (Yes, even *Treasure of the Four Crowns*.)

Around this same time, Tarantino became friends with another Video Archives clerk named Roger Avary. Avary was also an aspiring screenwriter and wrote a piece called *The Open Road*, which Tarantino would expand and use in his screenplays for *True Romance* and *Natural Born Killers*. It was suggested in later years that Tarantino had a bit of the plagiarist in his working habits, but at the time, Avary, Tarantino, Hamann, and all the other guys he ran with considered themselves collaborators—guys throwing ideas against the wall to see what stuck. Avary and Tarantino worked up a comedy routine about the gay subtext of *Top Gun* that they would perform regularly at Video Archives, adding to it as it developed. After Tarantino became famous, he did the monologue in a movie called *Sleep with Me* and failed to mention to anyone, including Avary himself, that it was Avary who had come up with the original idea. When he accepted the Golden Globe for *Pulp Fiction*, he also failed to mention that a third of that movie was a reworking of an Avary screenplay called *Pandemonium Reigned* that he had bought from Avary in order to create the Bruce Willis segment. Later that night, he started toward Avary's table, but Avary's wife, Gretchen, headed him off by yelling "Fuck you!" (In Tarantino's defense, he also helped Avary with his 1994 directorial debut when Tarantino and Bender executive-produced *Killing Zoe* for his former colleague.)

WHENEVER SOMEONE BECOMES FAMOUS overnight—Tarantino did go from pauper to king in about six months—there's bound to be a certain amount of resentment from the people left behind. One of those people was Cathryn Jaymes, the manager who had worked for him for eight years at the time *Reservoir Dogs* broke through. She set him up with the two Hollywood companies that would guide his career for the next decade—the William Morris Agency, which signed him, and Miramax Films, which locked up distribution rights to his films—and then, just before *Pulp Fiction* came out, Tarantino had his William Morris agent call her up and fire her. Her total income from Tarantino after ten years: $40,000. (For *Reservoir Dogs*, she had agreed to take only 5 percent of Tarantino's income instead of the manager's customary 15 percent.) Tarantino's rationale for firing her: "I don't need a manager anymore."

Stories like this started a backlash against Tarantino that was almost coincident with his rise to fame. Jami Bernard wrote a book-length unauthorized biography that concluded, "For all his brilliance, sweetness, and sudden bouts of kindness, he is also selfish, grandiose, unreliable. An only child, he doesn't share his toys." Yet how could he not be affected by the hype, with Dennis Hopper calling him "the Mark Twain of the nineties" and a critic for *Entertainment Weekly* saying, "He's the greatest American screenwriter since Preston Sturges"? *Reservoir Dogs* in 1992 played at the most prestigious festivals in the world—Sundance, Cannes, Telluride, and Toronto—and at each one he was feted like a conquering hero. When he was interviewed onstage at the British National Film Theatre in January 1995, there was not a ticket to be had in all of London. What was ignored in all the fuss is that *Reservoir Dogs* was not really a total critical success—it got raves but it also got pans—and it was definitely not a commercial success. Its total theatrical take was around $2.8 million, and the only reason it started to make money in later years was that it sold an astounding 900,000 videocassettes, and in the United Kingdom its video release had been blocked for two years, which made it possible for art houses to play it every weekend and continue to make money. (The film was actually more popular in Great Britain than in the United States, earning an astounding $6 million at the box office, breaking six London house records, being called "the best film ever made" by a *Daily Mail* columnist, and being produced as a touring repertory play. For the movie's tenth anniversary, local stores even did a brisk business in *Reservoir Dogs* action figures, complete with a cop with a removable ear.)

Harvey Weinstein, the president of Miramax, had snapped up the domestic distribution rights to *Reservoir Dogs* as soon as he saw it at Sundance—LIVE kept foreign rights—but Weinstein told Tarantino that it would be a tough commercial sell. "What do you think about taking the torture scene out?" he asked him. Of course, Tarantino went ballistic, a bullheaded argument ensued—and Tarantino won. The movie wasn't altered in any way.

"I knew we were down to one thing," said Weinstein later. "If you cut out the ear scene, you have a popular hit. If you leave it in, you lose the women. Thirty seconds would change the movie in the American marketplace."

What Weinstein got out of the deal was not cash, but the prestige of being Tarantino's distributor. From that time forward, they were joined at the hip. ("I'm the Mickey Mouse of Miramax," Tarantino once said.) Tarantino was actually paid a million dollars by TriStar Pictures to write *Pulp Fiction*, but when he handed in the script, president Mike Medavoy decided not to make it, deeming it too weird and violent for the mainstream. Weinstein snapped it up, made it for $8.5 million, and proceeded to sweep the Cannes Film Festival and win award after award with what turned out to be a monster hit. A case could be made that Tarantino's first two films are actually what transformed Miramax from a small but lively distributor of independent films into the dominant "prestige" studio in Hollywood, similar to United Artists in the twenties or Orion Pictures in the seventies.

IN LATER YEARS, TARANTINO WOULD SAY THAT he didn't care what the critics thought about him—especially after he was repeatedly hammered for his acting—but when *Reservoir Dogs* came out, he cared desperately. His favorite critic in the world was Pauline Kael. He'd read her *When the Lights Go*

Down as a textbook on filmmaking and he was crestfallen when she retired from reviewing just as he was starting production on his movie. He was not the kind of guy who "never reads reviews." He was the kind of guy who *always* reads the reviews, and reads *all* the reviews. So no doubt he was pleased to see Camille Nevers, in *Cahiers du Cinema*, enthusing over the "raw theatricality" of *Reservoir Dogs*, a film that "hits first and thinks later." But he also would have seen Ella Taylor's article in *LA Weekly*. "As an exuberant flirtation with genre," she wrote, "*Reservoir Dogs* is a fabulous accomplishment; but when it pushes to extremes, it becomes an exercise in spurious, sadistic manipulation. . . . The torture scene infuriates me because it has no point other than to show off its technique, and to jump-start our adrenaline, which takes some doing these days; we've grown so numb to images of brutality that they have to be jacked up to fever pitch to stir us at all."

Siskel and Ebert echoed the sentiment when they gave the film "two thumbs down," and inevitably Tarantino was asked to defend his use of extreme violence and race-baiting dialogue. And since he loves to talk, he got plenty of opportunities. "Violence is part of this world, and I am drawn to the outrageousness of real-life violence," he told Graham Fuller in *Projections 3: Filmmakers on*

"I STEAL FROM EVERY SINGLE MOVIE EVER MADE. I LOVE IT."

Filmmaking. "It isn't about people lowering people from helicopters onto speeding trains, or about terrorists hijacking something or other. Real-life violence is, you're in a restaurant and a man and his wife are having an argument and all of a sudden the guy gets so mad at her, he picks up a fork and stabs her in the face. That's really crazy and comic-bookish—but it also happens; that's how real violence comes kicking and screaming into your perspective in real life. I am interested in the act, in the explosion, and in the entire aftermath of that. What do we do after this? Do we beat up the guy who stabbed the woman? Do we separate them? Do we call the cops? Do we ask for our money back because our meal has been ruined? I am interested in answering all those questions."

And yet, when Tarantino philosophizes about his films, it doesn't ring true. It's precisely the cinematic qualities of the violence that he celebrates, not "all those questions" about what society should do about it. I think he actually undercuts his films when he attempts to make them somehow socially redeeming. Asked about his affection for the word "nigger," he says, "The minute any word has that much power, everyone on the planet should scream it. No word deserves that much power." Yes, that's the common defense of its use, but in fact he uses the word in contexts that have no purpose other than humor. I don't see anything wrong with that—they're movie characters—but you start to get the impression in Tarantino's public utterances that he's going down a self-justifying road that could kill his talent.

THE OTHER THING THAT TARANTINO HAS BEEN criticized for is theft—theft of plots, of characters, of material, of shots. In Hollywood, the ability to steal can sometimes be a badge of honor, so that's nothing new. What's strange is Tarantino's reaction to it. Right after *Reservoir Dogs* came out, Tarantino gave interview after interview in which he named his favorite films, favorite directors, people who had influenced him. He has somewhat weird tastes in film—for example, he likes Jim McBride's remake of *Breathless* better than Godard's original, because "it's in color"—but, when asked for influences on *Reservoir Dogs* itself, he named everyone from Roger Corman to Brian De Palma to Sergio Leone. He told French interviewers that his favorite movie was Godard's *Bande à Part*—he even named his production company A Band Apart—but he sometimes told American interviewers that his favorite movie was *Rio Bravo*. At one point he said, "This movie is my *The Killing*"—referring to the Kubrick film. He said his idea of naming the characters after colors was something he got from the French New Wave. It sounded like "tough-guy existentialism" to him. (Yet it's difficult to imagine that a film geek wouldn't have known that the same color-code names are used in the seventies thriller *The Taking of Pelham One Two Three*.) He cited Howard Hawks, *One-Eyed Jacks* (the only film directed by Marlon Brando), and *Blow Out*. At a horror festival in Spain—where the torture scene had fifteen walkouts, including Wes Craven!—he referred to *Taxi Driver* but backed off of comparisons to Martin Scorsese because, he said, Scorsese is "almost a stone around young filmmakers' necks. So many new films are aping Scorsese. I don't want to be a poor man's Scorsese." Then he made a goofy speech about the brilliance of *Fandango*. "Kevin Reynolds," he said, "is going to be the Stanley Kubrick of this decade. *Fandango* is one of the best directorial debuts in the history of cinema. I saw *Fandango* five times at the movie theater and it only played for a fucking week, all right?" Among his other favorites, he said, were *Big Wednesday*, *Where Eagles Dare*, *Days of Thunder*, and *Rolling Thunder*. In the actual published screenplay of *Reservoir Dogs*, he specifically thanked Jean-Luc Godard, Andre De Toth, Chow Yun-Fat, Leonard White, Roger Corman, and Timothy Carey.

In other words, he was all over the lot with his list of influences, loves, and film-geek connections. Yet he had given a totally different list to Josh Becker of *Film Threat* when he was actually making the film, and what he said at the time bears repeating: "It's like the films of Jean-Pierre Melville, *Bob the Gambler*, *Le Doulos*, which is my favorite screenplay of all time, with Jean-Paul Belmondo, it's fantastic. He did *Le Samourai* with Alain Delon. He made, like, the coolest gangster films ever. They're, like, fantastic. His films were like he took the Bogart, Cagney, the Warner Bros. gangster films, all right, he loved those, and a lot of times he just took the stories from them and did them with Belmondo or Delon or Jean Gabin and just gave them a different style, a different coolness, you know, they had this French Gallic thing going through it, yet they were still trying to be like their

American counterparts, but they had a different rhythm all their own. Then I took those movies and threw an L.A. right-now into them. So it's like a crossbreed, giving birth to this, giving birth to this [sic] . . ."

This is perhaps the closest he comes to the truth of how he developed *Reservoir Dogs*, although it's strange that he would mention Jean-Pierre Melville before the film comes out and then not give him credit after the film is a success. Perhaps the reason is that he wasn't admiring Melville's style so much as he was admiring his ability to steal from American films and impose a French quirkiness on it that makes it seem to be a whole new film. Because, as would soon be revealed, Tarantinto didn't take "those movies" from the French gangster era and "throw an L.A. right-now into them." He took one particular movie, not from France, but from the opposite side of the planet, and infused it with an L.A. right-now.

The movie was a Chinese-language film called *City on Fire*, and it came out in 1987 just as Hong Kong action movies were becoming immensely popular among film geeks. (It would be nine more years before Jackie Chan's *Rumble in the Bronx* made them popular among the general public.) In *City on Fire*, a gang of robbers with code names—just like Tarantino's—run away after their jewelry heist goes bad. The heist is bungled because one of the men, a psychopath, started shooting—just like Mr. Blonde. An undercover cop gets wounded during the heist by a frightened innocent bystander, who is in turn killed by the cop—as in

Following pages: Harvey Keitel as Mr. White.

THE CRITICS WHO HAVE DISSED IT—

FOR VIOLENCE,
FOR CYNICISM,
FOR SELF-CONSCIOUS ARTINESS—

ARE LOOKING FOR MORAL AND PHILOSOPHICAL CONTENT
IN A FILM THAT HAS NONE.

IT'S A HORROR FILM,
BUT INSTEAD OF ONE JASON VOORHEES,
WE HAVE EIGHT OF THEM.

Tarantino's movie. The cops had been lying in wait for the gang, because they were tipped off by the wounded undercover cop—just like Mr. Orange. But during the getaway, the wounded cop is taken care of by an older gangster who empties a pair of guns through the windshield of a patrol car—very similar to what Mr. White does. The gang meets in a disused warehouse. Once they know they've been set up, they call the big boss—a boss similar to Joe Cabot. The big boss shows up, accuses the wounded man of being a cop and draws his gun. A four-way standoff ensues. The older gangster protests that the wounded man is innocent—just as Mr. White defends Mr. Orange.

There are additional parallels—the documentary realism, the sudden violence—so obviously the whole structure and plot of Tarantino's movie is taken directly from *City on Fire*. Is this a crime? Not at all. He obviously pulled a Jean-Pierre Melville and simply put an L.A. hipster overlay on a Hong Kong story. What's strange is that, in his hours and hours of interviews, and in his encyclopedic attempts to name all his influences, he never cites *City on Fire* or its director, Ringo Lam, as one of them. Yet he's a self-described film geek who does admit to owning the *City on Fire* poster, and in the published screenplay, one of the people he thanks is the famous Hong Kong actor Chow Yun-Fat, the star of *City on Fire*. Why the star but not the director?

Many people wondered the same thing, and in 1994, one of Tarantino's fellow film geeks—Mike White, twenty-two-year-old manager of a Blockbuster Video in Riverview, Michigan—made a twelve-minute short film called *Who Do You Think You're Fooling?* that splices together footage from both movies. It got a lot of attention at the New York Underground Film Festival in March 1995, especially after it was pulled from public viewing, reportedly due to pressure from Miramax. (White didn't have copyright permissions to copy the two films.)

When a reporter finally managed to ask Tarantino about it, he said White's film was "a film-geek thing to do." Asked if he based his movie on *City on Fire*, he responded strangely. "I love *City On Fire*," he said, "and I have the poster for it framed in my house. It's a great movie. I steal from every movie. I steal from every single movie ever made. I love it. If my work has anything, it's that I'm taking this from this and that from that and mixing them together and if people don't like them then tough titty, don't go and see it, all right? I steal from everything. Great artists steal, they don't do homages."

Why the angry tone when talking about *City on Fire* but the reverent gee-whiz tone when talking about Godard, or Pierre-Melville, or the two dozen other filmmakers he named in the course of his year-long publicity tours on behalf of *Reservoir Dogs*? At one point, Miramax Pictures got equally defensive about their star director being criticized and issued a public statement to *USA Today* through spokeswoman Marcy Granata: "Quentin has always been really open about the movies to which he was making homage, including *City on Fire*."

But actually the opposite was true. He was really open about all the movies he was stealing from—remember, he doesn't make homages—except the one that he stole from most directly and most comprehensively. If he had just dropped the name *City on Fire* into the mix, along with *Taxi Driver* and *The Killing*, then I doubt anything would have been made of it. Instead, it became a raging controversy on the Internet, with White taking a lot of flack for being a "Tarantino hater" (which he was not), and Tarantino looking like he had something to hide. Strangely enough, the mainstream media wasn't too interested in the controversy at all, although by that time Tarantino had publicly trashed Oliver Stone for ruining his *Natural Born Killers* script, so Stone's producer Don Murphy weighed in with some epithets of his own: "Quentin doesn't have a single bone of originality in his body. Any that he has have long since died of loneliness."

Since Tarantino doesn't want to describe exactly how he used *City on Fire*, I think it's fair to speculate about why he didn't thank Ringo Lam. First of all, *City on Fire* was a recent movie. It was a Hong Kong hit just three years before Tarantino wrote *Reservoir Dogs*, and it had been available in the states for a much shorter time, but only in bootleg copies or at Chinatown cinemas. Perhaps

Tarantino felt bad about stealing from something that was a current box-office hit. Then there's the matter of Ringo Lam himself. Lam wasn't a universally revered international director like John Woo. *City on Fire* was only his second film, and his first one had been finished just two years before—*Cupid One* (1985). He was only six years out of film school and just seven years older than Tarantino. Perhaps Tarantino felt a twinge when he stole from a director of his own generation who was still struggling. (Lam has had an up and down career, but has survived through friendships with Chow Yun-fat and, later, Jean-Claude Van Damme.) In fact, at the time Tarantino wrote the script for *Reservoir Dogs*, Lam had had three flops in a row, two of which were international projects that were supposed to make him famous outside Hong Kong. It never really happened. Or perhaps Tarantino feared a lawsuit—not really likely, since Hong Kong filmmakers aren't very legalistic about where they get their own plots. Or perhaps it was simply the Hitchcock syndrome. Hitchcock was always notoriously stingy about giving credit to his writers, because he wanted the films to be regarded as his own. Writing was, in fact, probably the only thing Hitchcock couldn't do.

At any rate, if you look at both films, you can see that Tarantino doesn't have anything to be

"THAT'S HOW REAL VIOLENCE COMES
KICKING AND SCREAMING
INTO YOUR PERSPECTIVE IN REAL LIFE."

ashamed of. He made the material his own. No one else could have made *Reservoir Dogs*. But in his own mind, perhaps he thinks he got away with something—that it's somehow more honorable to steal from a film noir rarity from the fifties than from a director who's just like him but living in another country. My suggestion would be that, in the future, he not call it "homage" or "stealing" but, taking a word from the music industry, "sampling." He is, after all, "the first rock-star director," according to Jeff Dawson, author of *Quentin Tarantino: The Cinema of Cool*.

Reservoir Dogs is not just a promising first movie. It's a great movie that I think will age well. And because of its popularity, and the fact that it came out at the height of the video age, it has already been analyzed and parsed far more than many movies decades older. I won't go into all the aspects of it—the innovative use of seventies schlock music, the use of wide-screen long shots in intimate scenes, the use of banal dialogue as edgy counterpoint to the seriousness of scenes, the brilliant scene-within-a-scene-within-a-scene when the undercover cop is practicing his "amusing anecdote," the use of real time as screen time in the warehouse—but I do want to mention the "Who Killed Nice Guy Eddie?" debate.

In the final scene of the movie, there's a four-man Mexican standoff. Joe Cabot pulls a gun on the wounded Mr. Orange, certain that he's the rat. Mr. White pulls his gun on Joe Cabot, equally certain that Mr. Orange is innocent. Nice Guy Eddie pulls his gun on Mr. White, furious that his father is being threatened. The three guns remain drawn for a long time as they try to reason, and then threaten, their way out of the situation. Then shots ring out in such quick succession that you can't be sure of the order, and the three men standing all go down. But if you play the scene in slow motion, there are only three shots, and yet there are four men wounded by those shots. Joe Cabot shoots Mr. Orange. Mr. White shoots Joe Cabot. Nice Guy Eddie shoots Mr. White. But Nice Guy Eddie dies as well—so who kills Nice Guy Eddie?

The answer is that there was a mistake made during the filming. Joe Cabot was supposed to shoot Mr. Orange, and then Mr. White was supposed to pull the trigger twice, shooting both Joe Cabot and Nice Guy Eddie, even as he was hit with Nice Guy Eddie's bullet. But the blood squib on Nice Guy Eddie was detonated before Mr. White could fire the second time. Chris Penn, the actor playing Nice Guy Eddie, went ahead and collapsed to the floor at the same moment that Harvey Keitel, the actor playing Mr. White, collapsed, as though they had killed each other, even though Keitel's gun was still pointed at Lawrence Tierney. After the mistake was discovered, Tarantino looked at the footage, thought about it, and said, "Leave it. They'll talk about it forever."

He was right. We're still talking about it. That's what makes Quentin Tarantino a great director. And if you don't understand what I'm talking about, then you're just not enough of a film geek to get it.

FOR FURTHER DISTURBANCE

Ten years after his breakthrough film, Quentin Tarantino's body of work is not that extensive. Besides *Reservoir Dogs*, he has two noir screenplays that were directed by other people—Tony Scott's TRUE ROMANCE (1993) and Oliver Stone's NATURAL BORN KILLERS (1994). (Scott changed the ending of *True Romance*, and Stone changed *Natural Born Killers* to something Tarantino scarcely recognized.) He wrote a supernatural horror film, FROM DUSK TILL DAWN (1996), that was directed by his friend Robert Rodriguez. All three of these screenplays had been written prior to *Reservoir Dogs*, as was his script-doctor work on PAST MIDNIGHT (1992), a Rutger Hauer thriller. He is also responsible for uncredited rewrites on IT'S PAT (1994) and the blockbuster CRIMSON TIDE (1995).

His second film as a writer-director, and biggest hit to date, was PULP FICTION (1994), another contemporary film noir starring John Travolta, Uma Thurman, and Samuel L. Jackson, which won the Palme d'Or at the Cannes Film Festival and became the biggest selling book version of a screenplay in history. He contributed one segment to the anthology film FOUR ROOMS (1995) and then made the retro blaxploitation thriller JACKIE BROWN (1997). And that was it for the nineties. As

this book went to press, he had just finished principal photography on his next opus, KILL BILL, scheduled for release in 2003.

Watching all the films that have influenced Tarantino's moviehound mind is impossible, but supposedly the first film that inspired him was Charles Barton's ABBOTT AND COSTELLO MEET FRANKENSTEIN (1948). Other influences include Jonathan Demme's women-in-prison classic CAGED HEAT (1974), Jean-Luc Godard's BREATHLESS (1960), Jim McBride's BREATHLESS (1983), Godard's BANDE À PART (1964), Brian De Palma's BLOW OUT (1981), all the films of Sergio Leone including THE GOOD, THE BAD AND THE UGLY (1966) and ONCE UPON A TIME IN AMERICA (1984), Stanley Kubrick's THE KILLING (1956), Martin Scorsese's MEAN STREETS (1973), Scorsese's TAXI DRIVER (1976), Howard Hawks's RIO BRAVO (1959), Marlon Brando's ONE-EYED JACKS (1961), John Milius's BIG WEDNESDAY (1978), Brian Hutton's WHERE EAGLES DARE (1968), Kevin Reynolds's FANDANGO (1985), Tony Scott's DAYS OF THUNDER (1990), and John Flynn's ROLLING THUNDER (1977).

Tarantino cites two Jean-Pierre Melville films, LE DOULOS (1961) and BOB THE GAMBLER (1955), as his main inspiration for *Reservoir Dogs*, and calls *Le Doulos* his favorite screenplay of all time. But undoubtedly there were at least two other sources. The idea of color-coded criminals is first used in THE TAKING OF PELHAM ONE TWO THREE (1974). And the principal source was probably Ringo Lam's CITY ON FIRE (1987), a Hong Kong action flick starring Chow Yun-Fat that has a sequence very similar to the plot of Tarantino's movie. Mike White's twelve-minute short showing similar scenes from the two movies is called WHO DO YOU THINK YOU'RE FOOLING? (1994), and it's officially a prohibited item, since White doesn't own the copyrights, but it's easily available through Internet trades. White followed it up with a five-minute sequel called YOU'RE STILL NOT FOOLING ANYBODY (1997), revealing all the movies Tarantino borrowed from for *Pulp Fiction*. Ringo Lam's other

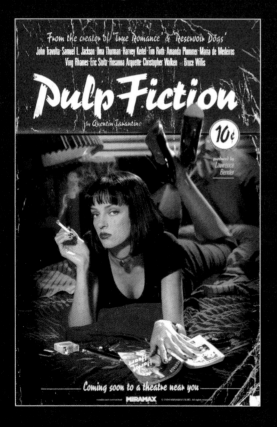

hits include the sequel, PRISON ON FIRE (1987), WILD SEARCH (1989), PRISON ON FIRE 2 (1991), and FULL CONTACT (1992), all starring Chow Yun-Fat. After the big-budget hit BURNING PARADISE (1994), Lam came to America in 1996 to direct MAXIMUM RISK (1996), but didn't get along with Jean-Claude Van Damme and publicly criticized his acting. Back in Hong Kong, he had another big hit with FULL ALERT (1997), then, oddly enough, continued to make movies with Van Damme, including REPLICANT (2001) and THE MONK (2003).

Tarantino's other unacknowledged influence is Louis Malle's AU REVOIR LES ENFANTS (1987), the movie he could never pronounce when he was clerking and took to calling *Reservoir Dogs*.

After *Reservoir Dogs*, Tarantino and his partner Lawrence Bender were big dogs in the independent-film world, and they used that power to encourage other young filmmakers. Bender produced Boaz Yakin's FRESH (1994). Bender and Tarantino executive-produced KILLING ZOE (1994), the directorial debut of Tarantino's friend and video-store coworker Roger Avary. Avary would go on to direct MR. STITCH (1995), which had a cable-TV premiere, and RULES OF ATTRACTION (2002), the adaptation of Brett Easton Ellis's novel. Prior to meeting Tarantino, Bender had produced Scott Spiegel's INTRUDER (1988). During this time, Kevin Smith, the director of CLERKS (1994) and MALLRATS (1995), was touted as the second video-store film prodigy.

Reservoir Dogs also jump-started Tarantino's acting career, which had been languishing for years. In SLEEP WITH ME (1994), he plays a whacked partygoer who does the speech about the homosexual subtext of TOP GUN that he and Roger Avary had performed together for years. In *From Dusk Till Dawn* he plays a sadistic killer, and he also appears (in a cameo role) in another Robert Rodriguez film, DESPERADO (1995). Other small roles included the voice of Panhandle Slim in THE CORIOLUS EFFECT (1994), Johnny Destiny in DESTINY TURNS ON THE RADIO (1995), LITTLE NICKY (2000), and a cameo as a bartender in his friend Alexandre Rockwell's SOMEBODY TO LOVE (1994). It was Rockwell's IN THE SOUP (1992), starring Steve Buscemi, that beat out *Reservoir Dogs* for the top prize at the 1992 Sundance Film Festival. Beginning in 1998 Tarantino made a number of appearances in documentaries, as himself, capitalizing on his cachet as a film expert in BAADASSSSS CINEMA (1998), GOD SAID, 'HA!' (1998), JACKIE CHAN: MY STORY (1998), FOREVER HOLLYWOOD (1999), and ALL THE LOVE YOU CANNES (2002).

A DAVID CRONENBERG FILM

CRASH

Love in the dying moments
of the twentieth century

JAMES SPADER   HOLLY HUNTER   ELIAS KOTEAS   DEBORAH KARA UNGER and ROSANNA ARQUETTE

"CRASH" written by **DAVID CRONENBERG**   based on the novel by **J. G. BALLARD**   produced and directed by **DAVID CRONENBERG**

music by HOWARD SHORE   edited by RONALD SANDERS   production design by CAROL SPIER   director of photography PETER SUSCHITZKY

co-producers STEPHANE REICHEL and MARILYN STONEHOUSE · executive producers JEREMY THOMAS and ROBERT LANTOS

NC-17   NO CHILDREN UNDER 17 ADMITTED

At the beginning of his career,
as a young English major at
the University of Toronto,

David Cronenberg said,
"I want to show the unshowable.
Speak the unspeakable."

A ND THEN HE STARTED MAKING FILMS— increasingly horrific, increasingly disturbing films that were frightening not because he was the first person to show exploding heads on screen (even though he was) but because of what was going on inside those heads. Cronenberg was the first director to make the human body itself the source of all horror. He took the Frankenstein myth and made it universal. He created entire worlds in which everyone is Dr. Frankenstein and everyone is also the creature. Cronenberg doesn't like to be called a horror director or a science-fiction director. His films have been shown in both grind houses and art houses, at drive-ins, at black-tie Cannes Film Festival screenings, and in museums. *The Dead Zone* and *The Fly* were both mainstream hits, while *The Brood, They Came From Within*, and *Videodrome* had cult audiences, and *Dead Ringers* and *Naked Lunch* were appreciated mostly by intellectuals. And yet they all make up a body of work that's almost one continuous film. I don't think there's any director in the world whose obsessions have been repeatedly reexamined so thoroughly in every work he does.

These are intensely personal films of ideas, even though we don't always know exactly what the ideas are. One thing we do know is that everywhere you look in a Cronenberg film, there are restless people unable to cope with technology, disease, infection, and the phantasms of their own minds, and their confusion makes them sick unto death. Cronenberg is a species that we all thought was extinct. He's an existentialist. His 1999 film is even called *eXistenZ*, in case we didn't already get it. But of all the films he's made so far, the most revolutionary was also the simplest. It's called *Crash*, and people have no idea what to do with it.

When *Crash* premiered at Cannes in May 1996, it was booed by the audience in the Palais du Festivals, and many people walked out entirely. At the usual raucous Cannes press conference, critics asked him to explain what he was doing. Was it pornography? Was it antipornography? Was he pushing a cultural message? At the end of the festival he was given a Special Jury Prize "for originality, for daring, and for audacity." Shortly thereafter it was revealed that two jury members were so appalled by the film that they refused to endorse the prize or any other recognition it might receive. *Crash* had been produced by Fine Line Features, part of Turner Entertainment, but when Chairman Ted Turner screened the film, he flew into a rage and vowed that his company would never release it. The MPAA ratings board gave it an NC-17, virtually demolishing its chances for any wide release, since most newspapers refuse advertising for NC-17 films. Yet Fine Line didn't even appeal the rating. "By accepting the NC-17 rating, we are acting in a responsible manner," said Fine Line President Ruth Vitale, almost apologetically. "This is a film that was made by adults for adults; this is not a film for children and therefore children should not be permitted to see it. Fine Line is wholly in agreement with the MPAA and will not challenge the rating for exploitative purposes." It opened in Canada in October 1996 to a firestorm of protest, denunciations, and negative reviews. None of that prevented it from becoming the highest grossing Canadian film of the year and winning five Genies (the Canadian Oscar). After delaying and hemming and hawing, Fine Line finally released it in a limited run in the United States in March 1997. Just when a jaded filmgoing public thought it had seen everything that could possibly be seen, Cronenberg had created something truly subversive.

ONE REASON IT'S SUBVERSIVE IS THAT IT deals with two subjects that are found in almost every big Hollywood film—sex and car crashes—but it reverses our perspective. The sex is seen as empty, without consequence, and arousing only when it becomes so kinky that you can't imagine the mind even going there. And yet the mind does go there, and in spite of yourself, you can't help but identify with it. The car crashes, on the other hand, bring not death and destruction but life itself—or, more accurately, life through death. The main characters can experience feeling—and orgasm—only through life-threatening, steel-crunching, body-mangling car crashes. It's the kind of idea that, when you first hear it, sounds utterly silly, but when you experience it—through the cool, flat directness of these people who will push every limit—it becomes engrossing. This is that rarest of films, the kind that actually changes your own ideas of what it means to be human. If you let it, of course.

Many people didn't. When Cronenberg first showed the sparse seventy-seven-page script to his agent, the agent said, "Do not do this movie. It will end your career." Christopher Tookey, in the *Daily Mail* of London, said the film was "the point at which even a liberal society should draw the line" because all it offers is "the morality of the satyr, the nymphomaniac, the rapist, the pedophile, the danger to society." Tookey was especially upset by the sex scenes, because "the initially heterosexual characters lose their inhibitions [and] they experiment pleasurably with gay sex, lesbian sex, and sex with cripples." (Since the "cripple" is Rosanna Arquette, wearing leg braces and a full-body support suit over her fishnet stockings and scarred legs, her sex scenes are among the hottest in the film—which would seem to be the kind of thing that the handicapped-rights era would applaud.) Alexander Walker, in the *London Evening Standard*, called it "a movie beyond the bounds of depravity," containing "some of the most perverted acts and theories of sexual deviance I have ever seen propagated in mainstream cinema." And even *The New Yorker*, normally a tub-thumper for experimental film, weighed in with a nasty review. "People are right to be shocked by *Crash*," wrote Anthony Lane, "but for the wrong reasons. What it shows you, even in scarred closeup, is only mildly nauseating compared to what it insists in telling you." He went on to call it a "road movie, blue movie, black comedy, and a load of white noise about nothing."

I would say it's none of those things. I think it's a love story. It's a love story told through sex scenes. Almost everything we know is conveyed through the sex itself. Critics are always saying that the problem with pornography is that it doesn't mean anything; it's just a succession of one sex scene after another. But now Cronenberg makes a film that is all sex, all the time, and every coupling is so fertile with meaning that he can be said to have created the first sex film in which there's not a single gratuitous moment. In mainstream Hollywood movies, the sex scene can usually be removed or simply implied and the film will still make sense. In this film, the whole story is told through sex, and the removal of any sexual moment would make the film impossible to understand.

The film opens, in fact, with three sex scenes, one right after the other. Early audiences, not accustomed to a story being told this way, were made vaguely uncomfortable, wondering, "When is the movie going to start?" In the first scene, a beautiful woman named Catherine caresses herself against the wing of an airplane in an austere hangar, and as she starts to move we see an anonymous man come up behind her and strip off his shirt. Her eyes are glacial as she licks the cold metal and the man kisses her butt and prepares to enter her. In the second scene, a harried film producer named James Ballard ducks into the camera room with his assistant and doesn't even bother to remove his clothes as he ravishes her naked body, expertly and without emotion. In the third scene, we're in the sterile apartment of Catherine and Ballard, overlooking the cloverleafs and gray concrete of a busy freeway. As Ballard runs his hand up under her dress, she tells him where she had sex that day, but confesses that she didn't come. "What about your camera girl?" she asks him. "Did she come?" He fondles her more intently as he answers, "We were interrupted." They have emotionless sex, never looking into each other's eyes, as she says, "Maybe the next one. Maybe the next one."

OBVIOUSLY WE'RE NOT IN KANSAS HERE. The film seems futuristic, perhaps the very near future, with a race of people so drained of feeling that they can't reach orgasm and their bodies only respond when their minds can touch something forbidden. But nothing is forbidden. This couple has done it all, seen it all. They can't find any new way to connect. All of that changes when Ballard, driving through heavy freeway traffic

---

Following pages: Holly Hunter brings James Spader to life.

while trying to read at the same time, veers off into the oncoming lane and has a head-on collision. A man in the other car flies through *both* windshields and lands in the seat next to Ballard, dead. The woman in the other car fumbles at her shoulder seat belt, then rips her blouse open, exposing a breast. There's no way to know what the gesture means. Is she hysterical? Was it a mistake? She and Ballard stare into each other's eyes, not comprehending but feeling something. Even this moment, the violent climax of the first act, is a sex scene.

Both victims are taken to a hospital for airline-crash casualties, where Ballard learns that the woman is a doctor named Helen Remington and that her dead husband was a chemical engineer for a food company. Ballard also encounters a spooky guy named Vaughan who shows him grisly accident photos and carefully examines all of Ballard's wounds. Catherine comes to Ballard's hospital bed and, calmly and clinically, recites all the gory details of his accident, caressing him between the legs as she does. He has an orgasm this time, and you get the impression it's the first one he's had in a long time. A few scenes later, he meets Helen Remington in the garage where their wrecked cars have been hauled and ends up giving her a ride to the airport. When he gets cut off in the heavy traffic, he runs up on the curb and they both feel the rush of a near collision. "We're close to the airport garage," she says. "It won't be busy this time of day." When he parks in the garage, she climbs onto his lap, facing him, with the steering wheel against her back, and they have sex hard and fast, this time with even more lust. That night, Ballard has passionate sex with his wife in exactly the same position.

The intensity of the sex increases with each successive scene, but it's increasing because of its connection to technology, in the form of the car, and body mutilation, in the form of their various wounds and injuries. The actors remain quiet, direct, and emotionless throughout, as though they're all sleepwalking. Only when they see the pain and destruction of the car crashes do they come alive. I can't imagine that anyone who really watched the first ten minutes of this movie could fail to understand that we're moving through a world where the rules of passion are turned upside down. Everything is about touching death. The colors used for the lighting and the costumes— browns, reds, purples, grays, blacks, blues—are the colors of bruised skin. Even the cars are painted those colors. We're in a world where tattooing and piercing have been taken to their ultimate level, where the mutilation of the body has become the only means of vitality. And Ballard and Catherine,

...the assigned reader scrawled on the manuscript, "This author is beyond psychiatric help. Do Not Publish!"

The categories of

gay, straight, and bisexual

don't seem to apply to this movie.

The kind of sex they're having is

not in the manual.

our two lovers, are determined to push through until they find that vitality.

Crash is based on a 1973 novel by the respected British writer J.G. Ballard, best known for his autobiographical *Empire of the Sun*, which was made into a 1987 movie by Steven Spielberg. Like many of his stories, this one is about an exhausted civilization. (When he first submitted it to his British publisher, the assigned reader scrawled on the manuscript, "This author is beyond psychiatric help. Do Not Publish!") The main character, who Ballard named after himself, is fascinated by a festering wound of a man named Vaughan, who can only achieve sexual release by crashing into people on the freeways around Heathrow Airport. He keeps searching for the ultimate orgasmic fantasy—ramming his car into a Rolls Royce carrying Elizabeth Taylor and causing a spectacular celebrity crash—but he kills himself trying to pull it off, and Elizabeth Taylor is unharmed. Cronenberg chose not to use the Elizabeth Taylor angle, probably for legal reasons, and instead turned Ballard into an evangelist who studies and reenacts all the celebrity death crashes in history, from James Dean to Jayne Mansfield. (The movie came out a year before the Princess Diana crash or else surely that would have been included.) Cronenberg also moved the locale to his hometown of Toronto, which is even better than London because it looks like the most generic of cities. It could be anywhere or nowhere. Anytime and no time. The characters have no families, no friends, no children, no ties, no real connection with anything outside themselves. They stare outward at the bleak landscape that seems composed entirely of freeways, garages, pillars, pylons, crash barriers, parking lots, gas stations, and wrecked cars, and they all have the sense that there are more cars each day, that the cars are "gathering" for some reason.

Even though Cronenberg used 200 vehicles and 60 stunt drivers, crashing 25 automobiles during 18 nights of shooting, the actual crashes are strangely unexciting. There is no slow motion. They happen with the confusing split-second sudden impact of real life. But the camera lingers on the aftermath—the twisted metal, the twisted limbs. Cronenberg himself drives a Ferrari and was an amateur race-car driver in the sixties—he even made a road-racing film called *Fast Company*—and he has a feel for this material. The most spectacular accident is the one staged by Vaughan for his little cult of spectators, whom he calls his "partners in psychopathology." He recreates, in minute detail, the death crash of James Dean on September 9, 1955, when he slammed his Porsche Spyder head-on into a 1950 Ford Tudor driven by college student Donald Turnupseed. Stunt drivers reenact the crash, and Vaughan himself plays Rolf Wutherich, an engineer from Zuffenhausen, Germany, who was in the passenger seat of Dean's car. This scene, in which Ballard falls under the spell of Vaughan, is a key to the rest of the movie. Vaughan has a scientific "project." Elias Koteas plays Vaughan as half mad scientist and half street hustler. Vaughan is the Dr. Frankenstein figure, but instead of creating monsters from scratch, he's a performance artist who works with found objects, and he lives in a world where, unlike Dr. Frankenstein, nobody thinks he's crazy.

Although we don't know exactly what the "project" is, we know that Vaughan has the secret of what Ballard is beginning to understand—that the car crash, as he tells the crowd, is "a liberation of sexual energy that mediates the sexuality of those who have died with an intensity impossible in any other form." Vaughan himself drives the "hero car," a 1963 black Lincoln convertible like the one in which JFK was assassinated—because that, after all, was "a special kind of accident." As Helen, then Ballard, then Catherine are all drawn into Vaughan's strange world, gathering to watch Volvo crash-test videos and becoming increasingly turned on by his quest for the merging of man and machine, the movie becomes both a thriller—how far will they go and how badly will it end?—and an upside-down love story. The closer everyone gets to the deranged Vaughan, the more passion they feel for one another.

This is not the kind of movie that big stars usually sign on for—their agents would probably say the same thing that Cronenberg's did—but one reason it works is that James Spader, as Ballard, and Holly Hunter, as Dr. Helen Remington, are genuine movie stars, and when we see genuine movie stars, we have a certain set of expectations for the way they'll behave. All of those expectations are frustrated. The number-one "walkout" scene is when Ballard finally has sex with Vaughan. The two men go together to get their bodies tattooed with car emblems, with Vaughan requesting that his be "ragged and dirty," then have sex in a convertible, kissing each other's tender fresh tattoos. For all the clamor about the perversions in the movie, including an earlier scene in which Ballard makes love to Rosanna Arquette's suture wound, it's this scene, where Ballard kisses the facial scars and chest tattoos of Vaughan, that grosses everyone out. It's certainly not the first homosexual act seen on the screen, but it's the moment of maximum passion in this movie, and something about it makes the men who identify with Spader turn away from the movie's premise. Yet everything has been building toward that moment, including a riveting scene in which Catherine and Ballard have sex while she fantasizes about what Vaughan's scarred body looks like, and especially what his damaged penis must be like. All of the turning points of the film are actually sex scenes, as the cast members couple in various combinations in their search for life and feeling. The only "normal" person in the movie is a salesman at a Mercedes-Benz dealership. But when Rosanna Arquette asks him to help her into the car so she can test it for its handicap access, he gets a glimpse of her fishnet thigh under her leg braces and is suddenly not so normal anymore. The categories of gay, straight, and bisexual don't seem to apply in this movie. The kind of sex they're having is not in the manual. And each scene raises the stakes, whether it's Vaughan having brutal sex with Catherine in the back seat while Ballard drives through a car wash and watches them in the rear view mirror, or when Rosanna Arquette offers her open wound to Ballard. The effect is to make the

James Spader told Cronenberg that the script scared him— and that's why he wanted to do it.

viewer first go, "Whoa! Don't go there," followed by "But he has to go there."

Cronenberg has always been highly respected in Hollywood despite working primarily in the low-budget world. (*Crash* cost only $6 million.) At various times he's been offered jobs directing *Top Gun*, *Witness*, *Total Recall*, *Beverly Hills Cop*, *The Truman Show*, *Aliens 4*, and, most curious of all, *Flashdance*. (Studio president Dawn Steele kept bugging him to do *Flashdance* for her, but he finally said, "I would destroy this!") To his credit, he's turned down all those paychecks to do the kind of movies that he truly believes in. "I didn't even do *Fly 2*," he says, "so why would I want to do *Aliens 4*?" When he first read the novel *Crash*, in the eighties, he put it down halfway through and decided he couldn't film it. But it's the kind of story that percolates in the mind and keeps gnawing at the subconscious. When he went back to the book, he had an epiphany. "Since I see technology as being an extension of the human body," he said, "it's inevitable that it should come home to roost."

Even the author of the book was amazed by Cronenberg's adaptation. "The film goes farther than the book I wrote," said J.G. Ballard. "What is so powerful about it, and its performances, is that they start where the book ends. They take for granted the strange logic that unfolds. There's no attempt to make the events being shown explicable in conventional dramatic terms. It's one of the best films on sexuality, violence, and the motor car."

Bernardo Bertolucci, the Italian director, went even farther, calling it "a religious masterpiece," and saying that "it doesn't have a single vulgar moment." For a viewpoint from the other end of the spectrum, cult director John Waters said, "*Crash*, to me, is the best art movie ever made, and I mean that in a great way—what art movies really used to be." And yet these were exceptions. Julie Gerstel, film critic for the *Toronto Star*, was so confused that she gave it a rating of "either one star or five stars." The only explanation, I think, is that people were put off by the formal inversions—the refusal to judge the motives of the characters, the use of sex as a character-development device, the refusal even to give the movie a closed ending. Fortunately, Cronenberg has never been shy about talking about his own films, and he gave a very revealing interview to *Film Comment*. "I'm questioning a lot of things that are, certainly in Hollywood terms, the immutables of film narrative," he said. "First of all, that you must have a narrative. Secondly, that it must go in a certain way. Thirdly, that your characters should be sympathetic and should evolve and you should tie everything up, all those 'well-made play' kind of things that Hollywood has been so successful selling over the years—a perfectly legitimate thing to do. But when you're not doing it and your audience's expectations are formed by that, they don't know what to do."

Even the actors who eagerly signed on for the project weren't entirely sure about what to do. James Spader told Cronenberg that the script scared him—and that's why he wanted to do it. Holly Hunter called and begged for the part even before the script had formally been sent out, but once on the set, she wanted some rehearsal time, as all the actors did, since they were all going to be having sex with one another. The most nervous was Deborah Kara Unger, as Catherine, who was the youngest and least experienced of the group—and the most frequently naked. At the Cannes press conference, one reporter made note of that fact, and asked Cronenberg why he didn't use more full-frontal male nudity, implying that he would have liked to have seen more of James Spader. "I can address that," piped up Spader. "It has more to do with geography. Most of the time we were fucking, and when you're fucking you don't see the penis."

Many critics noted that almost all of the sex was from the rear—a conscious device that Cronenberg used to make the actors disconnected. They're looking at something as they have sex, but never at each other. And yet this is what ultimately makes the journey of Ballard and Catherine a love story. At the beginning, they can't experience each other at all; their only connection is through fantasies involving other people. By the end of the movie, they've had the ultimate experience. Vaughan has tried to ram their car against an eighteen-wheeler, but instead he goes out of control, jumps a barrier,

lands on top of a bus, and dies in a fiery explosion. Ballard goes to the auto graveyard to claim the now useless 1963 black Lincoln of Vaughan's. (He doesn't claim the body. He claims the body's life force.) In the next scene, we see Ballard driving like a crazy man—and then roaring up behind his wife's convertible. He bumps her hard and she goes out of control and down an embankment. Ballard finds her overturned, smoking car and sees her body thrown out onto the turf. He leans over and whispers her name. She stirs. "I think I'm all right." He takes her tenderly in his arms and fondles her. "I think I'm all right," she repeats, a single tear coursing down her cheek. We think for a moment that she's trying to reassure him that she's alive, but the opposite is true. "Maybe the next one, darling," he tells her with real emotion. And he enters her from behind. "Maybe the next one." Catherine and Ballard are together at last. Even in its final moment, the film turns Hollywood inside out. No wonder people hated it. No wonder people love it.

FOR FURTHER DISTURBANCE

David Cronenberg's movies are all easily available, with the exception of his first four "student" films—TRANSFER (1966), about a psychiatrist stalked by a patient; FROM THE DRAIN (1967), about a war veteran strangled by a plant that grows up out of a bathtub drain; STEREO (1969), based on his novel; and CRIMES OF THE FUTURE (1970). From his earliest efforts, he was obsessed with the bizarre, the morbid, and the war between mind and body. Taken together, his work forms one of the most consistent directorial visions of anyone working today. He's a true auteur, and there's something to be said for watching the films in order, since his work seems to develop in concert with his inner life.

His early movies were all intense studies of the way the body wars against itself, with the sole exception of FAST COMPANY (1977), which was a racing movie made to indulge Cronenberg's passion for automobiles. THEY CAME FROM WITHIN (1975), starring Barbara Steele, is a story about parasites that are designed to help heal sick human organs, but they get out of control and go on a rampage, leading to gory special effects that alarmed the Canadian Parliament. (The movie actually prefigures the AIDS crisis.) RABID (1977), starring porn queen Marilyn Chambers in a proto-*Alien* shocker about venereal vampirism spread by a monstrous creature that burrows out of her armpit, and THE BROOD (1979), with Samantha Eggar and Oliver Reed in the ultimate mutant-pregnancy fable, are among the finest horror movies of the seventies.

With SCANNERS (1981), about the telepathic powers of an underground society, Cronenberg begins to explore the relationship between the body and technology. (*Scanners* also includes the famous exploding head scene.) He goes even further with this theme in VIDEODROME (1983), starring James Woods, in which television becomes the ultimate mind-control weapon. The modest success of these two films set up his biggest box-office hit, the 1986 remake of THE FLY, starring Jeff Goldblum and Geena Davis in the story of a scientist who accidentally gets fused with a fly and mutates into a horrible, pus-excreting creature. (Cronenberg himself appears in a cameo as the gynecologist.) DEAD RINGERS (1988) is another Hollywood movie, starring Jeremy Irons in a study of identical twin gynecologists that didn't really break through at the box office.

In 1992, he made NAKED LUNCH, the William Burroughs drug novel that was previously considered unfilmable, yet his weird take on the ultimate hallucinogenic story won eight Genie Awards, helped considerably by the cast of Peter Weller, Judy Davis, Ian Holm, Julian Sands, and Roy Scheider.

Cronenberg has twice worked as a director for hire, first on the adaptation of Stephen King's THE DEAD ZONE (1984), which is one of the best of the early King movies, starring Christopher Walken as the accident victim cursed with the ability to see into the future. He detoured into big budget movies with the film version of M. BUTTERFLY (1993), once again using Jeremy Irons, this time as the French diplomat obsessed with a Chinese diva who turns out to be a man.

J.G. Ballard, the author of the novel *Crash* is based on, is also known for his autobiographical EMPIRE OF THE SUN, which was made into an award-winning 1987 movie by Steven Spielberg.

After *Crash*, Cronenberg wrote and directed EXISTENZ (1999), with Jennifer Jason Leigh as the

inventor of a bio-engineered game played by plugging a living game pod directly into the central nervous system through an umbilical cord inserted into an orifice carved in the player's back. By this time, Cronenberg's vision had gone from the body against nature to the body against itself to the body against science to the body as just another cog in an organic ecology that is, by its very nature, deadly. He followed that up with the short film CAMERA (2000), which won several Canadian awards, and then made SPIDER (2003), starring Ralph Fiennes, Miranda Richardson, and Gabriel Byrne in the story of an acute schizophrenic losing his grip on reality as he tries to survive outside a mental institution. *Spider* is based on a novel by Patrick McGrath and, as this book went to press, had not yet been released in the States.

Cronenberg has also appeared frequently as an actor in recent years, always acquitting himself well, notably in Clive Barker's NIGHT BREED (1990), BLUE (1992), TO DIE FOR (1995), BLOOD AND DONUTS (1995), EXTREME MEASURES (1996), THE STUPIDS (1996), RESURRECTION (1999), STEVE MARTINI'S THE JUDGE (2001), and JASON X (2002). In addition, he's the subject of two documentaries—DAVID CRONENBERG: LONG LIVE THE NEW FLESH (1986) and DAVID CRONENBERG: I HAVE TO MAKE THE WORLD BE FLESH (1999)—and also appeared in the documentary THE AMERICAN NIGHTMARE (2000). Other small roles include INTO THE NIGHT (1985), BOOZECAN (1994), HENRY & VERLIN (1994), TRIAL BY JURY (1994), THE GRACE OF GOD (1997), and LAST NIGHT (1998).

A haunted Christopher Walken in *The Dead Zone*.

SELECTED BIBLIOGRAPHY

This bibliography is by no means a complete record of all the works and sources consulted. It lists only the major sources of general interest to the reader who wants to pursue a more in-depth survey of these films. A decision was made to omit Internet sources, since the Web sites often change.

Allen, Thomas B. *Possessed: The True Story of an Exorcism*. New York: Doubleday, 1993.

Bernard, Jami. *Quentin Tarantino: The Man and His Movies*. New York: HarperPerennial, 1995.

Berry, Skip. *Gordon Parks*. New York: Chelsea House Publishers, 1991.

Bey, Logan. *Hong Kong Action Cinema*. Woodstock, N.Y.: Overlook Press, 1995.

Bisland, Peter. *Easy Riders, Raging Bulls: How the Sex-Drugs-and-Rock'n'Roll Generation Saved Hollywood*. New York: Simon & Schuster, 1998.

Blackburn, Greta. "The Star: Linda Blair." *Fangoria* (Jan. 1987): 20–23, 59.

Blatty, William Peter. *If There Were Demons, Then Perhaps There Were Angels: William Peter Blatty's Own Story of* The Exorcist. New York: Screenpress Books, 2001.

———. *The Exorcist*. New York: HarperCollins, 1971.

Bosco, Scott. "A Look Back at *The Exorcist* Effects: Mechanical Effects Man Marcel Vercoutere Describes the Horrifying Illusions He Created for the Satanic Horror Classic." *Fangoria* (Dec. 1983): 28–31.

Brottman, Mikita. *Meat Is Murder: An Illustrated Guide to Cannibal Culture*. London: Creation Books International, 1998.

Canby, Vincent, Janet Maslin, and the Film Critics of *The New York Times*. The New York Times Guide to the Best 1,000 Movies Ever Made. Peter M. Nichols, ed. New York: Times Books, 1999.

Chan, Jackie, with Jeff Yang. *I Am Jackie Chan: My Life in Action*. New York: Ballantine Books, 1998.

Cohen, Danny. *Horror Movies*. Greenwich, Conn.: Bison Books, Corp., 1984.

Cronenberg, David and Chris Rodley, ed. *Cronenberg on Cronenberg*. New York: Faber & Faber, 1997.

Dawson, Jeff. *Quentin Tarantino: The Cinema of Cool*. New York: Applause, 1995.

Evans, Peter. *Bardot: Eternal Sex Goddess*. New York: Drake Publishers, Inc., 1973.

Everson, William K. *Classics of the Horror Film: From the Days of the Silent Film to* The Exorcist. New York: DIANE Publishing Co., 1974.

Friedman, David F. with Don DeNevi. *A Youth in Babylon: Confessions of a Trash-Film King*. New York: Prometheus Books, 1990.

Gallagher, John A. "The Exorcists: Max von Sydow & Jason Miller." *Fangoria* (Jan. 1987): 24–25, 61.

Gentry, Clyde. *Jackie Chan: Inside the Dragon*. Dallas: Taylor Publishing Co., 1997.

Goldberg, Lee. "The Director: William Friedkin." *Fangoria* (Jan. 1987): 30–32, 59.

Gordon, Alex. "Pit and Pen of Alex Gordon: Dissecting a Horror Classic." *Fangoria* (Jan. 1987): 14–15.

Gutman, Israel, ed. "Buchenwald." In *Encyclopedia of the Holocaust*. New York: Macmillan Publishing Company, 1990.

———. "Koch, Karl." In *Encyclopedia of the Holocaust*. New York: Macmillan Publishing Company, 1990.

Hacker, Carlotta. *Great African Americans in the Arts*. New York: Crabtree Publishing Company, 1997.

Hackett, David, trans. *The Buchenwald Report*. Boulder, Colo.: Westview Press, 1995.

Kauffmann, Stanley. "Stanley Kauffmann on Films: *The Exorcist*." *New Republic* (Feb. 9, 1974): 22.

Kermode, Mark. "Speak of the Devil . . ." *Fangoria* (Mar. 1994): 14–21.

———. *The Exorcist* (Bfi Modern Classics). London: British Film Institute, 1998.

Kohn, George C. "Albert Dekker: Kinky Finis." In *Encyclopedia of American Scandal*, edited by George C. Kohn. New York: Facts on File, 1989.

———. "Deep Throat: The Sexual Brutalization of Linda Lovelace." In *Encyclopedia of American Scandal*. New York: Facts on File, 1989.

Kracauer, Siegfried. *From Caligari to Hitler: A Psychological History of the German Film*. Princeton, N.J.: Princeton University Press, 1947.

Landay, Eileen. *Black Film Stars*. New York: Drake Publishers, Inc., 1973.

Landis, Bill. "Herschell Gordon Lewis Today." *Fangoria* 17: 23–27.

Leab, Daniel J. *From Sambo to Superspade: The Black Experience in Motion Pictures*. Boston: Houghton Mifflin Company, 1973.

Loder, Kurt. "Night Creatures." *Rolling Stone* (July 1984): 91–98.

Maynard, Richard A. *The Black Man on Film: Racial Stereotyping*. Rochelle Park, N.J.: Hayden Book Company, Inc., 1974.

McCabe, Bob. The Exorcist: *Out of the Shadows—The Full Story of the Film*. London: Omnibus Press, 1999.

McCarty, John. *The Fearmakers: The Screen's Directorial Masters of Suspense and Terror*. New York: St. Martin's Press, 1994.

———. *The Sleaze Merchants: Adventures in Exploitation Filmmaking*. New York: St. Martin's Griffin, 1995.

Meikle, Denis with Christopher T. Koetting. *A History of Horrors: The Rise and Fall of the House of Hammer*. Lanham, Md.: The Scarecrow Press, Inc., 1996.

Muller, Eddie and Daniel Faris. *Grindhouse: The Forbidden World of "Adults Only" Cinema*. New York: St. Martin's Griffin, 1996.

Palmer, Randy. "At Home with Herschell Gordon Lewis." *Fangoria* 26: 50–52.

———. "Before Cronenberg . . . Before Romero . . . There Was . . . The Wizard of Gore." *Fangoria* 4: 18–21.

Peary, Danny. *Cult Movies 2: 50 More of the Classics, the Sleepers, the Weird and the Wonderful*. New York: Dell Publishing, 1983.

Peary, Gerald, ed. *Quentin Tarantino: Interviews*. Jackson, Miss.: University Press of Mississippi, 1998.

Pines, Jim. *Blacks in Films: A Survey of Racial Themes and Images in the American Film*. London: Studio Vista, 1975.

Rhines, Jess Algeron. *Black Film/White Money*. New Jersey: Rutgers University Press, 1996.

———. "The Political Economy of Black Film." *Cineaste* (Summer 1995): 38–40.

Robinson, Jeffrey. *Bardot: An Intimate Portrait*. New York: Donald I. Fine, Inc., 1994.

Rovin, Jeff and Kathy Tracy. *The Essential Jackie Chan*. New York: Pocket Books, 1997.

Scappernotti, Dan and David McDonnell. "The Make-Up Artist: Dick Smith." *Fangoria* (Jan. 1987): 26–29, 66.

Schaefer, Eric. *"Bold! Daring! Shocking! True!": A History of Exploitation Films, 1919–1959*. London: Duke University Press, 1999.

Skal, David. J. *The Monster Show*. New York: Faber & Faber, 2001.

Stanley, John. *John Stanley's Creature Features Movie Guide Strikes Again: An A to Z Encyclopedia to the Cinema of the Fantastic*. Pacifica, Calif.: Creatures At Large Press, 1995.

Svehla, Gary J. and Susan Svehla, eds. *We Belong Dead: Frankenstein on Film*. Baltimore, Md.: Midnight Marquee Press, Inc., 1997.

Travers, Peter. *The Story Behind* The Exorcist. New York: Crown Publishers, 1974.

Tidyman, Ernest. *Shaft*. New York: Bantam Books, Inc., 1971.

Vadim, Roger. *Memoirs of the Devil*. New York: Harcourt Brace Jovanovich, 1975.

Winter, Douglas E. "The Author: William Peter Blatty." *Fangoria* (Jan. 1987): 16–19, 68.

INDEX OF FILM TITLES

TEXT AND PHOTO CREDITS: Anchor Bay Entertainment: pp. 166–7, 172–3, 178; © Arrow Productions, for ordering please call 1-702-438-1549: pp. 132–3, 153, and "Theme from *Deep Throat*"; Courtesy of the Academy of Motion Picture Arts and Sciences: pp. 24–5; Photofest: pp. 10–1, 16–7, 21, 22, 40, 42–3, 48, 52, 54–5, 62–3, 71, 72–3, 76–7, 81, 82, 83, 100–1, 107, 110, 112–3, 118–9, 129, 131, 154–5, 158–9, 165, 166–7, 185, 187, 192, 198, 200–1, 212, 213, 214–5, 232–3, 238, 239, 240–1, 246, 253; Popcorn Movie Posters / Anvil Archive: pp. 41, 132–3; © Royalty-free/Corbis: front cover; Something Weird Video: pp. 9, 41, 84–5, 90. "Theme from Shaft," words and music by Isaac Hayes, © Copyright 1971 Irving Music Inc. (BMI). International Copyright Secured, All Rights Reserved; © Video Dimensions: pp. 24–5.